FREEDOM'S
DETECTIVE

Also by Charles Lane

Stay of Execution
The Day Freedom Died

FREEDOM'S DETECTIVE

The Secret Service, the Ku Klux Klan and the Man Who Masterminded America's First War on Terror

CHARLES LANE

HANOVER
SQUARE
PRESS

HANOVER
SQUARE
PRESS

Recycling programs
for this product may
not exist in your area.

ISBN-13: 978-1-335-00685-1

Freedom's Detective

Library of Congress Cataloging-in-Publication Data has been applied for.

HanoverSqPress.com
BookClubbish.com

Printed in U.S.A.

For Bruce and Ann Lane

FREEDOM'S DETECTIVE

CONTENTS

PROLOGUE: Patrick County, Virginia, 1869 13

1. "Something terrible floats on the breeze." 20

2. "You will all be blown to hell in short order." 37

3. "He has worked his way through the labyrinth of lies." 63

4. "A powerful instrument for good or evil." 96

5. "The government secret agents were everywhere upon their track." .. 144

6. "I am radically opposed to any organized system of espionage." 208

7. "Suspicions come from Heaven." 248

ACKNOWLEDGMENTS 275

SELECTED BIBLIOGRAPHY 279

NOTES 293

INDEX 337

If men were angels, no government would be necessary. If angels were to govern men, neither external nor internal controls on government would be necessary.

—James Madison

Let lawyers, judges and sentimentalists say what they will, rogues can only be fought successfully with their own weapons, and any strategy resorted to by the officers to bring them to justice is in my judgment perfectly justifiable.

—Hiram C. Whitley, Chief,
United States Treasury Secret Service Division, 1869–1874

He had a summoner ready at hand,
No slyer boy in England, for a band
Of spies the fellow craftily maintained
To let him know where something might be gained.
One lecher he'd abide, or two, or more,
If they could lead the way to twenty-four.

—Geoffrey Chaucer, *The Canterbury Tales*

PROLOGUE

Patrick County, Virginia, 1869

Hiram Coombs Whitley sat on his horse and gazed down upon the rushing waters of the Staunton River. The mountain rains, which had fallen so abundantly in that spring of 1869, had turned it into a foaming torrent. The water was so high that it almost touched the low-hanging branches of trees on either side. Now Whitley had to decide whether to cross over from the north bank, where he sat in his saddle, to the south.[1]

He had reached this spot, deep in southern Virginia, on a mission from the new administration of President Ulysses S. Grant, inaugurated a few weeks earlier, on March 4, 1869. President Grant's commissioner of Internal Revenue had sent Whitley to crack down on the distillers in the Virginia backcountry who insisted on making and distributing alcohol without paying the federal excise levy. Congress had enacted the tax in 1862, to help fund the Union war effort. Consequently, it had not been enforced in Virginia, or anywhere else in the South, prior to the Confederacy's surrender in 1865. For white southern backwoodsmen, making untaxed moonshine was not just a livelihood, but also a way to show defiance of the victorious Union. For the federal government, the deployment of revenue agents like Hiram C. Whitley was not just about tax collection, but about establishing its writ across the entire territory of the United States.

Whitley knew that his destination, the moonshiners' stronghold in Patrick County, Virginia, lay on the other side of the white water. It was likely that illegal distillers were counting on the flooded streams of the region to protect them against the likes of him and his companions: two United States Army soldiers, a local guide, and a twenty-year-old clerk in the Treasury Department's Lynchburg, Virginia, branch office, who had met Whitley as he passed through on his way to Patrick County from Washington, and volunteered to join his expedition.

The young man's sense of adventure might have reminded Whitley of himself as a youth. He had left his home on the Ohio frontier many years before, while still a teenager, and he had never really stopped moving since. He had worked on fishing boats out of Gloucester, Massachusetts; slung hash at a makeshift Kansas restaurant; traded sugar and molasses on the Red River of Louisiana; and, of course, he had served the United States as an agent of federal law.

Through these experiences, Whitley had formed an appreciation for the American wilderness and the physical challenges it presented. He had grown from a skinny, bowlegged kid into a sinewy thirty-seven-year-old man, with piercing blue eyes, high cheekbones, and a vaguely menacing dark brown goatee. He had developed the skills with horses and firearms that helped make him useful to the government: he arrived at the Staunton River not only as a representative of the Treasury Department, but also as a deputy United States Marshal, carrying a sheaf of blank warrants authorizing him to arrest any violator of the tax law he might encounter. More than that, he had developed a thoroughly jaded view of human nature, and how it could be manipulated to his advantage, honestly if possible—but through deception if necessary, and convenient.

Two local men, members of the pacifist Church of the Brethren who had lodged and fed Whitley's group the previous night, approached Whitley as he contemplated the roaring Staunton. Solemnly, they advised him that it would be too dangerous for him and his fellow representatives of federal power to try to swim their horses across.

Whitley hesitated. Were these pious men trying to cover for the moonshiners? And what if they were? The water certainly looked life-threatening. Adventuresome as he might be, he had not risked his neck for the Union cause on any of the Civil War's great fields of battle. Rather, his had been what was known as "secret service": intelligence work, in the back alleys and no-man's-lands of the Union-occupied South. Some of these operations had been violent, to be sure, but at least they allowed for a measure of planning and control.

He turned to his local guide. "You have the best horse," he commanded. "Go in and swim the river first." The man refused.

The intrepid young clerk stepped forward and volunteered to try it on his mount. "Go it," Whitley said. "And we will follow suit."

Only when he saw the clerk plunge his horse into the water, and make it safely across, did Whitley decide that he, too, could make the attempt.

Soon, his entire party was on the south bank of the Staunton, dripping wet but ready to take on the moonshiners. Moving from point to point like a small Civil War raiding party, Whitley's team smashed some thirty illegal stills with axes, in just a couple of weeks.

Their most effective weapon was the element of surprise, enhanced by Whitley's knack for the strategic lie. Riding up to one still, Whitley's team caught a dozen of the locals filling jugs with rye and apple brandy. As they tried to flee, he shouted, "Boys, I have you surrounded by United States soldiers. There are over a hundred of them. All of you step up here and give in your names." Believing that there was a company of troops concealed in the surrounding woods, the men did as Whitley ordered. He seized an ax and proceeded to destroy the copper boilers and winding "worm-pipes" the moonshiners had so carefully assembled to produce their booze. Then he filled out the arrest warrants for his frightened captives.

In Whitley's opinion, illegal distilling could not be so rampant in the area without official connivance. The local representative of the federal tax-collecting agency was a native Virginian who lived in a nearby village called Liberty. Whitley proceeded to the village and arrested the man.[2]

A mob assembled outside the lodge in Liberty where Whitley and his crew were holding their detainee overnight, pending his transfer to a jail at Richmond, Virginia. An emissary from the crowd gave Whitley an ultimatum: if he and the other "damn Yankees" did not release the detainee, the people of Liberty would storm the building and take him themselves.

Whitley responded coolly, "Go tell your friends that if they offer to come up these stairs to interfere with us, the prisoner will be shot and thrown out of the window."

This bluff, too, worked; the crowd dispersed. Whitley continued the next day to Lynchburg, where he and his party rested, and he glanced at the newspapers for the first time in days.

He could hardly believe what he was reading. The Grant administration had announced a new chief for the Treasury Department's Secret Service Division: Hiram C. Whitley.

Officials had formally selected him on May 6, but, unable to contact him while he was in Virginia, they decided to give the information to the press, and let the news find him.[3] Now it had.

Established just four years prior to Whitley's appointment, the Secret Service was a new unit with a new, and, for the federal government, essential, mission: the detection and suppression of counterfeiting. It was the first civilian detective bureau the United States government had ever organized in peacetime.

Whitley had spent only a little of his previous career dealing with the particular breed of criminal that trafficked in fabricated currency, but for a federal lawman of his background, this was still a plum appointment, a dream come true, really. It would give Whitley command of an undercover outfit, and he certainly did know something about undercover work. It was what he lived for.

He rushed to Washington on the next train, arriving on May 12. As procedure required, Whitley first submitted a detailed report on his Virginia trip to the commissioner of Internal Revenue. Then he handed in his resignation. The commissioner tried to dissuade him. "I have got a special fund," he said, "and will pay you any reasonable money to remain with me."

Whitley was not interested. "I would rather be chief of the Secret Service," he explained, "than president of the United States."

The commissioner could see there was no changing Whitley's mind. He took him to the secretary of the Treasury, George S. Boutwell, who had signed Whitley's letter of appointment six days earlier. "This is the most active man of my bureau," the commissioner announced.

Treasury officials were impressed with Whitley's report, which contained abundant evidence that federal revenue officials in Virginia had been corrupted by the moonshiners. They immediately fired the man in charge of assessing taxes for the district through which Whitley had just passed.

That assessor had gotten his job at the behest of a powerful member of Congress from the president's own Republican Party. Incensed at the sudden downfall of his protégé, the politician went to the White House and demanded the assessor's reinstatement.

In those days before the federal civil service's professionalization, President Grant had the final say on matters of patronage. He agreed to intervene personally on this one.

Grant summoned Hiram C. Whitley and questioned him extensively on his report, which lay open on the president's desk, heavily annotated in Grant's handwriting. He seemed persuaded that Whitley had made the right judgment, but he had a lingering concern.

"Is there anyone down there…that you can recommend for an assessor?" Grant asked Whitley.

Whitley had to think fast. Another quality that had characterized him—for better and for worse—throughout his career was an absolute refusal to concede any point in an argument, no matter how seemingly insignificant. He did not have a substitute in mind for the official he wanted fired, yet he was loath to see the incumbent remain in office simply because he couldn't think of an alternative.

"No, Mr. President, I am unacquainted on that point," he began—and then his mind suddenly went back to that moment on the north bank of the Staunton, when he had dared the young clerk to lead the way across the perilous water. Perhaps he could help himself, and the president, by promoting the kid. He told Grant, "The sharpest and most earnest man I met while there was the young fellow…who first swam the river."

Grant brightened. He recalled the incident from Whitley's report. "I read about that," he said, "and I think he will make a good assessor."

"He is not quite twenty-one years of age," Whitley cautioned.

"I will waive his age," the president replied, ringing a bell and summoning an aide to take an order appointing the man.

For the commander-in-chief to side with Whitley against a lawmaker from his own party showed remarkable confidence in the new Secret Service head. Grant, though, not only esteemed Whitley's work for the internal revenue commission. The president also knew of Whitley's performance on behalf of the federal government in a case a year earlier, a murder investigation, of pivotal importance both to Reconstruction, the federal effort to remake Southern society and politics along more racially egalitarian lines, and to Whitley's own career. In that case, Whitley had taken on a criminal organization that was no less deeply rooted in the South than the moonshiners, yet far, far more dangerous.

1

"Something terrible floats on the breeze."

Nothing could be seen on the empty streets of Columbus, Georgia, during the early spring nights of 1868, except what the moon might faintly illuminate. The only sounds were the familiar calls of toads and insects, mingling with the murmur of the Chattahoochee River, as it flowed over a dam, powering the town's textile mill.

Around the middle of March, however, it became evident that something strange must be going on amid the late-night languor. Several local men awoke in the morning to find menacing signs and symbols nailed to their front doors: crude sketches of skulls, or bones, scrawled on yellowing paper, along with written demands to leave town—or face death. One day, the Columbus tax assessor discovered a threat attached to a bundle of actual bones, dangling from his front doorknob.

Rumors spread that spirits of Confederate soldiers killed in the recently concluded Civil War were swarming through the late-evening atmosphere, crying for blood and revenge.

The local newspaper, the *Daily Sun*, published lurid editorials heralding a new organization. "The Ku Klux Klan has arrived," the *Daily Sun* announced. "And woe to the degenerate."[1]

"Something terrible floats on the breeze," the editorial went on, "and in the dim silences are heard solemn whispers, dire imprecations against the false ones who have proved recreant to their faith and country. Strange mocking anomalies fill the air. Look out!"

The paper did not identify the "false ones" or "the degenerate." It was hardly necessary: only Republicans, members of the party that had stood for the Union, and against slavery, during the Civil War, received the threats. Their hero, the assassinated President Abraham Lincoln, had defeated the Confederacy, and helped emancipate millions of African Americans. Now, three years after Lincoln's death and the South's surrender at Appomattox, his political heirs—white and black—advocated greater equality between the races, the cause for which so many Union soldiers had fought and died.

Columbus's leading Republican was George W. Ashburn, a tall, gray-haired fifty-three-year-old—one of the minority of white Southerners who opposed secession before the war. Even more unusually, Ashburn had avowed that slavery was evil and that "Africans were human beings," as a friend would later recall.[2] Ashburn's beliefs prompted him to quit his job as a plantation overseer. Thereafter he sought work as a schoolteacher but no whites would hire him.

During the war, Ashburn left Columbus and joined Union General William Rosecrans's Army of the Cumberland in Tennessee, as an intelligence officer. After the Union triumph, Ashburn returned to his hometown and became an outspoken Republican. "I only hope to live to see Georgia reconstructed and to lay my bones in soil consecrated to liberty, within her borders," he wrote a fellow veteran of General Rosecrans's force.[3]

In late 1867 and early 1868, Ashburn served as an elected member of a state convention charged with drafting a new Georgia constitution. The proposed document guaranteed black men the vote, among other reforms. Many thought the state legislature to be chosen under the new constitution would select Ashburn to represent Georgia in the United States Senate, given his large following among newly freed and enfranchised African Americans.

All but a few whites in Columbus considered Ashburn a traitor to his region and his race, and the new constitution an evil blueprint for "Negro rule." When Ashburn returned to town after the convention ended on March 17, 1868, his enemies threatened to kill any white person who offered him housing. The prestigious Perry House hotel lodged Ashburn for a night, but asked him to leave the next day, citing other guests' objections to his presence. Brushing off a friend's recommendation that he leave Columbus to save his life, Ashburn boarded with Hannah Flournoy, a formerly enslaved black woman who rented a three-bedroom shotgun-style home two hundred yards from the Perry House.

There, Ashburn received an anonymous death threat, in a letter illustrated with a drawing of his body lying in a coffin marked "K.K.K."

Ashburn summoned fellow Republicans to his room and displayed the ghoulish message, along with similar missives other Columbus Republicans had received. He passed them around, joking, "Boys, here's your death warrants." The group "had quite a laugh, merely thinking them some rebel bombast," a participant later recalled.[4] They dismissed the Ku Klux Klan as a mythical conspiracy, a scare tactic by their political foes, the local white supremacist Democratic Party, whose leaders included Confederate veterans, cotton planters, merchants, and the editors of the *Daily Sun*. There was a company of Army troops stationed in town; Republicans confidently believed it would deter their antagonists.

It was indeed rational, in early 1868, for George W. Ashburn and other Republicans in the South to feel optimistic about Reconstruction.

That had not always been the case, to be sure. Lincoln's ex-pressions on how to deal with the postwar South suggested that he supported voting rights for at least some African Americans, but his plans never had a chance to ripen. His murder on the night of April 14, 1865, left Reconstruction up to his vice president and successor, Andrew Johnson, a Tennessean and a prewar Democrat. He had been made Lincoln's running mate as a gesture of bipartisanship, and because he was a rare pro-Union, antislavery Southerner. Those opinions reflected his class resentment toward the planter elite, not sympathy for people of color, however. In the early months of his accidental presidency, Johnson offered Southern states renewed member-ship in the Union, without substantial reform to their prewar system of racial hierarchy beyond nominal abolition of slavery. Their legislatures, dominated by former secessionists and former Confederate Army officers, enacted "black codes" limiting the rights of newly freed African Americans so rigidly as to restore slavery in everything but name.

Northern Republicans rejected President Johnson's policy, because it cheated African Americans of true freedom, and left Southern Democrats, most of them former rebels, in control of the former Confederate states—with a chance eventually to le-verage that power into control over the federal government, too. When the Republican-dominated Congress returned in Decem-ber 1865, after a nine-month recess, it immediately set about overturning Johnson's plan. The lawmakers refused to seat the Southern states' newly elected representatives or senators, who included no fewer than six former members of the Confederate cabinet, four former Confederate generals, fifty-eight former members of the Confederate Congress, and former Confeder-ate Vice President Alexander H. Stephens, who came to Wash-ington as a would-be senator from Georgia.[5]

Congress enacted major laws over Johnson's veto, one ex-tending the power of the new Freedmen's Bureau to aid newly emancipated people, the other a Civil Rights Act, which made all African Americans United States citizens and prohibited states from denying them equal rights. To entrench the Civil Rights Act's statutory equalization of citizenship in the nation's basic law, Congress passed the Fourteenth Amendment to the Constitution in 1866, then submitted it to the states for ratification.

Republicans campaigned on this program in the 1866 midterm elections. Voters rewarded them with veto-proof majorities in both houses of Congress. In 1867, Congress passed three Reconstruction Acts, over Johnson's veto. The laws grouped ten of the eleven formerly seceded Southern states into five military districts, with each district governed by an Army general and patrolled by several thousand troops. (Tennessee had already returned to the Union through a separate process.) The ten states would be excluded from congressional representation pending the rewriting of their constitutions by state conventions.

The conventions, in turn, would be elected by black and white male voters, except for former Confederate leaders, who would be ineligible based on their past role in the rebellion. Then voters would go to the polls again in April 1868, to ratify the constitutions in statewide elections. Only after its voters ratified a new constitution, and its legislature ratified the Fourteenth Amendment, could any of these ten former Confederate states be restored to the Union and send representatives to Congress.

By early 1868, it seemed Congress might indeed accomplish what had come to be called "radical" Reconstruction. Originally an exclusively Northern antislavery movement, the Republican Party would achieve national viability, based on black votes in the Southern states. That, in turn, would help sustain the great legislative achievements of the postwar Republican Congresses—equal rights, regardless of race or caste, for every man in every state. What had been an agglomeration of fractious states would at last be a true nation-state, steered by a federal government responsible for security and the economy, and, above all, rededicated to the Declaration of Independence's self-evident truth, "that all men are created equal."

The vast majority of Southern whites reacted with fury and horror. The war had destroyed their plantations and towns; now radical Reconstruction threatened the basic principle of their society, white supremacy. How to resist, though, was less clear. Another attempt at secession and armed revolt was unthinkable. The sporadic, uncontrolled violence across the South in recent months had proven counterproductive: in mid-1866, for example, whites attacked and murdered African Americans and white Republicans in Memphis, Tennessee, and New Orleans, Louisiana, achieving nothing except a Northern backlash and a landslide in favor of the Republicans in November. As for trying to compete with the Republicans for African American votes, that would have required the Democrats to concede that their presumed racial inferiors had a right to participate in the first place.

There was another alternative: subversion.

The Ku Klux Klan began as a club for a half dozen bored Confederate Army veterans in tiny Pulaski, Tennessee.[6] It formed during the Christmas season of 1865, when it still seemed Johnson's view of Reconstruction could prevail. American men had a penchant for freemasonry, fraternities, and secret societies, and at first the Klan—whose strange name derived from the ancient Greek *kyklos* ("circle"), and whose costumes and rituals seemed contrived mostly for amusement—typified that tendency.

As the Republican plan for Reconstruction took hold, however, Klan "dens" mutated into white supremacist vigilante groups targeting African Americans, Freedmen's Bureau officials, and white Republicans. They would don frightening masks and disguises, often hoods crowned with animal horns, to imitate those that supposedly protruded from the devil's head, and ride through the Southern nights, shooting and whipping their victims, and burning African American schools, churches, and homes.

During Reconstruction, Ku Klux Klan costumes served two purposes: to conceal the wearer's identity and to terrify victims. (*Collection of the Buffalo History Museum*)

The Ku Klux Klan remained relatively obscure and mostly limited to Tennessee until early 1868, when it became clear to the South's white supremacists that the political transition provided for under the 1867 Reconstruction Acts was indeed going forward, and their strongest defender in Washington, Andrew Johnson, was likely to face an impeachment attempt by the Republican Congress.

Former Confederate officers led by cavalry chieftain Nathan Bedford Forrest of Tennessee hatched a plan to take over the Ku Klux Klan and convert its sporadic violence into an organized terror campaign. Their goal would be to disrupt radical Reconstruction through intimidation of Republican voters and politicians, starting with the 1868 elections. The new Klan leaders formalized the hierarchy of the "Invisible Empire," as it would come to be known, with a "Grand Wizard," Forrest, at the top, commanding rank-and-file "ghouls" initiated in secret grips, passwords, and rituals.

A slave trader before the Civil War, and a commander of forces notorious for massacring surrendered black Union soldiers during the conflict, Forrest nevertheless remained at liberty to start a railroad and an insurance firm after Appomattox. Business gave him a plausible rationale to travel through the defeated region and to recruit white Democrats, many of them Confederate veterans, to the Klan conspiracy. New Klansmen swore to support "a white man's government," and to maintain absolute secrecy about Klan activities, upon pain of death.

In early March, Forrest came to Columbus.[7] The town had avoided the worst of the havoc Union General William Tecumseh Sherman's armies wreaked on Georgia, but a late Union cavalry raid—a week after Appomattox—left its textile and arms factories, powered by the Chattahoochee River, in ruins. By Forrest's visit the town had rebuilt the old Eagle Mills textile plant and renamed it the Eagle & Phenix Mills, a tribute to its emergence from the ashes of war. Leading white citizens, mostly Confederate veterans in their late twenties and early thirties, nevertheless seethed with resentment over the South's defeat and horror at living on equal terms with their erstwhile slaves.

They proved receptive to Forrest's appeal. Unlike more open forms of resistance, the Ku Klux Klan threatened radical Reconstruction at its most vulnerable point: its lack of support among white Southerners. The white population could be the sea, wide and deep, in which the Klan would swim. As in the rest of the South, what little organized police presence there was in Columbus and surrounding Muscogee County would itself be drawn from this pool of sympathetic manpower. Klan terrorists would be invulnerable to detection and punishment by the local Army garrison or any other federal authority as long as their code of silence held.

Within days of Forrest's sojourn in Columbus, the first threats against Ashburn and other Republicans appeared on their door-posts, and in the pages of the *Daily Sun*.

After their meeting in George W. Ashburn's room, Republicans, white and black, returned to the public spaces of Columbus, rallying in advance of the two-day state constitutional referendum on April 20 and 21, 1868; a new governor, state legislature, and local governments would be chosen then, too. On March 28, 1868—a Saturday—two thousand people, most of them black, filled the town's main square to nominate candidates, and to hear a campaign speech from Henry McNeal Turner, the famous African Methodist Episcopal bishop.

Born free in South Carolina, Turner had gone on to serve as the first black chaplain of the United States Colored Troops during the Civil War. That Saturday afternoon, he seemed to revel in telling the crowd that the mysterious skeletal remains found dangling from the Republican tax assessor's office door were not the remains of a Confederate soldier, as the accompanying Ku Klux Klan leaflet claimed, but the skull and neck bones of a harmless turtle. Like the Republicans who had assembled with Ashburn a few days earlier, Turner's audience roared with laughter.

On Monday evening, March 30, another crowd, numbering eighteen hundred, gathered at Columbus's Temperance Hall to hear Turner once again. This time, Ashburn stood with him on the speaker's platform.[8]

The Temperance Hall meeting had been over for a little more than an hour, the moon had set, and clocks had just struck midnight, when Hannah Flournoy heard a knock at the door of her home.[9] She rose from her bed, pulled on a dressing gown, and shouted to the unexpected caller to identify himself. "Mary Tillinghurst" was the reply, audible through the closed front door, but uttered in a weird falsetto, as if the visitor were trying to disguise his voice. Suspicious, Flournoy refused to open up.

In the next instant, five armed men broke down the door and swarmed her parlor. They were draped in dark clothing, their hands gloved and faces partially covered by pasteboard masks, like those worn at genteel antebellum costume balls. The intruders lit a candle and demanded to know where they could find Flournoy's boarder, George W. Ashburn.

Stunned, Flournoy did not respond. The men pushed past her. Startled out of his bed by the commotion, Ashburn grabbed a pistol and threw a rough cloth coat over his nightshirt. Another houseguest pleaded with Ashburn to give him the gun, and even tried to wrest it from Ashburn's hand, to use it in self-defense. Ashburn held on to the weapon, insisting no shooting would be necessary. The intruders probably wouldn't hurt them, he said.

"Who comes there?" Ashburn called, hastily lighting a candle and placing it on a small bedside table. Then, he opened his chamber door.

"There's the damned shit!" one of the assailants cried, and in that same moment, he and several other masked men opened fire.

Ashburn cried out, "Stop, stop!" and fell under a hail of bullets.

Shots hit the Republican activist on his left leg and in the buttocks, wounding him badly but not mortally. One intruder kneeled next to Ashburn's bleeding frame, aimed his gun through the legs of the bedside table behind which Ashburn lay—and shot him between the eyes.

"Come on, boys," the assassin said. As the gang fled, two more masked men came in from outside and peered briefly into Ashburn's room, confirming the kill. Then they, too, hurried out.

The brazen assassination of a key Republican politician in the South shocked the whole country. Prior to George W. Ashburn's murder on March 31, 1868, Northern newspapers knew, and reported, little about the Ku Klux Klan. After what appeared to be the Klan's first major political murder, the victim of which was a white politician, they could not get enough of the story.

THE KU KLUX KLAN AT WORK—THE ASSASSINATION OF THE HON. G. W. ASHBURN, IN COLUMBUS, GEORGIA, ON THE 31ST ULT.—SEE PAGE 27.

Ashburn's assassination shocked the country. A popular New York–based weekly captioned this artist's rendition of the crime "The Ku Klux Klan at Work." (*Frank Leslie's Illustrated Newspaper*)

The attempted decapitation of Georgia's Republican Party could only be the work "of a secret conclave who have spread themselves throughout the entire South," the *Cincinnati Daily Gazette* warned. It was "a blow at the Government—a blow at every loyal man."[10] A Detroit newspaper called Ashburn's killers "the most villainous secret political organization which has ever existed in this country, if not any country."[11] The *New York Times* called for a beefed-up military presence in the South, suspension of habeas corpus, and the trial of Klan offenders by "drumhead court-martial."[12] Suddenly, the success of Congress's plan for Reconstruction did not seem so assured; it might hinge on the federal government's ability to dismantle that "secret political organization."

In Columbus, men of color grabbed their shotguns or hunting rifles and stood watch over the homes of their white Republican allies. Some spoke openly of taking revenge, even of setting the town on fire. "As Mr. Ashburn was the political leader of the colored people here," the commanding officer of the eighty-man Army company in Columbus telegraphed his superior officers the day after the assassination, "great excitement has prevailed among them, and I had feared a collision with the whites." He ordered troops to patrol the city around the clock.[13] Republicans, led by Henry McNeal Turner, circulated through the black community, advising against retaliatory violence.

Between the deterrent effect of Army troops, and the calming words of politicians, a measure of order prevailed. Republicans and soldiers agreed, however, that discovery and punishment of the guilty parties would have to be swift, lest the uproar triggered by Ashburn's murder persist—and the violence spread.

On the morning after the crime, the mayor and town council of Columbus passed a resolution condemning the murder and pledging a thorough investigation. They offered a $500 reward for information and promised to expand the police force. Authorities convened a coroner's jury made up of seven local dignitaries. The jury, accompanied by the Muscogee County prosecutor and the county physician, proceeded to the Flournoy place for an inquest.

Ashburn still lay in a pool of blood in his bedroom, his shattered head wedged against the back wall. The doctor poked and prodded the politician's body, confirming that three shots had struck him, though there were eight bullet holes in his coat, various indentations in the walls and furniture, and four spent projectiles on the floor. He ruled that the fatal wound was the one in Ashburn's forehead, from which a piece of his brain still protruded.

With the dead man sprawled next to them, the coroner's jury called witnesses. After four hours of testimony, however, the inquest issued only a vague verdict: "George W. Ashburn came to his death by pistol balls through the body, fired by persons unknown to this jury."[14]

The *Daily Sun* admitted to regarding Ashburn's departure from politics "pleasurably," though the paper duly expressed "profound regret" at the manner of it. According to the *Daily Sun*, the real scandal was that "strenuous and active exertions have been made by some negroes and some of his white followers to lay this bloody deed at the door of some of the best and most exemplary young men of our city." Ashburn's own supporters had probably killed him, the *Daily Sun* implied, perhaps due to an argument between him and Henry McNeal Turner at the Temperance Hall.

The "negroes of this section," the *Daily Sun* warned, should reflect on Ashburn's violent death, and "take heed from the terrible fate of one who hoped to riot in the ruin of his kind."[15]

Captain William Mills, commanding Company G of the Army's 16th Infantry Regiment in Columbus, observed these events with a mixture of incredulity and alarm.

The federal legal authority for his unit's presence in Columbus, the Reconstruction Acts, empowered him "to punish, or cause to be punished, all disturbers of the peace and criminals." On April 2, the Army's supreme commander in Washington, General Ulysses S. Grant, sent a telegram from the War Department in Washington to General George Meade, the hero of Gettysburg now in charge of the military district encompassing Georgia, Alabama, and Florida, at his Atlanta headquarters: Grant recommended trying Ashburn's killers before a military commission, if civilian authorities in Georgia proved unable or unwilling to dispense justice. On April 3, Meade endorsed Grant's telegram and forwarded it to Mills.

Though they were all white Democrats—holdovers from the whites-only elections under President Andrew Johnson's version of Reconstruction in 1865—the local officials of Columbus assured Mills they would investigate and prosecute the Ashburn murder. Given the obvious hatred Columbus's Democrats harbored for Ashburn, and the fact that he had been the target of repeated death threats from the Klan, Mills assumed the killer or killers came from among the town's white population and could be identified swiftly. Certainly the confidential reports that he and his fellow officers received after the crime from the town's African Americans supported that impression.

Mills decided to give local officials a chance. At first, it seemed that they might keep their promises. When the mayor and town council offered their $500 reward, Mills persuaded the Army to put up an additional $2,000 as a gesture of cooperation.

Yet after he sat in on the farcical coroner's jury inquest, and read the *Daily Sun*'s intimidating message for the black population, Mills concluded that he was being dealt with in bad faith. The entire situation, he wrote to a superior officer, reeked of cover-up, or at least "apathy and indifference."[16]

Indeed, most whites' attitudes were uglier than that, as Mills learned during Ashburn's funeral procession. Company G supplied a squad of soldiers, plus a fife and drum team, to escort the parade—hundreds of African Americans marching beside Ashburn's coffin under a large American flag—to the Muscogee Depot on the eastern edge of town, whence it would be sent to his wife for burial in Macon, Georgia.[17] As the solemn throng moved through the streets, white women standing along the route applauded. "Thank God that he is dead!" one of them cried.[18]

Mills decided the time had come to use his full powers under the Reconstruction Acts, as Grant and Meade had strongly hinted he should do. On April 6, he ordered his troops to detain ten men whom he had reason to believe were involved in Ashburn's murder.

Angry white citizens flocked in protest to Mills's temporary headquarters, the Muscogee County courthouse, where he confined the detainees. Women in their Sunday best wept and wailed for their release. Lawyers appeared, demanding to know the Army's legal authority for the arrests.

On the advice of Meade's top military lawyer, Mills offered the men and their supporters a compromise: each would be released in return for a $2,500 bond, and a promise to report for trial before a military commission composed of Army officers. It was a substantial sum, but four hundred white residents of Columbus pooled their funds and supplied the bonds. On April 10, 1868, four days after they had entered jail, the suspects exited.

Mills's brief crackdown accomplished one important objective: to deter the Klan and keep Columbus peaceful through the April 20–21 election. Some sixteen hundred men, mostly black, cast ballots in the town. The overwhelmingly Republican African American voters had been subjected to bribes and intimidation by white Democrats, but did not succumb. Black students from a local school operated by Northern missionaries helped voters read their tickets marked with the names of Republican candidates, thwarting a Democratic plan to trick them into voting for the party of white supremacy.[19] The constitution that George W. Ashburn had helped to write won statewide ratification; some one hundred eighty-eight thousand registered voters, evenly divided between the two races, also elected a new Republican-heavy legislature and a Republican governor.[20]

This hardly guaranteed that the peace in Georgia, or elsewhere in the South, would hold through the November presidential election, when Grant was likely to be the Republican candidate. If the Ku Klux Klan got away with murdering an author of the charter under which Georgia was to govern itself, no ordinary Republican, black or white, could feel safe.

For all these reasons, Meade was almost desperate to crack the case. It was also a matter of personal pride: Ashburn's murder had caught him embarrassingly unawares. General Meade was new to Atlanta, having arrived on New Year's Day, 1868. He knew that Republicans in Georgia and Alabama had received menacing notes; unconfirmed news of lynchings had also come his way. He had no inkling a terrorist organization was incubating in his jurisdiction. He proceeded with a planned visit to his troops in Florida, and therefore was not even in Georgia when the Klan struck in Columbus. He had had to compose a telegram to Grant explaining that; and he was acutely aware of the Northern press coverage.[21]

He decided that the Army must gather enough evidence to identify all the members of the conspiracy to kill Ashburn, and to prove their guilt beyond a reasonable doubt, before a military commission. This required expertise that Mills, for all his determination, did not possess.

"I desire to have sent to me, without delay, an experienced detective to aid in detecting the Ashburn murderers," Meade telegraphed Grant on April 13, 1868. "Can such a person be sent?"[22]

Five days later, a War Department investigator, William H. Reed, reached Columbus—only to find himself stymied. Klan terror silenced black witnesses who had initially been willing to talk to the Army. As for whites, their leaders favored the conspiracy "heart and hand," Reed wrote Meade on April 22, 1868. His discreet inquiries showed that "the aim of the citizens is to put the blame on" Ashburn's Republican friends, "which I am satisfied they will perjure themselves to do."[23]

Reed telegraphed Meade seeking help: he knew a detective who might be able to succeed where he had so far failed. The man had experience in the South, having been an undercover agent for the occupying Union Army in New Orleans during the Civil War, penetrating the city's rebel spy rings and criminal gangs. After the war, he had helped Republican leaders of the House of Representatives dig up evidence of possible impeachable offenses by President Andrew Johnson. He had a reputation as a master infiltrator and interrogator.

At the moment, this detective was in Kansas, pursuing bootleg whiskey distillers for the commissioner of Internal Revenue. Meade wired the commissioner, asking to borrow his man. "He cannot come too soon," the general implored. When the commissioner hesitated, Grant intervened, insisting the Ashburn case took precedence.

On April 23, 1868, the commissioner's order clicked westward from Washington to Kansas over the telegraph wire: Stop what you are doing and get to Georgia. Five days later, when an eastbound train pulled out of Atchison, Kansas, the detective, Hiram C. Whitley, was on board.[24]

2

"You will all be blown to hell in short order."

The United States Army and the Treasury Department had to haggle over Hiram C. Whitley's investigative services because he was one of the relatively few professional undercover operators available to the federal government or, indeed, to any level of law enforcement, at that time. Prior to the Civil War, the only federal law enforcement agencies were small outfits dedicated to protecting the mails and collecting custom duties. United States Marshals arrested criminals suspected of violating a handful of federal criminal statutes, and helped execute federal court orders. The commissioner of Internal Revenue, and his agents, came on the scene in 1862.[1]

These federal forces derived their limited authority from enumerated powers granted in the Constitution: to provide postal service, impose tariffs, and levy taxes. They depended on appropriations from Congress and cooperation from local authorities—county sheriffs, usually—who retained the primary responsibility for crime fighting. The sheriffs, in turn, relied on posses drawn from the armed citizenry. Full-time police departments first appeared around 1830, in large cities, crime being mostly an urban problem. These forces fielded no full-time detective bureaus until

Boston established one in 1846, followed by New York in 1857, Philadelphia in 1859, and Chicago in 1861.[2]

In all of this, the United States differed from the more developed and centralized states of Europe. In London, the first full-time anti-theft patrol, the Bow Street Runners, began in 1749; followed by the Metropolitan Police under Robert Peel in 1829. Napoleon of France had his political spies under Joseph Fouché. In 1812, Eugène François Vidocq founded the French La Sûreté Nationale, a semiclandestine detective force targeting common crime in Paris. A brilliant and ruthless innovator, Vidocq had a long career as a forger, con man, prison inmate, and failed merchant before he put his talents at the service of the state. Most of his detectives were also ex-criminals, consistent with Vidocq's dictum that police must "set a thief to catch a thief."

Vidocq led the Sûreté until 1827, after which he wrote a memoir. It was an international bestseller; the first English translation reached American shores in 1836. Vidocq was the inspiration for detective characters in the popular works of Edgar Allan Poe and Honoré de Balzac. By midcentury, detective fiction was in vogue in the United States, while the *National Police Gazette*, founded in 1845, provided lurid tales of crime, and dramatic accounts of the lawmen who tried to bring the perpetrators to justice.[3]

As much as they enjoyed reading about Vidocq's exploits, or even admired him and his American imitators, Americans also harbored misgivings about applying Continental detective methods to their society. Europeans viewed law enforcement through the lens of their absolutist political tradition, which assumed the existence of a central state with authority over the entire national territory and a monopoly on the legitimate use of force. Americans took pride in their more libertarian republican traditions, which arose in opposition to European monarchy, and expressed itself both in the Constitution's limitations on federal power, and in the Bill of Rights—with its prohibitions against self-incrimination and unreasonable searches and seizures. The big exception, of course, was the elaborate system of surveillance and armed patrols, drawn from local white populations, that kept African Americans, both enslaved and free, under constant pressure, especially in the South.

Attitudes changed somewhat after the Civil War broke out, when, of necessity, the federal government employed undercover agents for purposes that ranged from spying on the Confederacy, and its Northern sympathizers, to combating fraudulent military contractors. The Scottish-born postal-agent-turned-private-detective Allan Pinkerton lent his skills and those of his agents to the Union cause: he protected President-elect Abraham Lincoln and broke up an assassination plot against him as he traveled by rail from Illinois to Washington for his inauguration in early 1861. Later Pinkerton gathered military intelligence for the Army of the Potomac under General George McClellan. The flamboyant Union detective Lafayette Baker—sporting a lapel badge declaring "death to traitors"—broke up a ring of pro-Confederate postmasters in southern Maryland, ran spies for Secretary of War Edwin Stanton, and hunted the Lincoln assassination conspirators in April 1865.[4]

In this respect, as in many others, the Civil War fostered the expansion of federal power and the formation of an American nation-state. Yet as the war ended, many Americans still felt that federal covert surveillance, even in the name of revenue collection or public safety, ran contrary to the small-government ideology upon which the country had, in part, been founded. They often recoiled at the methods to which detectives inevitably resorted: paying underworld contacts for information; wearing disguises and snooping on citizens; sting operations, or "put-up jobs," as they were called; and, notoriously in the case of Lafayette Baker, torture. "It is easy to see that such a force, necessarily recruited from a class in society whose moral tone is somewhat below par, while on the one hand it may now and then contribute to the detection of crime, is a constant menace to everything most valuable in a republican government," the *New York World* editorialized in 1867.[5]

The newspaper had a point: in America, as in France, many a detective had come to his profession after a previous career on the margins of the law. How else, indeed, was he to acquire his expertise? Lafayette Baker, whose unsavory past included helping San Francisco's bare-knuckled "committee of vigilance" rid the city of alleged criminals in the 1850s, was one example.

Hiram C. Whitley was another.

Shortly after dawn on January 25, 1859, a two-wagon convoy rounded a curve in the muddy road cutting through a grove of trees just north of Lawrence, in the Kansas Territory.[6]

John Doy, a local doctor, and his son Charles drove the first of the horse-drawn vehicles; one of Doy's neighbors held the reins of the second. Distributed between the wagons were thirteen passengers—eight men, three women, and two children—all of African descent. All had been living freely in Lawrence, an antislavery stronghold in the territory so bitterly and violently contested by pro- and antislavery forces that people called it "bleeding Kansas."

Two of the black men had never been enslaved, but had been born and raised free in Northern states. They worked as cooks in a Lawrence hotel. In recent weeks, however, raids by slave catchers from nearby Missouri had plagued Lawrence. Attackers forcibly carried African American captives east across the Missouri River, to the Show-Me State, where slavery was the law of the land, and they could be "returned" to "masters," or sold like so much livestock to the highest bidder. If the black captives presented documentation proving that they were free, their captors often shredded or burned it on the spot.

John Doy organized an effort to help black residents escape to safer places farther north, with the help of Lawrence "Free State men" including John Brown—the fierce abolitionist already contemplating the attack he would later make on Harpers Ferry, Virginia. Just a few days prior to the Doy party's expedition, in fact, Brown had departed for Canada with a group of escaped slaves. The Doy party's destination was closer: Holton, Kansas, where their charges would be transferred to another abolitionist guide and taken to the free soil of Iowa.

The predicament arose in part from the Fugitive Slave Act, which Congress enacted and President Millard Fillmore signed in 1850, as part of a last-ditch legislative compromise to keep North and South together. Meant to appease Southern fury at the increasing numbers of enslaved African Americans escaping North with the aid of abolitionists, the statute represented a vast expansion of federal law enforcement. Not only did it require United States Marshals to capture and return fugitive slaves; it required citizens of all states, North or South, to assist marshals when summoned to do so. And it authorized slaveholders to appoint "agents" to track down their "property" for them, again with the assistance of federal commissioners specially appointed to approve the necessary documents.

It was all legal and efficient on paper; in addition to its moral defects, however, the Fugitive Slave Act showed that the United States remained unlike France and other European states in its limited capacity for centralized surveillance and law enforcement. The statute attempted to adapt the American paradigm of semiprivatized local law enforcement, the sheriff's posse, to a national mission. In practice, that mission—shutting down what had come to be known as the Underground Railroad—was highly unpopular in the North, where the law met often furious opposition. Rather than channel the sordid business of slave capture into a proper, lawful system, the Fugitive Slave Act seemed to incentivize more, and more brutal, freelance "slave-hunting."

John Doy and his companions were about to experience that firsthand. As they negotiated the bend in the road, they were set upon by twenty men on horseback, who had been waiting in ambush behind a high hill and were now galloping toward them—weapons drawn. Leading the charge were Missouri-based slave catchers. Doy recognized some from their previous assaults on Lawrence.

Flummoxed and outgunned, Doy stalled. He demanded that the mounted men blocking his way exhibit the requisite documents—"process," in the argot of the day—from a federal commissioner, proving their authority to stop his wagons and seize his passengers.

As he argued, Doy suddenly spotted a familiar face among his assailants. He recognized the young man as one of thousands of "emigrants" from Massachusetts to Lawrence, many inspired by the goal of populating the Kansas Territory with antislavery citizens who would vote for its admission to the Union as a Free State, under the "popular sovereignty" provision of the 1854 Kansas–Nebraska Act. The young man ran a restaurant in downtown Lawrence, which he had started by dishing out food on a wooden plank laid across two barrel tops. To all appearances, he shared the views of his neighbors and clientele.[7] At every opportunity, he voiced support for abolition, even contributing five dollars to the community's "fund for freedom." Now, there he was, among the Missourians, abetting their seizure of freedom-seeking black men, women, and children.

The familiar face belonged to Hiram C. Whitley. And it was now clear to John Doy and his companions that Whitley had not been their friend, much less loyal to the antislavery cause. He was a traitor who had given the Missourians advance notice of Doy's mission, then joined them in waylaying the wagons— no doubt motivated by the cash bounty slave holders or traders usually offered for black people captured in Kansas.

"What? You, here, Whitley? A Free State man!" Doy spluttered. All that he could think to do was repeat his question, "Where's your process?"

"Here it is," Whitley replied—whereupon he produced a revolver and tapped its barrel against the abolitionist's forehead.

Hiram Coombs Whitley was indeed a product of New England's free soil, born in the tiny hamlet of China, Maine, on August 6, 1832.[8]

His father, William Whitley, was a native of Glasgow, Scotland, whose parents took him with them to America shortly after his birth in 1796. While still a teenager, William Whitley did battle for the United States against the British Empire in the War of 1812; he later learned medicine. After years practicing as a country doctor, William Whitley married Hannah Dixon McCoombs, a native of the rugged Maine coast who was sixteen years his junior but shared his Scottish roots. From a harsh girlhood experience, the starvation her part of Maine endured during the War of 1812, she learned a fierce love of the United States, and preached it to her son Hiram from an early age.

In 1839, the Whitleys joined what was then a large flow of New Englanders to promising lands in the Great Lakes region. The family settled in Kirtland, a village twenty-five miles northeast of Cleveland famous as the home Joseph Smith, the Mormon prophet, had chosen for his Latter-day Saints when they abandoned Western New York in 1831. During the national financial panic of 1837, a Kirtland-based Mormon-run financial institution collapsed; and, amid unrest in the church, Smith departed for a new Zion farther West, taking most of his two thousand followers with him.

By the time the Whitleys arrived, Kirtland was inhabited mainly by the "old" settlers who preceded the Mormons, though the Saints' red-roofed temple, completed in 1836, still towered over their homes and farms. William Whitley established a new medical practice, earning enough to send young Hiram to school at the Western Reserve Seminary, which, despite its links to the Presbyterian Church, briefly rented out the top floor of the former Mormon temple, before moving to a permanent site in town.[9] Young Hiram was evidently a good student; he learned elegant penmanship and acquired a vigorous, expressive writing style.

Bright though he was, Whitley did not entirely relish learning. Still less did he aspire to the career for which the Western Reserve Seminary prepared its young charges: teaching school. To the contrary, he was restless, pranksterish; he enjoyed racing, wrestling, and playing hooky. He was also interested in money, and from his early teens he earned a few dollars each month as a part-time hired hand on local farms.

One spring day in 1850, seventeen-year-old Hiram C. Whitley was lazing, barefoot, by the side of a road rather than attending his final year of classes at the seminary. A man approached him with an opportunity to earn five times as much money as he was getting at the local farms. All Whitley had to do was help the man drive cattle from the Cleveland area over the Allegheny Mountains to a market near Philadelphia. Without pausing to put his shoes on, Whitley said yes and was soon hiking beside the herd, helping move them during a nearly four-hundred-mile journey. Whitley wielded a long whip called a "black snake"; it had a bit of silk on the end that he learned to snap in the air, making a sound like a rifle shot that frightened wayward animals back into line.[10]

Whitley returned to Kirtland when the drive was over—sixteen dollars richer. The journey marked the end of his schooling, and of his stable home life. He would leave again and again on cattle drives over the Alleghenies, eventually completing the grueling round-trip more than a dozen times. In addition to the opportunity for financial independence, cattle driving put Whitley in regular contact with fresh mountain air and posed a physical challenge, both of which he loved. Just over five feet, ten inches tall, the young man was growing tough, both mentally and physically—more formidable than people might guess by looking at his slender frame.

Abandoning their hopes that he would become a teacher, Whitley's parents tried to steer him into a respectable alternative: agriculture. In 1854, when he was twenty-two, they sent him to a relative's farm near Canton, Massachusetts, twenty miles south of Boston. After a few months, however, Whitley again felt the familiar yen for adventure and rough travel. He struck out for the fishing port of Gloucester, where he found work on mackerel and cod-fishing boats, and pursued that dangerous, but poorly paid, career for the next two years.

In early 1856, Whitley found himself back in the Boston area, where, shortly before his twenty-fourth birthday, he married Catherine Webster Bates, the seventeen-year-old daughter of a carpenter from East Cambridge.[11] A minister of the liberal, antislavery Universalist Church officiated at the ceremony, in keeping with Whitley's Yankee bride's beliefs— but in implicit rejection of, or indifference to, Whitley's parents' Presbyterianism.

For Whitley, marriage to a woman steeped in egalitarian religious doctrine did not imply any spiritual conversion, though matrimony was a concession to convention. Whitley opened a saloon in East Cambridge, but business was slow due to competition from experienced, better-known establishments. In June 1856 Whitley approached a local citizens' committee to seek a catering contract for their annual dinner. He was told that the committee preferred to use a rival business, owned by one R. M. Campbell, which supplied the previous year's event. Whitley assured them he now owned Campbell's establishment, the latter having gone bankrupt and sold out to him. The committee hired Whitley.[12]

In truth, R. M. Campbell was still solvent and very much in business. What actually seems to have happened is that, to retire a debt, Campbell gave Whitley and a business partner the saloon they were now operating, but Whitley had felt entitled to more. When Campbell learned of Whitley's chicanery, he published an open letter in the *Boston Herald* declaring that Whitley had procured the catering contract through "absolute falsehoods." Campbell asked customers to shun Whitley and continue doing business with him.

Whitley did not apologize, as some men might have done, or keep a low profile until the scandal blew over. It was "not in his nature," as a Bostonian who knew him would later write, "to yield a single point, in controversy, where he feels assured of his position."[13] He published two open letters of his own, in which he not only denied Campbell's accusations but heaped invective upon him, insinuating that, if anyone was a liar, it was Campbell.[14] Whitley sarcastically thanked the "asinine" Campbell for disavowing a connection to him, saying that this was "an immense favor." He claimed to have evidence "in my possession" to prove his ownership of Campbell's business, and warned the competitor to "mind his own business, keep quiet, go to church regularly, and above all, *pay his honest debts!*"

This was probably a bluff; it seemed to work, though. Campbell fired off two more letters in the *Boston Herald*, but seemed hesitant to prolong the matter by taking Whitley to court. Campbell concluded his rebuttal with a final offer to Whitley: "I am ready to meet him face-to-face…and prove any assertions and brand him with his infamy, or failing to do so I am willing to bear all he can heap upon me."

Whitley never seems to have accepted this challenge. Instead, he declared in print that he would not "demean" himself by further dispute with Campbell, and, in the spring of 1857, left Massachusetts. He was bound for the Kansas settlement named in honor of the wealthy antislavery Boston businessman, Amos Lawrence, who had sponsored the first Free State emigrant groups in 1854. Whitley promised his new wife he would send for her once he got settled.[15]

Whitley did not have to shoot John Doy on that day in January 1859. Surrounded and outnumbered, the abolitionist and his companions surrendered. The "border ruffians," as Missouri-based raiders were known in Kansas, tied up John and Charles Doy, and W. F. Clough, the neighbor who had aided them by driving the second wagon, and packed them off to Missouri, where they were jailed and indicted for slave-stealing. One of the thirteen African Americans the Doy party had been attempting to take to free territory managed to escape; the others, though, wound up in the custody of slaveholders in Missouri who claimed them, or were sold to slave traders and taken to New Orleans.

For his part, Whitley slipped back into Lawrence after the ambush and resumed operating his eatery as if nothing had happened. He told no one what had really gone on prior to the Doy expedition: two slave catchers from Missouri had been scouting Lawrence in disguise for weeks. They had a clandestine meeting with their paid informers in the town a few days before the Doy expedition departed. Whitley had joined the conspiracy in return for a share of the bounty. And he had exploited contacts among Lawrence's black population to learn the details of Doy's plan, which he and his coconspirators then communicated to their confederates on the other side of the Missouri line, before Whitley ultimately joined them on the road outside town. Whitley felt perfectly confident that none of this damning information would ever come to light, because the Doys would soon be lynched or imprisoned in Missouri. True, the Missourians had released W. F. Clough, the driver of the second wagon, after only a couple of days in jail; he had promptly returned to Lawrence. That was no reason for Whitley to worry, however.

He had made a point of ingratiating himself with Clough during the kidnapping, by protecting him from more violent members of the Missouri gang. In addition, before turning him loose, the Missourians had paid Clough fifty dollars for his silence, possibly at Whitley's recommendation.

Whitley had not reckoned with the possibility Clough might double-cross him. When that erstwhile member of the Doy party got back to Lawrence, the town was in an uproar over the ambush and kidnapping, with many citizens convinced that the attack had been an inside job, and crying for violent retaliation. Remorseful, fearful of being targeted by the mob, or both, Clough identified Whitley as one of the men who had ambushed Doy's party.

On February 1, 1859, Whitley found himself under arrest on charges of kidnapping and highway robbery. During a preliminary hearing that day at the court in Lawrence, Clough testified in copious detail about Whitley's role in the ambush. Authorities produced Clough's stolen gun, which they had found hidden under Whitley's pillow at his home. The judge ordered Whitley held on $500 bond, pending trial.

A day later, local officials in Lawrence brought the prisoner to a meeting of the Lawrence town council—attended by an angry crowd of citizens.[16] Many in the assembly had survived an attack by pro-slavery forces in 1856 that left much of Lawrence a smoking ruin. Some of them, in turn, had joined John Brown and his sons in a bloody retaliatory raid against a pro-slavery settlement, Pottawatomie Creek. It was, in short, a vehemently antislavery crowd, embittered by horrific conflict, and accordingly eager to vent its fury on Whitley.

Perhaps thinking that he could talk his way out of this predicament, just as he filibustered R. M. Campbell back in East Cambridge, or perhaps just following his argumentative instincts, Whitley demanded a chance to speak in his own defense. The antislavery Kansans refused; one leaped atop a table and called for the meeting to declare itself a jury and try him on the spot. Someone else slammed the doors shut to prevent Whitley's escape. But the cries to hang the spy subsided when a member of the gathering pointed out, amid the chaos, that the court was still working on Whitley's case. Under the circumstances, a journalist present later reported, "many thought it would be improper at that time to lynch him."[17] As a compromise, the assembly appointed a committee to take Whitley's confession, then adjourned.

Hiram C. Whitley was not about to confess to anything. He posted the bond and fled Lawrence, for Pikes Peak, the mountainous region six hundred miles to the west, which was then still part of the Kansas Territory, and the scene of the most frantic gold rush to hit the North American continent since the California frenzy a decade earlier. Whitley hid out among prospectors and land speculators for the next six months, until he got word that it might be safe to come back to eastern Kansas and rejoin Catherine, his wife. She had arrived in Lawrence a few months after he did.

In late July, meanwhile, John Doy had broken out of jail in Missouri, aided by ten abolitionists from Lawrence, who rode across the border to extract him. The daring escape made headlines across the country.

Whitley, however, had not heard the news. On a hot afternoon in August 1859, as he was passing through Lawrence—probably planning to retrieve Catherine and move with her to another Kansas town more sympathetic to slavery, or to Missouri—a burly man with a thick black beard approached him on a downtown street.[18]

It was John Doy, burning with rage and bent on revenge. Doy tackled Whitley, stuck a revolver in his face, and told him he could either come clean or die.

Cornered, Whitley finally told Doy and a hastily assembled committee of Lawrence antislavery leaders about the plot to ambush the Doys and their African American charges the previous January. To be sure, he minimized his own role, identifying instead two other Lawrence men as masterminds of the conspiracy. The first was the town's former postmaster, who had indeed shown his true pro-slavery colors by helping to ambush Doy and deliver him to Missouri—then remained permanently in the latter state. The second was a less prominent man, an emigrant from New Hampshire who had lived in the abolitionist stronghold for years.

Doy and the others already knew about the postmaster's betrayal and defection, but were surprised to hear about the New Hampshire man. They refused to believe he had deceived them. They had watched with their own eyes as he helped the African Americans raise money, gather tools and provisions, and load John Doy's wagons.[19]

Whitley insisted he could prove the New Hampshire man's duplicity, if they would simply search his home. They would find a stack of letters containing orders from the Missourians in his trunk, Whitley said. Sure enough, when Doy and his friends went to the man's house, they discovered the documents. Confronted with the incriminating letters, the New Hampshire–born infiltrator confessed, including the shocking detail that he had treacherously bade the Doy convoy's African American passengers farewell as they pulled out of Lawrence, knowing full well what was in store for them. The abolitionists told him and Whitley to get out of Lawrence, and never come back.[20]

Hiram C. Whitley was lucky to be alive. If he wanted to stay that way, though, he would have to find a new home, preferably far away. As the now-admitted betrayer and kidnapper of abolitionist whites and freedom-bound blacks, he would be persona non grata in Lawrence, or any other antislavery settlement in Kansas. Having saved his skin by fingering the slave catchers' agent in the abolitionists' camp, he was now an informer in the eyes of the pro-slavery faction, and therefore not welcome in their Kansas and Missouri strongholds, either. Going back to Massachusetts, and Catherine's family, would certainly take him a long distance from all that trouble. Alas, people there might remember his ugly dispute with R. M. Campbell.

Whitley, accompanied by Catherine, headed south, for a fresh start in a part of the country where word of his involvement in the Doy case had almost certainly not yet reached: New Orleans. The port on the Gulf of Mexico was shot through with crime and corruption, and prone to deadly yellow fever epidemics. Yet New Orleans was more economically vibrant and more cosmopolitan than any other Southern city. And it offered Whitley another advantage, if news of his dubious conduct in Kansas ever did catch up with him. Southern states generally snubbed Northern requests to extradite slave catchers accused of illicitly trying to capture free blacks.

Taking up residence with his wife on St. Peter Street in the French Quarter, Whitley operated throughout 1860 as a kind of itinerant merchant, peddling his wares, mostly sugar and molasses, among the cotton plantations and steamboat landings that lined the Red and Mississippi Rivers, between New Orleans and Shreveport.[21] By this time, the entire United States was coming apart over the same conflict between pro- and antislavery forces that had bloodied Kansas during Whitley's time there. Louisiana, with its vast cotton and sugar plantations worked by thousands of enslaved African Americans, belonged firmly in the pro-slavery camp. Roughly a year after Whitley's arrival, on January 22, 1861, a convention of white politicians declared that the state would secede from the Union.

THE KANSAS NARRATIVE,

By

"A Plain, Unvarnished Tale."

When Hiram C. Whitley betrayed and ambushed abolitionist John Doy and his party of escaping African Americans, he had no idea Doy would not only avoid lynching or prison in Missouri, but would also publish a memoir of his experience.

Whitley stayed in the city, perhaps still fearing that his Kansas past would come back to haunt him if he tried to flee to federally held territory, as many other Northerners living in New Orleans had done, or perhaps unable to afford the trip. He voiced rebel sympathies and from time to time drilled with various military companies being assembled to wage war on behalf of the fledgling Confederacy—but each time his unit was about to be sent into battle, he managed to avoid service by feigning a disability.

For her part, Catherine felt as if she were under house arrest during rebel rule. Whitley, too, was under stress; so much so, perhaps, that he lost his temper and beat a fellow citizen with a cane, which landed him in Orleans Parish court on a charge of assault and battery "without due provocation."[22]

Fortunately for both of the Whitleys, the United States military reoccupied New Orleans before Catherine could succumb to depression, and while Hiram was still out on bail. The day the Union forces arrived—May 1, 1862—Catherine sat by her window gazing at a flagpole atop the United States mint, anticipating joyfully the national banner's reappearance.[23]

Her husband, however, was in Shreveport—the Confederate-ruled Red River steamboat hub seven hundred miles to the north—ostensibly on business. When Shreveport's authorities learned that the Union had retaken New Orleans, they immediately hatched a plan to prevent a Union riverine advance on their city: volunteers would drive the one-hundred-sixty-two-foot-long side-wheel steamboat, *Starlight*, a few dozen miles south along the Red River and scuttle it, turning the submerged vessel into a barrier against Union boats.[24]

Whitley signed up for the mission, but not because he wanted to help it succeed. Instead he saw a chance to get back to New Orleans, Catherine, and whatever opportunities might be in the offing under its new Union authorities. On the first night aboard the side-wheeler, as his supposed rebel comrades slept, Whitley stole a lifeboat and quietly paddled it away, aided by two of the *Starlight*'s African American crew; he promised to protect them in return for help reaching what was now the largest city in the South held by the forces of Abraham Lincoln.

Traveling on the water at night, sleeping in bushes on the riverbanks by day, Whitley and the two black men made it to New Orleans in less than a week, whereupon Whitley walked to the United States Army's makeshift headquarters at the St. Charles Hotel and presented himself as a source of intelligence on the rebel-held areas to the north.

He was in luck: the commanding general, Benjamin Butler, hailed from Massachusetts, Whitley's sometime home state. These common origins helped Whitley gain an audience, and to overcome the inevitable suspicions that he might be a Confederate double agent. To win the Union military's full confidence, however, Whitley proposed to put his knowledge of the Red River steamboat trade to work for them. The specific act of sabotage he suggested was audacious: to cross rebel lines at Alexandria, Louisiana, a commercial center on the Red River, two hundred miles northwest of New Orleans, and hijack the *New Falls City*, a three-hundred-foot steamboat that the Confederates were using to transport men and supplies.

Far-fetched though it seemed, Butler approved the mission, promising Whitley $20,000 if he succeeded, and warning him the Union would not come to his rescue if he ran into trouble. Retracing the same route he had just traveled to escape rebel territory, Whitley soon reached Alexandria, disguised as a rebel soldier and accompanied by a steamboat engineer from New Orleans whose assignment it would be to drive the boat once Whitley commandeered it. For several days, Whitley talked his way into the confidence of the watchman on the *New Falls City*, while his engineer companion lay low in a safe house. Finally, one of Whitley's drinking sessions with the watchman ended with the latter unconscious, as Whitley had planned. He summoned the engineer—who suddenly realized he had no idea how to drive the huge side-wheeler.

Whitley fumed but did not panic. Continuing to pose as a rebel, and drawing on his prewar experience trading along the Red River, he offered to help move a shipment of supplies to flooded-out rebel villages east of Alexandria. A merchant accepted Whitley's offer and gratefully arranged the necessary safe-conduct documents. Whitley then used the passes, not to resupply the Confederates, as promised, but to move through rebel-held territory between Alexandria and the Union lines, where he slipped across no-man's-land and returned to New Orleans.

When Whitley appeared again at the St. Charles Hotel, Butler laughed heartily at his tale. Disappointed Whitley had not brought him the steamboat, he was nevertheless impressed with the intelligence Whitley gained on his trip, and with the knack for survival and steady nerves he had demonstrated in procuring it.[25]

The general promptly assigned Whitley to the staff of the United States Army's provost marshal, the officer in charge of fighting crime, suppressing rebel sentiment, and ferreting out Confederate spies and saboteurs. During the second half of 1862, Whitley operated as Butler's all-purpose spy among the civilian population. When rebel sympathizers tried to hide silver and jewels in the city's cemeteries' unique aboveground tombs, protecting their wealth from Yankee taxation, Whitley exposed their plot and broke up a fake funeral before the "mourners" had time to "entomb" a coffin filled with necklaces, spoons, and candlesticks. When thousands of New Orleans residents claimed to be French or British citizens, entitled to protection against the Union from those foreign sovereigns, Whitley blew open a safe containing the city voting records proving they were Americans.

For the first time in his career, Whitley had to contend with counterfeiters. In October 1862 the city saw a surge in fake railroad tickets, suspected to be the handiwork of a gang led by Nicolas Gregorio, a Sicilian immigrant, and Andrew Feeley, a recent escapee from state prison. Whitley arrested one of their street dealers with phony tickets in his possession and offered the suspect his freedom if he would set up a meeting to buy more tickets from Gregorio with Whitley, in disguise, as his companion. As soon as the purchase was completed, Whitley arrested the gangster. In due course, he discovered an entire factory for the counterfeit tickets; Gregorio and Feeley were sentenced to two years each in prison.[26]

Not all such cases ended in convictions. When counterfeit two-dollar bills began to circulate, Whitley traced the phony money's origins all the way to General Benjamin Butler's own private secretary, an expert forger—whom Butler allowed to go free, sparing himself an embarrassing scandal.

And in New Orleans, for the first time, Hiram C. Whitley killed a man.[27]

Louisiana's state prison at Baton Rouge had been in the cross fire between Union and Confederate troops during 1862; many prisoners, including Andrew Feeley, managed to escape amid the confusion and destruction. After his success against the counterfeiters, the provost marshal assigned Whitley to capture an especially dangerous escapee, Pedro Capdeville, a convicted burglar, who was rumored to have killed fourteen men during his outlaw career.

By noon on January 6, 1863, Whitley had tracked a man he believed to be Capdeville to a French Quarter restaurant. Interrupting the suspect's lunch, Whitley announced himself as an officer of the law. The two struggled, and Whitley spotted what looked like a knife in his quarry's hand. He pulled back; the suspect broke free. Whitley fired his revolver at the man's back as the latter sprinted out the restaurant's back door. Following as fast as he could in the muddy unpaved street, Whitley cried out "Stop him! Stop him!" and fired again, from half a block away. The suspect fell, badly wounded. Whitley handcuffed him and took him to the city's Charité Hospital.

Whitley had escaped a sticky situation, but it was not clear that he had actually shot Pedro Capdeville. As he lay dying at the hospital, the man protested that he was a victim of mistaken identity. His name was Jean Louis Stella, he said, and he was a native of France. Stella was indeed the name he had given when Whitley, dressed in plain clothes, first demanded he identify himself in the restaurant. Just before he expired, the man admitted he had done prison time for larceny, but insisted he knew Capdeville well from his stint behind bars and that the latter had gone away to join the Confederate Army.

The shooting, in broad daylight on a busy street, caused an uproar; rebel sympathizers in New Orleans depicted it as yet more evidence of Union oppression. To soothe public opinion, the military authorities organized an inquest, at which three witnesses—the restaurant owner and two former policemen—testified that the man Whitley had killed was Jean Louis Stella *and* Pedro Capdeville. The latter name, they explained, was Stella's alias. With Whitley's quarry now dead and unable to contradict those claims, the detective was cleared of any wrongdoing.

Still, the episode demonstrated the risks to the Army of having agents like Whitley roam the city, serving the military but, as nominal civilians, not formally subject to military discipline. In 1863, another Massachusetts man, General Nathaniel Banks, replaced Butler as the Union commander in New Orleans. Under Banks, the Army decided to enroll Hiram C. Whitley formally in the ranks—as a major. Worried that the rebels might mount an attack on the Crescent City, the Army was recruiting reinforcements at the time, and Whitley's assignment was to train the new 7th Louisiana Volunteer Infantry, drawn mainly from the city's large population of free black and mixed-race men, known as the *gens de couleur libre*, or "free people of color."[28]

A spy, saboteur, and detective with no military experience, Whitley lacked preparation for leading troops. His subordinates, meanwhile, were drawn from a population with a long, proud tradition of self-sufficiency in New Orleans, going back to the city's founding by the French in 1718. One source of that pride was the military service that the Crescent City's free black men had rendered in the American victory at the Battle of New Orleans in 1815.

The only known photograph of Hiram C. Whitley as a United States Army officer during the Union occupation of New Orleans. (*Danforth W. Austin Family Collection*)

The pitfalls of this situation became evident soon after Whitley accepted his commission in July 1863, when three of his new soldiers of color balked at his order to dig latrines. Whitley ordered the men arrested, then instructed a nearby artillery unit to aim its guns at them, from a spot where the detainees could view the cannon pointed in their direction. "You see that battery?" Whitley barked. "It's trained on this camp, and if resistance is offered to my commands, you will all be blown to hell in short order."[29]

He then forced the men's hands behind their backs, and tied them together by the thumbs, holding the three soldiers in that painful position until they agreed to do his bidding. Two quickly yielded, but a third said he would rather die. He fainted in the brutal summer heat as Whitley stood over him.

As word of Whitley's methods spread, dissension rose in the ranks, and Whitley ringed the installation with loyal forces to prevent a mutiny. Finally, lower-ranking white officers came to him with a proposed solution: other soldiers had offered to do the digging he demanded, so there was no need to continue torturing anyone who had balked.

This troubled regiment lasted three months, until the threat of a rebel attack passed and the Army dissolved the unit in October 1863. For a brief time thereafter, Whitley held a provisional commission as a lieutenant colonel, but never actually served in any organized unit at that rank; he resumed working instead as an undercover agent. He repeatedly went on scouting missions in rebel-held territory and bloodied himself again, in a clash between rebel guerrillas and an Illinois cavalry unit that he was guiding through a contested area near Baton Rouge. The skirmish ended with seven Confederates dead.

In 1865, Whitley aided an Army investigation into procurement fraud among the forces headquartered in New Orleans. After the war, he auctioned off a stockpile of surplus federal military supplies in Texas—then returned to Cambridge, where he arrived in 1866, accompanied by Catherine and planning to establish himself in business again, in the hope that, at last, sufficient time had elapsed since his contretemps with R. M. Campbell.

He soon faced accusations that ranged from swindling an apothecary out of his shop to selling fake whiskey and diamonds. Though Whitley avoided criminal liability, local authorities stripped him of his pawnbroker's license. By 1867, Whitley had moved to Washington, looking for government work.[30]

In the nation's capital, his old connection to Benjamin Butler, and the latter's esteem for his abilities as an undercover man, served him well. Having been a member of Congress from Massachusetts before taking a leave from politics to fight the Civil

War, Butler was now back in the House of Representatives as one of the body's leading "radical" proponents of Reconstruction. His letter of recommendation secured Whitley a temporary appointment as a special agent for the Treasury Department, in which capacity he worked as an investigator for the House Republicans' effort, led by Butler, to impeach President Andrew Johnson.

That assignment led to a job interview for Whitley with yet another former Union general who was serving as commissioner of Internal Revenue. Brandishing Butler's recommendation, Whitley boldly declared he had knowledge of the illegal, untaxed whiskey-distilling epidemic that was so badly draining government finances and hampering efforts to pay off the Civil War debt. He offered to devote himself to the federal fight against it, without pay.

It was an audacious gesture, reminiscent of Whitley's initial meeting with Butler in New Orleans five years earlier, in which he had offered to hijack the *New Falls City*. Like that gambit, this one worked.

"I have made up my mind to give you a sixty-day commission, and try you," the commissioner told Whitley. "I want you to go to Kansas."

"Any place will suit me," Whitley instantly replied.[31]

Across the vastness of America, Hiram C. Whitley had traveled a mighty distance since his days at the Western Reserve Seminary. He had struggled for economic gain, on land and sea. He had spied on abolitionists before the Civil War and rebels during the conflict. He had run for his life across the Kansas Territory to Pikes Peak, and gunned down a man who was trying to do the same on the backstreets of New Orleans.

In that time, he had boldly and astutely used deception, or force, or his own undeniable charm, to take advantage of opportunities—and his fellow man. He could be a con artist, and a bully; and those aspects of his character had gotten him into one tight spot after another, then helped get him out.

Yet a young woman of religious principle, Catherine—a believer in high-minded causes like the abolition of slavery and the integrity of the American Union—saw something redeeming in him. She had placed her faith in Hiram C. Whitley, married him, and apparently felt committed enough to him to leave her family home on the Charles River and follow him, from the Great Plains to the Gulf of Mexico.

When it was time to make the most consequential political choice of his era, Whitley had thrown in his lot with the government of the United States, which was not only the winning side in the Civil War, but also the side people like his wife fervently regarded as the right one.

Having emerged from the cataclysm of Civil War larger and more powerful than ever before, the government, led by Abraham Lincoln's Republican Party, faced the enormous challenges of extending its writ, establishing law and order, and ordaining freedom, from the defeated South to the still-unconquered West.

The Republican authorities in Washington were building a nation, and forming a state, all at the same time. These men believed that the same federal legal authority that had been placed in the service of Southern slaveholders—through the Fugitive Slave Act and other measures—could now be turned to the Party of Lincoln's political advantage, and employed for the sake of national unity and human equality.

They did not necessarily know, or care, about every detail of Hiram C. Whitley's career. What they saw in him was someone who could get results.

At the same time, Whitley's amoral attitude toward the great issues of slavery and equality, so evident in his slave-hunting in Kansas and in his treatment of his troops in New Orleans, seemed to be evolving. The cruelty inflicted on enslaved people in Louisiana was so ugly that it could shock even his conscience, and, in one case, spur him to action.

In the first week of July 1863, just as the Union scored pivotal victories at Vicksburg and Gettysburg, James Walkinshow, a plantation overseer in Union-held Lafourche Parish, south of New Orleans, assaulted and stabbed an enslaved African American known as George. The overseer had accused George of working too slowly, then flew into a rage when the black man denied the white man's charge. "The Yankees have spoiled you niggers, but I'll be even with you," Walkinshow roared, reaching for his dagger. Exhausted and bleeding from the stab wound, George escaped to nearby woods, where Walkinshow found him, tied him up, and whipped him. When he had recovered enough to do so, George fled the plantation again and found his way to United States Army headquarters in New Orleans, where he presented his story to a detective on the provost marshal's staff.

That detective was Hiram C. Whitley. He took down the African American's complaint in copious detail, emphasizing the overseer's sadism. He then presented the case to a military court, where Whitley vouched for the black man's word against the white overseer. Walkinshow's lawyer objected that a slave had no right to complain against a free white man, but the military judge instructed him that this principle of Louisiana law had no validity in his court. Walkinshow would have to answer for his abuse of George's rights before the United States Army. The court sentenced him to six months in prison.[32]

3

"He has worked his way through
the labyrinth of lies."

Columbus's newspaper, the *Daily Sun*, had described the Ku Klux Klan as "large and powerful, and conducted upon such a system as to defy detection."[1] As of the moment Hiram C. Whitley's train pulled into the Georgia town on May 3, 1868— more than a month after George W. Ashburn's death—the *Daily Sun*'s claim appeared all too true. The Columbus Klan's secrets remained unexposed, the Republican politician's murder, unpunished.

Whitley strode the five blocks from the Muscogee Depot to Captain William Mills's headquarters at the courthouse, in the center of town. The two-story Greek Revival structure, built from red bricks set atop a massive stone half basement, certainly looked like what it was, at least for the time being: the stronghold of an occupying force. The building stood in the middle of a grassy field, which was dotted with soldiers' white pup tents and surrounded by a low brick wall.[2]

Whitley presented Mills a letter of introduction he obtained from General Meade the previous day, during a brief stopover in Atlanta. With that formality out of the way, Whitley settled in to discuss the case with the Army officer and William H. Reed, the War Department detective who had preceded Whitley to Columbus.

The evidence so far came from two main sources. The first of these was the testimony of African Americans from Columbus, supporters of the murdered Ashburn. On the day or two after the killing, they had come to the courthouse and offered statements to Mills and to Major John Leonard, the local representative of the Freedmen's Bureau, whom they especially trusted in part because he was supervising the construction of a school for black students.[3] Domestic servants of several white men, for example, said they had seen their employers going out in masquerade dress on the night of the murders. These reports, while useful as investigative leads, consisted largely of circumstantial evidence. The black informants had not actually seen the killings.

The second source was sworn testimony at the inquest conducted by the coroner's jury on the morning after the murder. Mills sat through it himself. The key witnesses were the men and women who had been in or near Hannah Flournoy's house at the time of the crime. The first was Flournoy herself. The second was Alexander Bennett, one of Ashburn's fellow white Republicans; he was the houseguest who tried to seize Ashburn's gun for self-defense as the attack began. Next came Amanda Patterson, a seventeen-year-old white female, who used the Flournoy house both as a residence and as a place to receive male visitors who paid her for sex. The fourth eyewitness was Thomas Johnson, an African American who lived in a cabin just a few yards behind Flournoy's place.

Taken together, their accounts created a sketchy, but coherent, narrative of the crime: a gang of masked men broke down Hannah Flournoy's front door; five of them stormed into Ashburn's room, opened fire, and left, joining an unknown number of accomplices who could be seen and heard moving around in the darkness outside the house, cutting off Ashburn's possible escape routes.

Crucially, two of the witnesses—Amanda Patterson and Thomas Johnson—said they had glimpsed the faces of one or more of the intruders, and recognized them. Patterson testified that one man's mask had fallen off, at which point she made eye contact with him and heard him snap, "Damn you, if you tell on me, I'll kill you." Judging by the quality and style of their clothing, Hannah Flournoy added, the intruders seemed to be well-to-do "dandy young gentlemen belonging to Columbus."[4]

The tone and tenor of the inquest suddenly changed when the mayor of Columbus and the Muscogee County prosecutor, both white Democrats, came in, accompanied by two Columbus policemen. The officers stepped forward and told the coroner's jury they had seen a large crowd gathered in a vacant lot outside Hannah Flournoy's shortly before midnight on the night in question. They had even heard the cocking of revolvers. This much corroborated what the first four witnesses had said. In every other detail, however, the police officers' testimony contradicted it. Both denied under oath that they could identify a single person they had seen. Indeed, one claimed he had not noticed whether anyone in the crowd was wearing a mask or other disguise, much less fine clothes, as Hannah Flournoy had insisted.

The prosecutor, a holdover from the local government elected when President Andrew Johnson controlled Reconstruction policy, demanded the initial four witnesses return to explain these discrepancies between their testimony and that of the lawmen. Intimidated, Amanda Patterson stammered out a new, vaguer story, claiming that she had been mistaken when she named the man who had dropped his mask. Alexander Bennett simply declined to say anything one way or the other. Thomas Johnson, the African American neighbor, refused to recant despite the pressure. Hannah Flournoy, however—undoubtedly trying to protect him, and herself—claimed, falsely, that Johnson could not possibly have seen anything because he had never left his cabin the whole night.[5]

Mills watched in disbelief as the coroner's jury accepted this welter of perjury, and issued its verdict that Ashburn had been killed by "persons unknown." He was even more astonished a few nights later when his soldiers intercepted the two police officers as they escorted a group of disguised men to Alexander Bennett's new temporary residence. Their intent, apparently, had been to assassinate this crucial witness.[6]

Whitley quickly surmised that Mills and Reed had a rough idea of the truth, and of who the culprits might be. The question, though, was how to crystallize their facts and logical inferences into hard evidence, capable of identifying named suspects and proving them guilty beyond a reasonable doubt.

Despairing of cooperation from Columbus's whites, Reed thought the best approach would be to build a case on testimony from blacks. African Americans worked in white-owned homes, factories, and fields; in those positions they could hear and see a great deal. For the time being, they might be too intimidated to provide more testimony to the detectives, much less in a public trial. "The great trouble is with the negro witnesses," Reed observed in an April 22 message to General Meade. "They do know, but are afraid to tell what they know."[7] With appropriate incentives, however, especially offers of protection from the Army, that could change.

Whitley saw the situation differently—more audaciously. African American testimony could bolster the evidence here and there, and it was in black citizens' self-interest to provide it, assuming that their legitimate fears of reprisal could be addressed. Yet no black person, not even Hannah Flournoy, had witnessed the actual shooting; none possessed detailed inside knowledge of the plot.

Therefore, Whitley concluded, the investigators would have to do what had so far seemed impossible: penetrate the conspiracy, and induce some of its members to turn state's evidence. They would have to attack the Ku Klux Klan's code of silence head-on, and break it.

Whitley focused his blue eyes on Mills and Reed and told them that it was time to be ruthless: if it was impossible to get anyone to talk in Columbus, then they should arrest both suspects and material witnesses and take them for interrogation to a different place, of the investigators' choosing, far away from the Klan-dominated town. In this secure location, Hiram C. Whitley would be in charge, not white supremacist terrorists, and "we could handle them in such a manner as to give sufficient evidence to convict them," as the detective explained in a telegram to Meade on May 4. "I sincerely believe, should these measures be carried out with severity and dispatch, that the whole affair would be brought to light."[8]

This plan obviously did not correspond to the usual norms of criminal procedure, according to which suspects could be arrested only after authorities had established some basis for doing so. Whitley took it for granted, however, that the Reconstruction Acts gave the Army authority to carry out his plan—to dispense with warrants and formal charges, and transport civilians under military guard to a military prison, where they would be held incommunicado. His plan even contemplated rearresting some of the men whom Captain Mills's company had previously detained in Columbus, then granted bail. Whitley assumed that the Army would allocate the scarce resources necessary for guarding and provisioning his proposed interrogation center. What's more, Whitley assumed that the Army would trust him, a civilian who came highly recommended, but whom General Meade and the rest of the Army hierarchy in Georgia barely knew.

It was not clear what this intense, self-assured detective, fresh from a job breaking up illegal distilleries out in Kansas, meant by handling detainees with "severity," though the word certainly had ominous connotations.[9] The Reconstruction Acts, under which Meade and his subordinates did indeed exercise power to detain, charge, and try civilians, specifically provided "that all persons put under military arrest by virtue of this act shall be tried without unnecessary delay, and no cruel or unusual punishment shall be inflicted." This language had been added to placate senators wary of the consequences of military rule for civil liberties.[10]

Still, the detective's logic was sound. The Reconstruction Acts intended to fill the chaotic postwar South's vacuum of legitimate civilian law enforcement with a measure of military justice, much as military provost courts had done in New Orleans during the Civil War. The Freedmen's Bureau, an agency of the War Department heavily staffed by Army officers, had empaneled military commissions to try crimes committed by whites against blacks.

Meade consulted his military lawyer and Mills. Both supported Whitley's plan, the lawyer because he could see nothing in the Reconstruction Acts to forbid it—Mills because he saw no realistic alternative. Though reluctant at first to sign off on the arrest of more than "two or three of the most prominent" suspects, Meade eventually agreed to take more people into custody. In a May 6 telegram to Mills, he authorized the detention of an initial group of up to seven suspects and witnesses identified by Whitley. Of those, the Army actually seized four—two suspects and two witnesses.

On May 14, the troops bundled these detainees, accompanied by Whitley and Reed, aboard a heavily guarded eastbound train.[11]

Their destination was Fort Pulaski, the United States Army's military prison on Cockspur Island, a flat, sandy scrap of land in the mouth of the Savannah River, fifteen miles east of the eponymous Georgia city. Meade had personally recommended the site to Whitley, and, given the detective's purposes, it was an appropriate choice. No one could get on or off Cockspur Island without the Army's knowledge. Fort Pulaski itself was a pentagonal structure whose walls, made from a total of twenty-five million red bricks, were eleven feet thick. The bastion was bristling with cannon and surrounded by a moat. It contained a series of four-by-seven-foot cells, in which the United States Army had held Confederate prisoners during the Civil War, after recapturing the place from the rebels.[12]

Over the next two weeks, detainees flowed from Columbus to Fort Pulaski, where Whitley kept them for the most part in solitary confinement, their guards under strict orders to allow no communication among prisoners, or between them and the outside world. Only two people—Whitley, and his detective partner, William H. Reed—enjoyed total access to the prisoners in their cells. By order of General Meade, the detectives had carte blanche regarding the detainees and their treatment.

Even his detractors acknowledged a certain relentlessness to Whitley that made him, if not exactly charming, then at least uncommonly persuasive. A colleague would later describe this quality as his "magnetic power," the "wondrous gift of controlling the passions, the inclinations, the thoughts, the secrets of other men."[13] Drawing on this trait, Whitley cajoled and threatened the detainees. He would place previously isolated prisoners in a cell together, then eavesdrop on their furtive conversations from a nearby hiding place, or through the walls of an empty next-door cell. He confronted them with evidence of their guilt, telling them they would never again see the light of day unless they confessed. He promised that if they did confess, and agreed to testify at the military commission, he could guarantee them a chance for a new life under the government's protection.

At first, Whitley's efforts produced little in the way of new information. "They are hard cases," he wrote Meade on May 18, "and nothing can be learned from them *with their consent*."[14] He asked for more time, emphasizing that if "we can get the right persons here, we can get evidence sufficient to convict them." He reminded the general that Amanda Patterson, the seventeen-year-old part-time prostitute who lived in Hannah Flournoy's house, could be the key to the case. She had witnessed practically the entire crime. At the inquest she had identified perpetrators by name, before recanting under pressure from Columbus's pro-Klan authorities.

"The woman Amanda...would be the most important one to bring here," Whitley wrote, "for we know she was there, and we believe she possesses the facts and will blow as soon as she is out of control of the rebels."

Patterson had avoided being taken to Fort Pulaski with the first group of detainees by claiming to be sick when Captain Mills's men called for her. Since she was a witness, not a suspect, and vulnerable to pressure from the Klan conspirators, the soldiers did not insist. This exercise of restraint was "all very well," Whitley informed the general, "but ought not to be allowed at this stage of the game. We want her bad." The detective wired a similar plea to Captain Mills, urging him to send Patterson to Fort Pulaski, as well as two suspects they had tried and failed to track down during the first round of detentions. Mills must "do it at once," Whitley asked, "as delays are dangerous at this stage of the case."[15]

Whitley was right: even as the detective wrote these messages, the Klan and its allies in Columbus were plotting to silence Amanda Patterson.[16]

With the Army having taken charge of the town and detectives prowling about, the conspirators understood that it would be risky to spill any more blood. They opted instead for a more subtle plan: manipulating forty-eight-year-old Republican Alexander Bennett, Patterson's former fellow occupant at Hannah

Flournoy's house, into getting the seventeen-year-old female out of Georgia.

Bennett had seen the entire crime. After George W. Ashburn refused to give him his gun, but before the Klan killers entered Ashburn's room, Bennett had ducked behind a rack of clothing; he watched the murder from this hiding place. The next day, he told Captain Mills what he saw, and he named several of the intruders.

Yet when it came time to testify publicly at the coroner's inquest, Bennett quickly lost his nerve. He balked at repeating the details—thus proving that he could be easily intimidated. He demonstrated this susceptibility again six weeks later, on May 11, when two of Columbus's leading citizens, cotton merchant William D. Chipley, the chairman of the Muscogee County Democratic Party, and Elisha Kirkscey, the county physician who had inspected George W. Ashburn's body at the inquest, arranged to have the sheriff arrest Bennett on a trumped-up charge: failing to pay for whiskey delivered to the little shop where he sold drinks by the glass.

Visiting him in jail, they pumped him for the names of black witnesses who had talked to the Army, and what they had said. They demanded that he give them a list of the white Republicans in town, plus Ashburn's private letters. The documents, they assured Bennett, would be returned to him if he helped Chipley and the Democrats persuade Captain Mills to return power to elected Democrats in Columbus.

If Bennett did not cooperate, they warned, he would rot in jail. If he did what they said, they could assure his release, and, Chipley added, he would have nothing to fear from "the Ku Kluxes."

Bennett refused to give them the list of white Republicans, but he capitulated to all their other demands. He told a jailer where to find Ashburn's letters: in a steamer trunk back at Bennett's permanent lodgings. After the jailer retrieved them and gave them to Chipley, the cotton merchant paid Bennett's fine, and the latter went free.

Just nine days later, the thoroughly frightened Bennett was approached at the barbershop by another cotton merchant, who asked if he knew that one of the men rumored to be on Captain Mills's arrest list, Robert Daniel, had been one of Amanda Patterson's regular visitors. That would certainly make it easy—too easy—for her to identify him, if the Army took her to Fort Pulaski. Bennett said he had seen Daniel call on Patterson, from time to time. The cotton merchant wondered aloud whether it might not be better, under the circumstances, to get Amanda out of town. Bennett said he didn't know. Well, there would be a lot of money in it for whoever persuaded her to go, the cotton merchant remarked as they parted.

Later that day, undoubtedly anxious about what was happening, Bennett sought solace in a downtown bar. A local banker found him there and brought up the same proposition that the cotton merchant had mentioned at the barbershop: a handsome reward for anyone who helped persuade Amanda Patterson to get out of Columbus.

Bennett did not have to be told a third time. On the night of May 20, he showed up at the Flournoy house, drunk and frightened. Amanda Patterson was still living there, and she was suffering, not from any physical ailment, but from paralyzing fear. Bennett pleaded with her to leave town with him. If they stayed, he told her, "the Ku Kluxes" would kill them. On the other hand, he said, if the "Yankees" took them to Fort Pulaski, they would surely die there. Their best option was to get out altogether. Rich men in Columbus had promised to bankroll a getaway, he said, if she would just agree to leave town, make a new start elsewhere—and never testify.

Amanda Patterson was still contemplating Bennett's offer two days later—May 22—when General Meade issued an order to Captain Mills. Whitley was right, he had concluded, the young woman should be sent to Fort Pulaski without further delay. The next day, soldiers took her into custody in Columbus, along with Robert Daniel and another suspected conspirator, and placed all three aboard a Savannah-bound train.

The Army had not acted a moment too soon.

Whitley had not only anticipated Amanda Patterson's vulnerability in Columbus, he had also formed the right intuition as to how the young woman would respond when removed from the threatening surroundings of her hometown. Lonely and austere as it was, Fort Pulaski was the first place in Georgia where men with power—Whitley and his military backers—possessed the ability and the willingness to protect her. The detective ordered this most despised and exploited member of Columbus's white community lodged in one of the few decent rooms at the fort, an officer's spacious quarters, with a view of the sea and a cozy hearth, and assured her that her safety would be guaranteed.

He informed her, less gently, that she would never get out of the fort unless she told him everything she knew about the Ashburn case, and agreed to repeat it under oath before an eventual military commission.[17]

Patterson did tell her story, just as Whitley had predicted. She seemed to be unburdening herself of all the tension that had accumulated during the weeks since Ashburn's murder. She recounted the bloody events at the Flournoy house. And she told Whitley of the lengths to which Alexander Bennett, clearly at the behest of the conspirators, had gone in recent days to persuade her to leave town and not testify.

Patterson let slip the fact that she had been given advance knowledge of the murder plot. A week before the assassination, conspirators had approached her at a doctor's office downtown, telling her they planned to kill the man they called "old Ashburn," and asking her to help them gain access to Hannah

Flournoy's house. She told Whitley she had begged them to leave her out of it—but she certainly had not taken any steps to warn Ashburn about the plot, mainly because the Klan threatened to kill her if she did. Patterson probably didn't realize it at the time, but this admission gave Whitley additional leverage. If she tried to back out of her deal to testify, he could have the Army charge her as an accomplice.

Most important, Amanda Patterson named names. The men who tried to persuade her to join the plot included two of those who later tried to pressure Alexander Bennett into taking her out of town: twenty-eight-year-old William Dudley Chipley, the chairman of the local Democratic Party and twenty-nine-year-old Elisha Kirkscey, the Muscogee County physician. Both men were Confederate veterans; Chipley's military résumé was especially dramatic. He was a former lieutenant colonel in a Confederate unit from Kentucky, wounded at the battles of Shiloh and Chickamauga and taken prisoner near Atlanta in the waning days of the war. Upon his release from the Union prison at Johnson's Island, Ohio, in mid-1865, he settled in Columbus, and married the daughter of a planter from Phenix City, Alabama, just across the Chattahoochee River.[18] "We are going to kill old Ashburn the night of the day he speaks" at the Temperance Hall meeting, Chipley had told Patterson.

She had also seen Chipley and Kirkscey at the Flournoy house on the night of the murder. Both were masked, but Patterson knew the prominent men of the town well enough to recognize them even in disguise. In addition, there was the one intruder who had accidentally dropped his mask: Christopher Columbus "Lum" Bedell, another Democratic businessman. He hissed a death threat to Patterson as the two made eye contact at the dimly lit murder scene. Bedell had repeated that threat to her in the weeks since. And Alexander Bennett had told Patterson "Lum" Bedell was one of the wealthy men who would pay for them to get out of town.

★ ★ ★

Patterson confirmed that three men the United States Army had arrested and locked up at Fort Pulaski were, as Whitley suspected, among those who had actually fired their weapons at George W. Ashburn on the night of the crime. One, James W. Barber, also a Confederate veteran and the Democratic clerk of the Muscogee County court, was detained with the first batch of four men to reach Fort Pulaski on May 15. The other two, George Betts, a twenty-three-year-old former policeman who worked as a fireman on the train that ran from Columbus to Montgomery, Alabama, and Robert Daniel, had been rounded up and transported to Fort Pulaski with Patterson.

After they had been at the fort about a month, during which time they had proven resistant to Whitley's interrogation methods, the Army ordered Betts and Daniel transferred to the McPherson Barracks, General Meade's headquarters in Atlanta, where several rooms had been converted to holding cells. Indeed, as of early June, the upper-class suspects Patterson had named—Chipley, Kirkscey, and Bedell—had been arrested and shipped to the McPherson Barracks, as well.

Chipley requested that Daniel, who not only worked for him at his cotton brokerage but also rented a room in his house, be allowed to stay with him, Kirkscey, and Bedell. They occupied a relatively commodious cell, which the Army granted these wealthy detainees in return for a cash bond.[19] This special favor undoubtedly also reflected the fact that Chipley had friends in high places. He had been raised in Lexington, Kentucky, the son of the city's leading physician. Since childhood, he had been close to a Democratic member of the House of Representatives from Kentucky, James B. Beck. Chipley had sent Representative Beck a letter claiming he had been "arrested and imprisoned without cause, by order of General Meade." Beck was a staunch white supremacist who called Reconstruction a scheme "to place the white men of the south under the domination of the negro."[20] Beck had Chipley's letter read aloud by the clerk of the House, and demanded to know under what authority the United States Army had arrested Chipley and his fellow Klan suspects.[21]

Chipley's gesture of favoritism toward Daniel was an obvious attempt to assure that he would not testify against him and the other ringleaders. Whitley, though, saw it as an opportunity to influence the man Chipley and his friends did not invite into their nice quarters: George Betts. "They're leaving you to be hung [sic] because you're poor," he told Betts. The big shots wanted it that way, Whitley added, because, once Betts hanged, he could never testify against them, and they would go free.[22]

Betts wavered. Whitley allowed Betts a visit from his father, reminding him, as he spoke with the older man, "the halter is still around your neck." The detective insisted that the well-to-do conspirators were planning to buy their way to freedom, while he took the fall.

Betts finally cracked—the first of the actual shooters to do so. He felt that Whitley, for the most part, was treating him as a friend. He agreed to testify for the prosecution in return for a guarantee of protection.

Betts told Whitley that Kirkscey had circulated through Columbus for weeks prior to the murder, offering not only him but several other men between fifty and a hundred dollars each if they would help kill Ashburn, not a dime of which, he noted bitterly, had yet been paid to him. Betts provided details of how the squad of masked men assembled in a vacant lot across the street from Hannah Flournoy's house before midnight, just as their leaders—Chipley, Kirkscey, and Bedell—had instructed. He recalled that a particularly motivated member of the mob, former Confederate soldier Robert Hudson, had cried out, "we'll give him hell," as they set out for the Flournoy place. Hudson was also the one who shouted, "there's the damn shit," when Ashburn opened the door to his candlelit bedroom.

And it was Robert Hudson who had kneeled on the floor to fire the mortal shot between the prostrate Ashburn's eyes.

Perhaps the most stunning information Betts provided was his revelation that the assassination conspiracy extended into Captain Mills's very own United States Army company.

Sergeant Charles Marshall, a twenty-seven-year-old Union Civil War veteran from New Jersey, had fraternized with Columbus's white Democrats almost from the moment the unit arrived in town. He shared their disdain for Reconstruction and the rights of African Americans, and was "highly thought of by our citizens," as a white supremacist newspaper put it.[23] In March 1868, at about the time of Nathan Bedford Forrest's visit, Kirkscey had confided to Marshall that he was planning to assassinate Ashburn. Marshall eagerly agreed to take part, in return for a promise of money, and a home in Columbus after his service commitment expired at the end of the year.

On the afternoon of March 30, the sergeant received a package at his quarters, containing a pasteboard mask and written directions to the assassination party's rendezvous point. Marshall sneaked away from the base to a downtown bar, where he fortified himself with drink—and got into a fight with a group of black men. George W. Ashburn arrived at the scene and broke up the altercation, upbraiding Marshall for mistreating the African Americans. Ashburn threatened to report him to Captain Mills, whereupon the sergeant slapped Ashburn and spat in his face.[24]

By the time he reached the vacant lot near Hannah Flournoy's house just before midnight, Marshall was furious at the Republican politician. Other conspirators handed him a gray English walking coat and a pair of trousers to wear over his blue Army uniform. Moments later, Marshall barged to the front of the mob, where he stood shoulder to shoulder with four of Columbus's white supremacists and fired his pistol at Ashburn.

The men on whose behalf he acted later rewarded the Army

sergeant with gifts including a solid gold pocket watch and one hundred dollars in cash, the latter presented to him by the mayor of Columbus. In the weeks following Ashburn's death, Marshall made little effort to conceal his political sympathies, going so far as to assist the Democrats at the April election by trying to deceive illiterate freedmen into casting ballots marked for the party of white supremacy. Captain Mills demoted him for this and, as further punishment, sent the sergeant on a month's unpaid furlough to his home in New Jersey.

The Army arrested Sergeant Marshall upon his return from furlough in late May. Whitley confronted him with George Betts's confession—and with the fact that Betts had agreed to name Marshall as one of the shooters, in return for immunity from prosecution. Marshall could have the same deal, Whitley told him, but only if he, too, told the truth. Otherwise, he would have to take his chances as a defendant. The sergeant resisted for three days, until—worn down by the detective and, he later asserted, plagued by his own conscience—Marshall confirmed everything that George Betts and Amanda Patterson had said.[25]

He supplied a chilling new detail: Elisha Kirkscey and "Lum" Bedell were the two men who looked into Ashburn's room after the shooting to verify that the bullets had struck their intended target.

By the final week of June, Whitley had assembled a powerful case for the military prosecutors, the heart of which would be the testimony of two shooters, George H. Betts and Sergeant Charles Marshall, and two eyewitnesses from within Hannah Flournoy's house, Amanda Patterson and Alexander Bennett. Whitley had arrested the latter in Columbus on June 1 and sent him to Fort Pulaski. Bennett had been a troublesome witness from the beginning of the case; immediately after Ashburn's murder he had told Captain Mills what had happened, then, fearing the Klan, he had prevaricated under oath before the coroner's jury inquest. Most recently, of course, he had agreed under Klan pressure to try to induce Amanda Patterson to flee. Intent on ending Bennett's evasions once and for all, Whitley and Reed told him that he had to cooperate or else he would be charged for trying to spirit Patterson away, and, as Whitley told him, "rot" in military confinement. Bennett capitulated.[26]

On June 27 General Meade approved formal murder charges against twelve men, nine of whom the United States Army had managed to locate and arrest: William D. Chipley, Elisha J. Kirkscey, and Christopher Columbus Bedell, who organized the plot; James W. Barber, William A. Duke, and Robert Hudson, who had actually fired at Ashburn; and Alva C. Roper, James L. Wiggins, and Robert A. Wood. Roper was in the mob that surrounded the house and prevented Ashburn's escape. Wiggins and Wood had staked out the Temperance Hall rally on the evening of March 30, to alert the others when Ashburn left. They had also supplied the group with masks and overcoats.

All of these men, the indictment said, had combined "feloniously, unlawfully, willfully and of their malice aforethought… to kill and murder" the leading Republican politician in Columbus.[27]

Hiram C. Whitley had proved that the Ku Klux Klan was not impenetrable after all.

General George G. Meade was a professional soldier not known as particularly sympathetic to the Republicans. Indeed, President Andrew Johnson had installed him as commander of the military district encompassing Alabama, Florida, and Georgia on New Year's Day, 1868, because he considered Meade less "radical" than his predecessor, General John Pope. The fact that an officer of Meade's reputation considered the evidence strong enough to warrant indictments caused no reflection or reconsideration among Georgia's white supremacists, however. To the contrary, they rallied even more fervently behind the defendants the state's Democratic newspapers now called "the Columbus Prisoners."

Their campaign to discredit Meade's military commission had two main themes. The first was the immorality of George W. Ashburn, a racial agitator who met his end in a place Democratic journalists insistently described as "a low negro brothel." Though he richly deserved death, the narrative went, the claim it had come at the hands of the Ku Klux Klan, or any group of honorable white men, was sheer Republican propaganda. Far more likely, the politician had been done in by his own party, which found him not much less obnoxious than Democrats did.

The second theme was the illegitimacy of the military-led investigation itself. The Democratic press portrayed the entire process as a "reign of terror," or military "tyranny," devoid of warrants, formal charges, and all the other usual constitutional protections.[28] Hiram C. Whitley had procured testimony against the Columbus Prisoners through force and bribery, under infernal conditions at Fort Pulaski and the McPherson Barracks. As the *Atlanta Constitution* put it in an editorial shortly before the trial began: "The prisoners are under the control of detectives and…they, acting under orders from the head of the army, are responsible for the fiendish malignity and racking tortures visited upon the victims who have fallen into their hands."[29]

Meade could scarcely believe that Georgia's white Democrats would vent their contempt on him, and his investigators, rather than on the people responsible for murdering Ashburn in cold blood. The general took the accusations personally; he was especially incensed because he had already had second thoughts about the grim conditions at Fort Pulaski, and began moving prisoners to well-ventilated wooden buildings at the McPherson Barracks at the end of May. Though the Army initially had to house them in makeshift cells only a few feet wide, they were provided more space as it became available. They ate what Meade's own soldiers did. William D. Chipley had used money and political connections to get especially favorable conditions, including, by the end of the trial, the right to leave the barracks and visit his wife, who complained of illness. "I cannot find from the testimony of the prisoners themselves that any of them have been treated with the slightest degree of cruelty," a *Chicago Tribune* reporter wrote after Meade allowed him to make an extensive tour of the base.[30]

Yet the cries of torture reached all the way to the White House, where President Johnson, newly acquitted of impeachment charges, received a delegation from Columbus, led by the editor of the *Daily Sun*. Ever solicitous of white Southern Democrats, President Johnson ordered General Grant to send an Army colonel, the brother of Secretary of War John Schofield, to investigate the accusations.[31] In response, General Meade asked his subordinates, Whitley included, for written reports on the detainees' treatment.

On June 27 Whitley replied to Meade, in his usual combative tone. The claims of prisoner abuse were "false in every particular, without even a shadow of foundation," he wrote, declaring himself eager "for an opportunity to contradict them; and when this case is tried let the sword of justice fall where it will, I am willing to stand all the bitter curses that have been heaped upon me, and the Government that I serve." The detective appended a letter, signed by the detainees at the McPherson Barracks, and purportedly written by Elisha Kirkscey, which praised Whitley for treating them all "very kindly indeed."[32]

Yet Whitley had to acknowledge that the word *kindly* did not apply to his treatment of all prisoners at all times. There had been, he admitted to General Meade, certain "exceptions."

Among the first four detainees to reach Fort Pulaski on May 15, James W. Barber was the biggest fish by far. Captain Mills had information pointing to Barber as one of the men who fired on Ashburn: a black carriage driver in Columbus had heard a half-drunk Barber boast on the day of the assassination that "we Ku Kluxes" would carry out their threats "in spite of men and hell," and that "Ashburn will be a dead man shorter than any of you have knowledge of."[33]

Whitley coveted Barber's confession. He entered his cell and told him the situation was hopeless. Not only did the Army have proof he was guilty, but, Whitley lied, others in the conspiracy had informed on him. He would be their fall guy—unless he cooperated.

Whitley's interrogations continued in this vein for a day, then two. Even in the isolation of the island fort, he could not make Barber talk.[34] A twenty-six-year-old Confederate infantry veteran, Barber had been severely wounded at Chickamauga in 1863; he saw action at the siege of Petersburg in 1864. These experiences defined his loyalties. The Ku Klux Klan oath of silence cemented them.[35]

Whitley turned to the second of the four men in his custody, a twenty-one-year-old by the name of Wade Stevens. A poor, sporadically employed leather shoe and harness maker, he was not made of the same stern stuff as Barber, and far less clearly implicated in the Ashburn crime. The detective ordered guards to put Stevens into Barber's cell. Then Whitley slipped into the empty one next door, and pressed his ear to the wall.

The pair's barely audible words implied that Barber did indeed possess guilty knowledge of the murder of "that son of a bitch Ashburn," as he referred to the Republican politician. Ashburn wouldn't be the last Republican to meet a bloody end, he swore. Otherwise, Barber astutely avoided incriminating details, and named no higher-ups in the conspiracy. Perhaps suspecting that Whitley was listening, he audibly scoffed at the detective's claim coconspirators had betrayed him. That was a "damned lie," Barber muttered. "All hell couldn't make me confess."[36]

Frustrated, Whitley approached the next two prisoners, who, unlike Barber and Stevens, were African American. Though obviously not complicit in Ashburn's murder, these freedmen were believed to know more about it than they were saying, based on their frequent contacts with the suspected white conspirators. Or so Captain Mills and William H. Reed had informed Whitley in Columbus. One of their sources, however, appears to have been Wade Stevens. And he had a grudge against one of the freedmen, fifty-one-year-old John Wells, for moving in with Stevens's widowed mother and siding with her in a dispute with her son over family property.[37]

Whitley did not know that. Based on what he had been told, Whitley believed Wells might be withholding valuable intelligence. He ordered soldiers to blindfold Wells and take him to a casemate—one of the alcoves in Fort Pulaski's defensive walls through which artillery pieces pointed outward. Wells could hear Whitley and the guards talking in stage whispers about shaving his head, a form of Civil War–era military punishment that was sometimes a prelude to worse. When his blindfold came off, Wells found himself seated in a chair, restrained by two burly soldiers, his hair full of barber's shaving lather—and a cannon pointing at him from across the casemate.

Whitley ordered Wells to talk, threatening to instruct a soldier manning the big gun to fire if Wells refused. Terrified, the freedman implored Whitley to spare his life. He poured out all the details he could remember about where he had been, and what he had done, on the night of the crime. He swore not only that he had no direct knowledge of it, but also that he had no idea who in Columbus might know about it. He begged Whitley to believe him, protesting that he was a churchgoer and would rather die than bear false witness.[38]

After about fifteen minutes, Whitley concluded John Wells was, indeed, telling the truth, and let him go back to his cell. But the detective was not quite finished. Whitley ordered guards to bring him the other black detainee, twenty-two-year-old John Stapler, who had been arrested as he drove his wagon through town. The sudden detention had forced him to abandon both the vehicle and his horse.

Whitley subjected Stapler to a mock execution much like the one he inflicted on Wells. "I have an order from General Meade to put you through," the detective growled, as Stapler stared at the barrel of a cannon. An Army officer, playing along with Whitley, pretended to refuse him permission to kill the prisoner; then "consented" to let him do it if Stapler still didn't cooperate after fifteen minutes. Whitley demanded that Stapler tell him everything he knew about the Ashburn murder. Stapler responded with protestations of ignorance. Whitley accused him of lying to protect "the rebels," but said he would not carry out the execution after all, and instead gave the freedman a day to go back to his cell and think it over.

Four days, not one, went by, with Stapler waiting anxiously in solitary confinement. Then soldiers returned for Stapler— not to deliver him to Whitley for more interrogation, but to place him in a cell with James W. Barber. As Whitley listened in, Barber urged Stapler, "Don't let them scare you. They can't prove anything. They'll let us go in a day or two."

When Stapler emerged from Barber's cell, the young African American insisted that Barber had told him only a few pleasantries, which Whitley knew from his eavesdropping to be untrue. In response, the detective took Stapler to a different part of Fort Pulaski, where the Army maintained punishment cells for soldiers who had committed disciplinary infractions. The sweatboxes, as they were known, consisted of closets built into the walls of the fort, not much wider than a man, and only two feet deep. Whitley forced Stapler into the tiny cell and slammed the iron door, which had a few small holes in it for ventilation. A half hour later, Stapler cried out that he had something to say. He admitted having seen Barber after the Ashburn murder, getting his beard shaved at a downtown barbershop, as if changing his appearance to avoid identification. Whitley, unsatisfied with that revelation, locked Stapler back in.

Thirty-three hours later, on the morning of May 17, Whitley's partner, William H. Reed, found to his amazement that Stapler was still locked in the sweatbox. Reed opened the door, and Stapler stumbled out, exhausted and perspiring, his legs visibly swollen from the heat, but still with nothing more to tell the detectives. Whitley admonished Reed that he should have left Stapler in longer, but Reed and the prison's military commander prevailed on him finally to let the freedman go.

Upon returning to Columbus June 7, John Wells told the story of Whitley's tactics around town, and the Klan's local defenders quickly got wind of it. They obviously had even less regard for the rights and dignity of African Americans than Whitley had demonstrated at Fort Pulaski; but they knew a propaganda bonanza when they saw one. White Democrats took Wells to a lawyer's office downtown and had him swear out an affidavit on June 11 describing the mock execution. The *Daily Sun* published it on June 14.

It did not take long for the rest of the Democratic press, in Georgia and elsewhere in the country, to embroider the story of torture by "infamous 'detectives,'" as one paper described Whitley and Reed.[39] Another Democratic organ claimed that "the dungeons of Fort Pulaski have reverberated with the half-stifled groans and screams of victims of a contrivance brought there for the purpose" of forcing them to confess. This purported torture machine consisted of "a box sufficiently capacious to admit the victim, and then arranged for compression by screws, by which a force could be brought upon the prisoner sufficient 'to squeeze the breath out of him.' It was also provided with a steam apparatus connected with the throttling box by pipes, and upon turning a faucet jets of steam were thrown in, which added materially to the anguish of suffocation."[40]

This was obviously a wild exaggeration, but there was a kernel of truth to it, as Whitley himself recognized by admitting his use of mock executions against Wells and Stapler in his letter to General Meade. Whitley's letter offered the general a twofold explanation. First, he had been led to believe by Captain Mills that the two black men "knew the whole affair," making it seem imperative to get them to talk. Second, Whitley believed, as he put it, that "they could be frightened out of it" and "took this method to scare them."

The detective claimed that he understood what he called "the negro character." Given the intimidation to which they had been subjected under slavery, he continued, they were "naturally more easily frightened into measures than white men."[41]

This was at least a backhanded acknowledgment of slavery's cruelty, which Whitley had witnessed and, in the case of overseer James Walkinshow, helped to punish, during his time in New Orleans. Still, Whitley partook of, and acted on, the racial prejudice and stereotyping of his time, even while trying to penetrate a conspiracy of white racists bent on restoring as much of the old slave system as possible. Even Captain Mills had pressured and threatened some African American witnesses he thought were not being candid with him, in the apparent belief that the only cure for Klan intimidation was to instill countervailing fear. Mills did not go so far as to point a cannon at anyone, however; this was Whitley's own tactic, which he had first used against the *gens de couleur libre* troops in New Orleans. Ever since he sarcastically tapped a revolver against John Doy's forehead in Kansas, Whitley seemed to get a certain thrill from holding people at gunpoint.

Hypocritical and opportunistic as the Georgia Klan's apologists' campaign to discredit the investigation campaign might be, Whitley had played right into their hands.

General Meade stood by the detective, and defended him publicly, pointing out that Whitley had mistreated the two black detainees but they were "in nowise injured."[42] As he declared in a cable to Washington, he was astonished and disgusted by the Ashburn murder, and by the efforts of professedly civilized Southern gentlemen to cover it up, which made it "most urgent that this trial should be carried on to the end by the military authorities."[43] Whatever Whitley's methods, the general could hardly disavow him without jeopardizing that objective.

The trial began in an airy, newly constructed meeting area in the McPherson Barracks military hospital at 10:00 a.m. on June 29, in front of an audience swollen by a large delegation from Columbus.[44] It was as if the whole violent, racially tinged saga of secession, war, and Reconstruction were being restaged as a morality play in that improvised court.

General Caleb C. Sibley presided over a seven-member panel of blue-uniformed judges. General Sibley served as assistant commissioner of the Freedmen's Bureau in Georgia, the highest-ranking bureau official in the state. The remaining six members included one of his subordinates at the agency, which white supremacists hated for its work ensuring that former slaves received wages and fair treatment from former masters. Indeed, there were initially three Freedmen's Bureau officials on the commission, but Meade replaced one of them, General Rufus Saxton—a well-known abolitionist from Massachusetts who had also commanded black troops during the Civil War—on the day before the trial, possibly because the defense would have objected to his inclusion.[45]

Leading the prosecution team was Judge Advocate General William M. Dunn of Indiana. A Republican member of the House of Representatives from 1859 through 1863, he had signed on as a military lawyer after leaving Congress. General Dunn recruited fellow Yale alumnus Joseph E. Brown, the Confederate-era governor of Georgia, as a civilian counsel to the prosecution. At the time of the Ashburn trial, Brown was a state supreme court justice, having joined the Republican Party believing that the white South's best hope was to cooperate in Reconstruction. Brown agreed to join the prosecution in return for a $5,000 fee and a promise that the commission would not impose the death penalty if the men were convicted.[46] Generals Meade and Sibley agreed, hoping that the employment of this distinguished Georgian as a prosecutor would help convince Georgia whites that the military commission was not an exercise in Yankee revenge.

The composition of the nine-lawyer defense team seemed intended to make the opposite point. The leader, Alexander H. Stephens, served in the U.S. House before joining the secessionist movement in Georgia and rising to the vice presidency of the Confederate States. Stephens's March 1861 "Cornerstone Speech" at Savannah declared that the Confederacy was "founded upon...the great truth that the negro is not equal to the white man; that slavery, subordination to the superior race, is his natural and normal condition."[47] For him, defending the "Columbus Prisoners" was a matter of principle, and an opportunity to promote his campaign for the United States Senate. Former Confederate General Henry L. Benning of Columbus, who had served on the prewar Georgia supreme court, joined Stephens, along with seven other prominent members of the Georgia bar.[48]

The prosecution case took up the first week of this clash of legal giants. The core of it was the testimony of Marshall, Betts, Patterson, and Bennett. As General Dunn and Joseph E. Brown led them through their narratives, Hiram C. Whitley looked on intently from the spectators' gallery, watching for any sign that the witnesses might falter, or change the stories they had told him, and that he had subsequently rehearsed with them in preparatory sessions at the McPherson Barracks.

Cross-examining the prosecution witnesses, Alexander H. Stephens tried to turn the proceeding into a trial of the detective who had elicited their testimony. He repeatedly demanded to know from Marshall and Betts how Whitley had gotten them to confess, suggesting that Whitley had either tortured them, or scripted their testimony, or that they were lying in return for favorable treatment from the government.

For the most part, though, the former Confederate vice president failed to shake their stories. All prosecution witnesses swore Whitley had not told them whom to implicate, but simply to tell what they knew of "the affair," as they referred to the Ashburn murder. Rather than punch holes in the prosecution narrative, Stephens's questions seemed unintentionally to elicit even more damning details about who and what the witnesses had seen in the Flournoy house, along with plausible protestations that they had hesitated to tell the truth previously, to local authorities in Columbus, because of their fear of "the Ku Kluxes."

The star prosecution witness was Charles Marshall, the United States Army sergeant who sided with the Klan and joined its invasion of Ashburn's home. He spent two grueling days on the witness stand. Despite his evidently despicable recent behavior, he proved formidable on the stand, seeming almost to atone by telling the truth. "A visible sensation overspread the court, counsel and spectators," a newspaper reporter noted, as the trim, black-mustached soldier confessed the details of the plot, and his own participation in it, "in the clearest and most direct manner."[49] On cross-examination, Stephens tried to get him to say that Whitley had demanded he implicate particular defendants, but Marshall steadfastly, and truthfully, denied it. Whitley had been far too careful to make that elementary mistake.

"He told me that if I knew anything about it I better make a full confession of the affair," Marshall testified. "He gave me the reason that it was my duty, sir, and proved to me that the evidence against me was sufficient."[50]

Stephens's cross-examination of Marshall "failed to shake his testimony in a single particular," the *Cincinnati Daily Gazette*'s correspondent reported. "The confession of two of the conspirators has swept the ground from under their feet and Stephens has been floundering about to recover himself ever since."[51]

On July 3, a Friday, the prosecution rested. On July 6, after the Independence Day weekend, the defense proceeded to put on its case. It consisted of a parade of alibi witnesses, friends and family members of the accused, who claimed the defendants were at home in bed, or miles away from Columbus, at the time of the murder.

Under cross-examination, the defense witnesses vented their contempt for lawyers who deigned to challenge their stories. Joseph E. Brown especially seemed to arouse the defense witnesses' ire, not diminish it as General Meade's officers had anticipated: one, a seventeen-year-old female, "manifested an antagonism for the prosecution more remarkable for its energy and its fire than for its politeness," a Northern journalist reported. As she left the stand, she shot Brown a look that was "painful to behold on the countenance of any living creature, much less in one of her age and sex."[52]

The defense testimony was transparently false, as prosecutors had no trouble showing on cross-examination. Each morning, as the defense prepared to resume this routine, one of its witnesses would return to court and request permission to amend a contradiction in which he or she had been trapped on the previous day.

In an especially damaging moment for the defense, a female member of defendant Elisha Kirkscey's household admitted she had rejoiced at the news of Ashburn's death. When Joseph E. Brown asked her if the women living under the accused's roof wished for the death of all the Republicans, a defense lawyer tried to object. Before he could get the words out, the woman said: "We do." The following day, she asked permission to rephrase her answer; she meant to say that the women desired only the death of Republicans such as Ashburn, "who were trying to excite the negroes against their former masters."[53]

Even some in the Georgia Democratic press conceded, albeit backhandedly, the strength of the prosecution's case. On July 10, after Whitley's witnesses had fared well under cross-examination, but the defense's had not, the *Macon Weekly Telegraph* tried to adapt previous categorical denials of Klan guilt to the facts emerging at the trial. Possibly, the paper reported, some of the defendants had paid a nighttime call on Ashburn, intending only to tar and feather him. Ashburn, in a panic, fired his pistol at the intruders, at which point they shot back in "quasi self-defense," the *Telegraph* explained.[54]

The defense team, too, must have realized that Hiram C. Whitley had assembled proof of their clients' guilt. Alexander H. Stephens's redundant cross-examination of prosecution witnesses, followed by his tedious barrage of implausible alibi testimony for the accused, hardly seemed calculated to impress the panel of military judges, and it didn't. As time went by, they were "evidently growing somewhat weary of the great mass of trifling and irrelevant matter introduced by the defense," the *Chicago Tribune* reported.[55]

The defense's dilatory presentation did, however, buy time for a political solution to the "Columbus Prisoners'" predicament.

The military commission proceedings coincided with the first session of the new Georgia state legislature, which had been elected in April, and met in the new state capital, Atlanta, on July 4. This body's key task was to be ratification of the Fourteenth Amendment—a precondition for Georgia's readmission to the Union under the Reconstruction Acts. Georgia white supremacists regarded the measure as an abomination, because it guaranteed African Americans citizenship and equal rights. Yet ratification did offer a certain potential consolation: once Georgia was back in the Union, and its civilian government restored, Democratic politicians could run for federal offices; civilian courts, subject to Democratic influence, and to Ku Klux Klan intimidation, would once again have jurisdiction over the Ashburn case and all other crimes.

Observing the trial, General Meade soon sensed that "every conceivable obstacle is being resorted to to produce delay, with the intention of taking the prisoners out of my hands...so soon as the state is supposed to be admitted," as he wrote to his superiors in Washington.[56] The general asked the War Department whether Congress could help him thwart this tactic by authorizing the Ashburn military commission to continue even after Georgia ratified the Fourteenth Amendment. General Grant consulted with Republican members of both the House and Senate—and informed Meade in early July that no such change in the law would be possible.[57]

Back-channel negotiations followed between one of Alexander H. Stephens's colleagues on the defense team and Democratic members of the Georgia House of Representatives: the purpose was to secure the Democratic votes needed to create a majority for ratification. Undoubtedly aware of the talks, the *Atlanta Constitution* admonished the party's politicians to "stand firm" against the hated amendment. "This is no time for policy or expediency," the paper declared.[58] Yet expediency, on behalf of the "Columbus Prisoners," carried the day. On July 21 the Georgia state legislature ratified the Fourteenth Amendment; the vote was 27–14 in the Senate, and 89–70 in the House of Representatives.[59]

On the same day, Meade ordered the dissolution of the military commission. Its last act was to grant the nine defendants bail on July 24. The day after that, William D. Chipley, Elisha Kirkscey, and the seven other men who had been on trial for conspiring to murder George W. Ashburn arrived at the Muscogee Depot in Columbus. Hundreds of people turned out to welcome them as heroes.[60] The prosecution's witnesses, meanwhile, fled with the Army's assistance to new homes far away.

★ ★ ★

The United States government had achieved a kind of stalemate in its first contest with the Ku Klux Klan. The new terrorist threat had not been defeated, but it had been exposed and condemned. Its members had escaped individual accountability for their crimes, but they had been unable to stop the political reforms called for under the Reconstruction Acts: a new state constitution, equal suffrage for black and white men, and ratification of the Fourteenth Amendment. These accomplishments were tentative, to be sure, given the Klan's impunity for the Ashburn assassination, the recalcitrance of white supremacist Democrats, and the prospect of future violence. Yet as the commission disbanded, there was still hope Republicans could overcome opposition to the "new birth of freedom" of which President Lincoln had spoken so eloquently.

As a participant in the Ashburn investigation later wrote:

To the unobserving mind the murder of George W. Ashburn would seem totally unavenged; but to him who sees in every great event the hand of an overruling Providence, evolving good from evil, a different conclusion must be arrived at. In his life, he fought manfully for the establishment of civil rights, and the political equality of the oppressed race of which he was the chosen champion. In his death that result was consummated, in the State of Georgia, sooner perhaps by years than it would otherwise have been without this sacrifice.[61]

By the time the case reached its denouement, the author of this assessment—Hiram C. Whitley—was long gone from Georgia.

The defense had made a motion to subpoena Whitley as a witness, and the prosecution had consented. But the detective was not eager to testify under oath about his investigatory methods, despite his defiant claim, in his letter to General Meade, that he would "stand all the bitter curses that have been heaped upon me." On July 16, he left for Washington, reporting to the commissioner of Internal Revenue and rejoining his wife, Catherine, who was waiting for him there.[62] He was still outside Georgia when the military commission disbanded.

Mixed as the results of the Ashburn case might have been for the federal government, it was a triumph for Hiram C. Whitley. His arrival in Columbus had been the turning point. Until he made his recommendation to create a separate interrogation center under military control, the investigation was stymied. After Meade adopted Whitley's stratagem, and gave him latitude to execute it, the truth, at last, came out.

The Republican newspaper that followed the trial most closely, the *Cincinnati Daily Gazette*, attributed whatever success the prosecution had to Whitley: "With rare tact, discrimination, and courage, he has worked his way through the labyrinth of lies," its correspondent concluded.[63]

Whitley had employed hardball methods; in two cases, he had gone beyond hardball to cruelty. The fact that the victims were African Americans, and that his mistreatment of them became public and revealed his own racial biases, was certainly appalling, and, given the nature of the case, ironic. Whitley's conduct had handed the Klan's defenders a propaganda coup.

Yet his excesses had not fundamentally undermined the evidence; the Democratic press's contention that the case had been built on tortured or suborned testimony was false, egregiously so. On the day he dissolved his military commission, General Meade mounted a vehement defense of his decisions, and of Whitley's methods, in a letter to General Grant. The detective "did operate on the fears of the negroes, Wells and Stapler," General Meade wrote, but "had the people of Columbus evinced or felt any horror of the crime, and cooperated in any way in detecting its perpetrators, much that was seemingly harsh and arbitrary might have and would have been avoided."[64]

With those pragmatic words, the hero of Gettysburg endorsed his detective to the man who was not only the highest-ranking officer of the United States Army, but also the new standard-bearer of the Republican Party for the November 3, 1868, general election—and very likely the next president of the United States.

4

"A powerful instrument for good or evil."

Ulysses S. Grant was indeed elected—in a landslide—to succeed Andrew Johnson as president. Hiram C. Whitley, with his record in the Ashburn case and in the battle against Virginia's moonshiners, made a logical pick for Secret Service chief when the new Grant administration chose him two months after the president's March 4, 1869, swearing-in. As much as the political leaders of the United States might have wanted Whitley to lead their anti-counterfeiting force, and as much as Whitley himself coveted the job—even more, he said, than the presidency—the nation's founders probably would have been surprised that such a position even existed.

The Constitution did authorize Congress to "provide for the Punishment of counterfeiting the Securities and current Coin" issued by the United States government. In that sense, the Secret Service resembled existing forces of postal, customs, and revenue agents—even the slave-catching commissions of the 1850s. Those bodies, too, had been established pursuant to one of the federal government's enumerated powers.

What would have astonished the founders was the fact that the United States had instituted a national paper currency at all.

Many of them took a dim view of paper money, due to the disastrous hyperinflation during the Revolutionary War. George Washington said paper money would "ruin commerce, oppress the honest, and open the door to every species of fraud and injustice."[1] James Madison called it a "wicked project."[2] The Constitution prohibited the states from creating "bills of credit," a kind of government IOU that the colonies had employed as currency. Therefore, when the Constitution referred to "securities" and "coin," it meant federal bonds and actual gold or silver pieces, the latter being the primary means of payment for federal taxes and tariffs.

Inevitably, though, the expanding nation needed more liquidity than limited supplies of precious metal could provide. States therefore evaded the ban on bills of credit by chartering private banks, hundreds of which then issued banknotes—commercially tradeable promises to pay, ostensibly backed by the state banks' own reserves.

Counterfeiters exploited the monetary anarchy. Fake state banknotes, many made in Canada and smuggled south, flooded the market. Printers on Cogniac Street in the tiny hamlet of Dunham, Quebec—just over the Vermont border—produced so much high-quality counterfeit that Americans began referring to all counterfeiters as "coniackers," or "coney men," and all fake money as "coney."[3]

Congress left suppression of these counterfeits up to the states. They had little success against a crime that was inherently difficult to detect, and even harder to prove in court, since anyone who passed a counterfeit bill could plausibly deny doing so *knowingly*. As it happened, Americans were not necessarily eager to crack down on counterfeiting. The robust demand for fake bills showed that coney men were meeting a public need for financial liquidity.

Financial decentralization, states' rights, and a strictly limited federal government, except to the extent it protected slavery—this policy mix reflected the influence in Washington of the Southern-based Democratic Party. When Southern states seceded in 1861, taking their senators and representatives with them, they plunged the Republican-dominated Congress and President Abraham Lincoln into a crisis, but also gave the Republicans an opportunity to deal with it according to the party's much more robust notion of federal power.

By late 1861, when it became clear that the Treasury did not hold nearly enough gold and silver to finance the military effort ahead, Congress and President Lincoln asserted the authority to expand money and credit, by selling hundreds of millions of dollars' worth of bonds, backed by tariff proceeds and taxes, including the new excise and income taxes, and, in February 1862, by establishing a national currency that had to be accepted in nearly all transactions. The National Banking Act of 1863 created federally chartered banks empowered to issue banknotes. That measure, coupled with a federal tax on state-chartered banks, effectively ended state banknote issuance.[4]

In essence, the Republicans had replaced the prewar system with a more centralized federal equivalent. It was a political exercise as much as a financial one. Republicans were asking the American people to place their confidence not just in their home states, but in the nation and its government—just as Republicans would, over time, replace narrow, state-based notions of citizenship with a nationalized concept, inclusive of emancipated African Americans in the South. "The policy of this country," Senator John Sherman of Ohio, an author of the new financial laws (and brother of United States Army General William Tecumseh Sherman), declared, "ought to be to make everything national as far as possible; to nationalize our country so that we shall love our country."[5]

Republican creators of the new monetary policy did not think counterfeiting would be a problem. Since there would be only a handful of standardized national bills, as opposed to hundreds of antebellum state-bank bills, citizens could learn to identify the genuine ones and reject the fakes. Printed on special "fiber paper" with unusual green ink, the money would also be technologically resistant to counterfeiting.

Such hopes quickly proved unfounded in practice. Ingenious but greedy engravers and printers found clever ways to copy both "greenbacks" and the new banknotes, as well as government bonds. The federal government had to exercise its constitutional power to fight counterfeiting more vigorously than ever before. Between 1862 and 1864, it used detectives affiliated with the War Department, headed by the flamboyant Lafayette Baker, to pursue coney men on an ad hoc basis. Then Congress appropriated $100,000 for the Treasury Department to spend on fighting counterfeiters. It was a significant sum of money, equal to ten times all previous appropriations for the purpose since the nation's founding; the department used it mainly to finance rewards for individuals or private detectives who fingered suspects to the United States Marshals.

Not until July 5, 1865—after the Confederate surrender at Appomattox—did the Treasury Department organize its own in-house anti-counterfeiting detective force, employed and supervised by the department's legal officer, Solicitor of the Treasury Edward Jordan. No new law enacted by Congress authorized this. Solicitor Jordan simply claimed the power to create the "division," as he called it, based on his own expansive interpretation of the anti-counterfeiting appropriations. It was a chaotic time, less than three months after Lincoln's assassination and his replacement by Vice President Andrew Johnson. Congress was not in session; if it had been, lawmakers might have balked at Jordan's idea.[6]

Jordan swore in the new force's first chief, William Patrick Wood, with no outside vetting or Senate confirmation. Wood was a Mexican War veteran, Union Civil War intelligence agent, and ex-superintendent of the Old Capitol Prison in Washington, which had housed both common criminals and Confederate prisoners of war. Wood's contacts with counterfeiters there made him an expert on the crime; he parlayed that into a job investigating wartime counterfeiting cases for the Treasury Department, prior to his 1865 appointment.[7]

Without an explicit congressional grant of authority, his detectives lacked the independent power to make arrests. If they wanted to detain a suspect, they had to call in the federal marshals; ask local police or sheriffs to deputize them; or, when they actually witnessed a crime in progress, attempt "citizens' arrests," based in common law. Still, Wood's Secret Service Division made aggressive use of these alternatives, arresting some two hundred counterfeiting suspects during the four years of the Johnson administration, and confiscating numerous engraving plates and stashes of coney.

The pursuit of more arrests, however, proved corrupting. In 1866, Wood offered twenty-five dollars for each counterfeiter taken into custody, which incentivized his men to frame innocent people—"put-up jobs" in the argot of the day. They sometimes extorted protection money from real crooks, or sold the counterfeit bills they confiscated. None of this was surprising, given that Wood recruited about half of his operatives from the underworld itself.[8]

In 1867, President Johnson pardoned dozens of convicted counterfeiters, partly to rebuke Wood for his tactics.[9] That same year, Wood appeared as an adviser to the defense at the trial of a notorious counterfeiter in New York's federal court. The defendant had been a paid Secret Service informant; Wood felt he owed him help. The judge denounced the "unseemly spectacle."[10] Agreeing, the *New York Times* called for a congressional investigation.[11]

Even if William P. Wood's tenure at the Secret Service had been less controversial, a new Republican president would have been unlikely to retain him, simply because he was associated with the hated Johnson. Republican leaders viewed the Secret Service's crime-fighting mission in the broader context of partisanship and policy. For them, debauchers of the national money threatened Republican plans for postwar nation-building just as surely as the Klansmen who had killed George W. Ashburn in Georgia did. The Klan challenged the national expansion of civil and voting rights to all citizens. The coney men undermined the federal government's control of the legitimate issuance of money.

President Grant's secretary of the Treasury, George S. Boutwell, was a Massachusetts man who, as a member of Congress, had helped establish the tax-collection bureaucracy that financed the Union war effort. He was a "radical" on Reconstruction and a close collaborator of Representative Benjamin Butler, the former Civil War general who had first put Whitley's talents to use for the federal government. Butler and Boutwell spearheaded the House of Representatives' impeachment effort against Andrew Johnson, for which Whitley and William H. Reed had provided undercover assistance.

Such men valued Whitley not only for his general prowess as a detective or his specific experience investigating counterfeiting gangs for Butler's Civil War occupation force in New Orleans. Equally if not more important was his long record of service to them and their causes. True, Whitley had a dark side; his inability to suppress it had marred an otherwise laudable performance in the Ashburn case. But that was not disqualifying in Secretary Boutwell's eyes. Though the secretary had made his career on the high principles of the antislavery movement, he also believed, as he once put it, that "there is a rough side to government, and there must be a quality of harshness in those who administer governments successfully."[12]

For public consumption, the Republican press presented the new Secret Service chief neither as a reliable Republican nor as

an avatar of necessary governmental "harshness," but as a re-
former. Under Whitley, a newspaper noted, the Secret Service
would end such abuses as his predecessor Wood's "pernicious
system of manufacturing criminals." The Secret Service was "a
powerful instrument for good or evil, according to the hands
that guide it," the paper suggested, and, led by Whitley, who
was "cool and collected and looks you straight in the eye when
talking to you," it could be a force for good.[13]

Whitley's direct supervisor would be Solicitor of the Treasury
Everett C. Banfield, who had replaced Edward Jordan. A Boston Brahmin and small-time Massachusetts politician, Solicitor
Banfield came to Washington intending mainly to serve his pa-
tron in the Bay State Republican Party, Secretary Boutwell. He
had little aptitude for, or interest in, keeping tabs on detectives.
The very idea of undercover work struck him as unseemly—"a
branch of business that I have no particular fondness for," as he
put it. Banfield gave Whitley wide operational latitude.[14]

He cheerfully approved Whitley's first major policy change:
to move Secret Service headquarters from the Treasury building in Washington to a tenement on Bleecker Street in Lower
Manhattan. This suited the new Secret Service chief in two
ways: it put distance between him and anyone in Congress or
the Grant administration who might try to probe into what he
and his men were doing; and it was closer to Cambridge, Massachusetts, where his wife, Catherine, now lived in a house she
shared with their respective mothers.[15]

The move made sense for the Secret Service, too: it placed the
detective force in the heart of New York's counterfeiting indus-
try, an area bounded by Houston Street, Broadway, the Bowery,
and Chatham Street. The shift could also be justified under new
legislation, enacted by Congress in the last days of the Johnson administration, which added "frauds upon the government" to the
list of crimes the Treasury Department could "detect" using appropriations previously devoted exclusively to counterfeiting. The

net effect of that law was to give the Secret Service responsibility for smuggling and tax evasion—both rampant in the port of New York. One of Whitley's successes in his first year as chief, in fact, was to break up a New York–based gang that specialized in removing used federal excise tax stamps from cigar boxes and wine bottles, reconditioning them, and selling them as new.[16]

Yet by the end of his first year in power, Whitley voiced frustration at his inability to make more progress against the Secret Service's principal target: counterfeiting. "We are having some pretty tough times with the counterfeiters," he acknowledged in a rambling, ambivalent report to Banfield on June 14, 1870, "notwithstanding I have but few men, there is good work going on. I have captured three men this week…but one of my men got a fearful beating, which gave me a setback, but the whole division is not yet dead."

In addition to the lack of personnel and violent resistance from the criminals themselves, Whitley blamed New York's federal court, where, he claimed, "for money, justice can be bought either by wholesale or retail." He tried, without success, to lobby for a special new court in New York dedicated just to his cases. Whitley sounded both angry and, uncharacteristically, depressed about the situation, though he vowed to overcome the obstacles. "I sometimes feel a little discouraged groping uselessly in the dark," he wrote Banfield, "but I trust there is a glimmer of light ahead… coming into contact with these things daily stirs me up to constant action."[17]

Whitley's fundamental problem—obtaining hard proof against the counterfeiters—was the same one that had bedeviled law enforcement since the days of rampant state banknote falsification. Counterfeiting, like gambling or prostitution, was a "consensual" crime. It harmed society, certainly. Yet the people who actually took part in it did so either voluntarily or unwittingly (in the case, say, of merchants who passed along fake bills thinking them genuine). They usually had neither opportunity nor incentive to report it to the police.

Like the Ku Klux Klan in Columbus, Georgia, counterfeiting gangs operated according to a strict hierarchy, enforced by a code of silence. At the apex of a typical organization sat a financier, who did not get his hands dirty actually making "queer"—as phony bills were then known—but who recruited the experts who did, and advanced them funds to design and produce the needed engraving plates, ink, and paper. Wholesale dealers purchased the notes from these illicit partnerships, usually for about 10 or 15 percent of their face value. Then the wholesalers sold the queer to "shovers," who scratched out a living exchanging the fake money for real goods or legitimate cash.

It was a compartmentalized structure designed to protect the higher ranks. Whitley fully understood that "the most successful and efficient mode" of action against such a group would be to penetrate it and to make its component criminals "work against each other," as he told Banfield in a June 16, 1870, letter. The way to do that, as he had learned firsthand in New Orleans, was to identify lower-level criminals, then coerce or persuade them to cooperate against their higher-ups. This, in turn, required associating with criminals, engaging in their factional disputes, selectively turning a blind eye to various misdeeds, and even paying shady characters for their cooperation, all of which could sully the federal government.

In Whitley's view, it was hopelessly naive to suppose that there was any alternative. "It is entirely impossible," he wrote, "to reach criminals, especially counterfeiters, without using men themselves not above the taint of suspicion, and the best and most reliable information ever acquired relative to counterfeiting comes from the disaffected counterfeiters." Through the skillful manipulation of informants and agents, Whitley promised, "strife can be kindled that is almost certain to end in the entire annihilation of the whole gang."[18]

He duly stipulated in a code of conduct he issued shortly after taking office that, in the Secret Service, "no person convicted of any crime could be made a 'regular' informer." Yet this seeming prohibition left room for the occasional use of any crooks except for the small, unlucky minority proven guilty in a court of law.[19]

The Secret Service chief shook off his depression and devised a plan to infiltrate counterfeiters. Its essential point was to create a Secret Service hierarchy through which to maintain interactions with the criminal class, but in a controlled manner, so as to prevent a repetition of the division's mistakes under his predecessor. At the top of this pyramid, orchestrating everything, would be Hiram C. Whitley. At the bottom would be Secret Service infiltrators and informants, drawn from the back alleys, saloons, and jail cells of America. They would be paid ad hoc, according to the "value" of their information. Whitley specifically reassured Solicitor Banfield that these spies would not be formally commissioned or salaried by the Secret Service, "so that it may not appear that the government employ" them.

The handling of underworld agents would be the job of the crucial middle cadre in Whitley's scheme. Whitley had in mind "men of judgment and character with a taste and tact for a class of business which…requires the utmost caution as well as firmness," as he explained to Banfield. Such men "are hard to find," he advised; they would not work cheap. To recruit and pay them would require a bigger appropriation than the $100,000 that Congress had approved on President Johnson's last day in office, and that Whitley had been obliged to stretch throughout his first year.[20]

Whitley's concept was unprecedented in American history: a permanent, semiclandestine national police bureaucracy, with its own system of ranks and promotions, and full autonomy to recruit, pay, and supervise informants within the civilian population. The Secret Service would be considerably smaller than the European detective and intelligence services, but its goals and methods would be similar.

This innovation would undoubtedly have been fiercely debated if Solicitor Banfield ever put it before Congress, which may be why he never did. Banfield assented to Whitley's concept, and backed the Secret Service's request for more money, without telling Congress exactly why it was needed. On July 15, 1870, Congress approved a 25 percent increase in the Treasury Department appropriation that had always been construed, but never declared, to authorize the Secret Service. The bill specified only that the money be used for "detecting persons counterfeiting treasury notes, bonds, and other securities; and coins, and other frauds."[21]

Freshly empowered, Whitley turned to assembling detectives with what he considered appropriate "judgment and character."

The Secret Service chief insisted publicly that, in contrast to the blatant patronage in the rest of the federal government, his force would be selected on merit, with partisan politics "out of the question."[22] In practice, he included no former Confederates or Southerners among his initial hires. Whitley could not risk bringing in anyone who was not unquestionably loyal to the United States government, much less who might harbor disagreements with the current administration. He favored Northerners, preferably Union intelligence veterans with some Republican leanings, if they had any partisan inclination at all.

Whitley's choice to head the Secret Service's San Francisco bureau, responsible for the vast territory of the West Coast, was Henry F. Finnegass, a deputy United States Marshal whom Whitley knew from their Civil War–era work together on General Butler's detective force in New Orleans. In Chicago, he hired Thomas Lonergan, who, though not yet thirty years old, had compiled an impressive academic and military résumé. Educated at Notre Dame and West Point, he served in an Illinois regiment during the war—losing part of his right hand in combat—then worked for Allan Pinkerton's private detective agency, before joining the staff of Chicago's Republican newspaper.[23]

Whitley would hire recent immigrants if they had some connection to the Union cause; in a detective, the ability to speak multiple languages and to adapt to different cultures were useful skills, he thought. Charles Anchisi was an Italian who had served as an officer of his native country's army in foreign wars during the 1850s. He arrived in the United States in November 1861, and soon signed on as a spy for the War Department, operating as far south as Richmond.[24] At the end of 1870, Whitley hired the police chief of Jersey City, New Jersey, Michael G. Bauer, who arrived in the United States from Germany in 1857. During the Civil War, Bauer served as an intelligence officer for a New Jersey regiment.[25]

CHARLES E. ANCHISI,
OPERATIVE, CENTRAL DISTRICT,
U. S. SECRET SERVICE DIVISION.

Charles Anchisi emigrated from Italy to the United States before the Civil War and became a Union spy. At the Secret Service under Hiram C. Whitley, he infiltrated counterfeiters in the Northeast. (*Memoirs of the United States Secret Service*)

Whitley did not attempt to rebuild the Secret Service from scratch, however. Wisely, given the need to preserve institutional memory, he tried to retain those of William P. Wood's veterans whose personalities and capabilities meshed well with his, and who had not committed egregious offenses during his predecessor's time. Two holdovers would, in fact, gradually become Whitley's closest confidants.

The first of these was Ichabod C. Nettleship, a meticulously well-organized bureaucrat who had helped Wood assemble the federal government's first files on counterfeiting suspects, an archive that Whitley would retain and, with Nettleship's help, greatly expand. Nettleship immigrated to the United States at the age of eighteen from Nottingham, England, arriving at New York in 1851 with a silver half crown coin in his pocket—savings from years of his labor as a child in a silk factory.

I. C. NETTLESHIP,
OPERATIVE, U. S. SECRET SERVICE,
CHIEF ASSISTANT TO COL. WHITLEY.

British-born Ichabod C. Nettleship started at the Secret Service under its first chief, William P. Wood, and stayed on to become Hiram C. Whitley's most trusted lieutenant. (*Memoirs of the United States Secret Service*)

Nettleship worked making saddles in Newark, New Jersey, until the Civil War broke out. He joined a New Jersey regiment, and eventually wound up on occupation duty in Union-held Alexandria, Virginia, just across the Potomac River from Washington. One of Nettleship's officers proposed that they go into the counterfeiting business together, and he feigned agreement while secretly informing on the officer to the Treasury Department. With his superiors' approval, Nettleship arranged to have the officer deliver him a supply of counterfeit bills, whereupon he arrested the man and turned him over to the military authorities. Impressed by this feat, Treasury officials asked the Army to let Nettleship join Wood's new Secret Service Division.

Whitley first met Nettleship at the Metropolitan Hotel, near the counterfeiting district at the corner of Prince Street and Broadway in Lower Manhattan, on June 25, 1869. He developed an instant appreciation for the potbellied Englishman's genial disposition. Whitley soon made Nettleship assistant chief, with responsibility for managing day-to-day finances and personnel matters at the Bleecker Street headquarters.[26]

Abner B. Newcomb had left the Secret Service in 1867 when Wood tried to frame him for taking a bribe to let a counterfeiter escape jail. Whitley reinstated Newcomb, earning his enduring gratitude and loyalty. Given Newcomb's experience and strong Republican credentials, it is easy to see why Whitley thought he deserved a second chance. Born in 1833 to a wealthy Boston merchant and his teacher wife, he moved to Rockford, Illinois, in 1857, where he spent the next two years as editor of the Republican Party's newspaper. Newcomb accepted the party's nomination for the Illinois state legislature in 1859, but withdrew from the race when his wife became ill. The couple moved to New York, where, in 1860, he published an exposé of inhumane conditions in the city's jails. As a sideline, he briefly worked undercover for the State Department, investigating the illegal transatlantic slave trade.

During the Civil War, Newcomb became a spy for the United States Marshals. Posing as a pro-secession newspaper reporter, Newcomb infiltrated a smuggling ring that was moving Confederate letters and messages through Northern states to Canada, whence they could be shipped to Confederate agents in Europe via the postal system of Great Britain, which controlled Canada at the time. Newcomb also monitored passenger ships arriving in New York from abroad, to spot incoming Confederate spies and sympathizers, until the war ended and Wood brought him into the Secret Service.[27]

Whitley eventually assembled a permanent crew of about twenty men; his ostensible boss Solicitor Banfield's only contribution to their recruitment was his signature on the men's commission papers. Whitley assigned the most capable and experienced members of his team as "chief operatives" in nine major cities: Boston, Chicago, Cincinnati, Detroit, Louisville, New Orleans, St. Louis, and San Francisco. In each branch office, the chief operative would be responsible for hiring an assistant, and for developing informants and agents within the counterfeiting gangs. Whitley granted them autonomy, subject only to his requirement that they account for every penny they spent—and describe every hour of their activity—in reports to him in New York. The remainder of the detectives worked directly under Whitley in New York.

During the second half of 1870, Whitley's force captured several notorious counterfeiters who had eluded the Secret Service under William P. Wood. Fred Biebusch, the dominant wholesale dealer of queer in the Midwest since prior to the Civil War, had been arrested dozens of times, but always beat the charges by bribing witnesses against him and—Whitley learned—paying off Wood's detectives. Whitley arrested Biebusch's top engraver in New York, far from Biebusch's base in St. Louis, kept him isolated, and promised him leniency, in return for testifying against Biebusch. The engraver agreed to cooperate; on the strength of his evidence, Biebusch was convicted and sentenced to fifteen years in prison.[28]

To hunt down Jim Boyd, a major New England coney distributor, Charles Anchisi and his assistant, fellow Italian immigrant Louis Del'Omo, toured the Northeast, posing as French-Canadian counterfeit dealers, until they contacted one of Boyd's trusted retailers, who eventually led them to Boyd at his house in Canada. Anchisi and Del'Omo enticed Boyd to follow them to New York by promising to buy $5,000 worth of counterfeit greenbacks. The Secret Service arrested him there.[29]

Though they did not realize it, with each of these skirmishes, Whitley and his men were drawing closer to a climactic confrontation with the man who secretly held sway over the most powerful and sophisticated counterfeiting ring on the East Coast.

On the evening of August 25, 1870, a crowd of New Yorkers gathered under a wooden shelter at the end of Tenth Street in Lower Manhattan, waiting to board the next steam-powered ferry boat across the East River to Greenpoint in Brooklyn. Amid the throng, a heavyset man with thick black eyebrows and a broad nose glanced nervously around him, taking advantage of his height, a couple of inches above six feet, to scan his surroundings.

He saw nothing particularly suspicious. A white-collared clergyman milled about nearby, as did a man dressed in the scruffy garb of a mechanic, puffing on a clay pipe—and so inebriated he could barely stand. The heavyset man concluded it would be safe to proceed with the mission that had brought him to the ferry landing: to meet a young ex-con, known to him as Jake Buck, who had arranged to buy $3,000 in counterfeit twenty-dollar bills, for the attractive price of $540 in genuine money.

The heavyset man spotted Jake Buck, recognizable by the cigar he always smoked, and winked at him, the prearranged signal to consummate their transaction. He moved a few steps in Buck's direction—whereupon the drunken mechanic and the clergyman tackled him, forced his hands behind his back, and locked a pair of iron handcuffs around his wrists.

Both "Jake Buck" and the drunken mechanic were undercover Secret Service men, and the clergyman was their disguised chief, Hiram C. Whitley.

The prisoner, Bill Gurney, a veteran distributor of counterfeit money, had been arrested a half dozen times by the Secret Service under William P. Wood, but always managed to beat the charges, due to a lack of evidence, legal technicalities, or outright bribery. This time, though, the detectives had trapped Gurney with $3,000 in counterfeit money bulging in his pocket.

Gurney's arrest culminated a weeks-long undercover operation, orchestrated by Whitley, in which a Secret Service man, posing as Jake Buck, had bought increasing amounts of coney, first from Gurney's underlings, and then—once trust had been established—from Gurney himself. The bills were copies of a twenty-dollar note issued by the National Shoe and Leather Bank, a New York institution that received its federal charter in 1865. Whitley considered the fakes especially skillfully made, and therefore especially dangerous.

Ever since they came on the market, he had been trying to determine the ultimate source of this unusually convincing queer. Now, with Bill Gurney in custody, he finally had his hands on someone who might know the secret, and who might divulge it under interrogation by the Secret Service chief.

It didn't take long. Locked up in Manhattan's Ludlow Street Jail, unable to afford bail, which had been set at $20,000, and facing between five and fifteen years in prison, Gurney was desperate to cut a deal with Whitley for some sort of leniency.[30]

He gave the detective the name of the man behind the spurious bills, and it was a shocking one: Joshua D. Miner.

As far as New York's public knew, "Jot" Miner was a paragon of the Manhattan business community, who had made a fortune building streets and water projects, as a contractor to the city government dominated by the Democratic Party's Tammany Hall political machine and its famous chieftain, William M. "Boss" Tweed. Miner had adhered to Tammany after an initial flirtation with the Republicans in the late 1860s.[31] He owned and operated one of the first steam drills capable of boring through rock, and employed more than one hundred fifty workers. As of 1871, the city owed Miner's company $100,000 for work it had performed on the Upper West Side of Manhattan, which included paving Ninth Avenue and constructing a sewer system under it.

Bill Gurney's revelations cast Miner in a different light, however: as the mastermind of a vast counterfeiting organization. Miner's legitimate, politically connected business fronted for his network of engravers, printers, and distributors, which fabricated and sold hundreds of thousands of dollars' worth of bogus banknotes.

JOSHUA D. MINER,
THE AUTOCRAT OF AMERICAN CONEY MEN.

To all outward appearances, Joshua D. Miner was a wealthy and respectable businessman, but Whitley knew he ran a counterfeiting ring and set out to destroy it. (*Memoirs of the United States Secret Service*)

As Whitley learned, Miner came from a long line of counterfeiters, going back to the era of the state banknotes. He was born in 1830 in rural Steuben County, New York, where both his father and his brother had run afoul of the law by distributing coney. His wife's brothers were shovers, too. For a time, Miner ran a sawmill in his home county, where he notoriously paid his workers in counterfeit. He tried to establish a branch of the family's illicit business in Cleveland, Ohio, during the 1850s, but the Cuyahoga County sheriff arrested him in February 1855 for possession of $7,000 in phony money. Miner spent three months in an Ohio penitentiary before escaping. In 1858, he secured a pardon from Ohio's governor, possibly in return for a promise to leave the state, which he did.

By 1859, Miner had made his way to New York City, where he went into ostensibly lawful business. Miner might have contented himself with this, but he seems to have regarded the United States government's development of a supposedly counterfeit-proof new currency during the Civil War as a challenge. In 1862, Miner made contact with Thomas Ballard, an expert engraver and chemist who worked for one of the companies that printed authentic banknotes. Funded by the wealthy contractor, Ballard developed engraving plates for the two-dollar, ten-dollar, twenty-dollar, and fifty-dollar notes issued by various federally chartered banks, as well as a process for making the special paper on which they were printed.

Miner and Ballard set up a clandestine money factory in Manhattan, and by the late 1860s they were turning out fake notes by the thousands, which circulated throughout New York and Pennsylvania. Miner's take was 10 percent to 15 percent of the spurious bills' face value.

Whitley realized that he had a chance to decapitate the biggest counterfeiting ring on the East Coast, which would be a greater coup for federal law enforcement than William P. Wood or any other detective had ever delivered. It could make him a hero.

Whitley's first move was to escort Bill Gurney up to Miner's mansion on 67th Street for a surprise visit to the counterfeiting magnate.

"Hello, old stick–in–the–mud!" Miner called out, spotting Gurney.[32]

To Miner's chagrin, Gurney introduced his companion as a Secret Service detective. "I am in trouble, and I need your help," he pleaded, playing his part just as Whitley had scripted it for him.

Miner spluttered a refusal. Whitley took the counterfeiter aside and explained that Gurney had told him all about Miner and his engraving plate for the twenty-dollar National Shoe and Leather Bank note. "I want it," Whitley demanded.

Miner pondered Whitley's proposition. He was not in business to do favors, not even for an erstwhile collaborator, and definitely not for the Secret Service. At this point, however, Gurney had exposed him; if Miner played his cards right, helping Gurney out of his jam might be the best way to save his own neck. He had never dealt with Whitley before. William P. Wood, however, had frequently agreed not to pursue counterfeiters who surrendered the tools of their trade. Perhaps Whitley might make a similar deal; a few months earlier, in fact, he had done so with the Midwestern counterfeiter Pete McCartney. McCartney showed the Secret Service chief spots in several states where he had buried engraving plates and large quantities of fake bills, in the hopes of receiving leniency—though he absconded after Whitley arranged for him to be released on bond pending trial, thus avoiding any conviction or sentence at all.[33]

Miner coolly lied, telling Whitley that he did not have the plates, but would try to find out where they might be. He agreed to see Whitley a few days later at the Astor House hotel, and asked the Secret Service chief to show good faith in the meantime by keeping Miner's name out of the papers. Whitley complied. When they met at the Astor House, Miner promised he would, indeed, hand over the plates, if Whitley could wait for another meeting, and continue to protect Miner from publicity. Whitley again agreed.

Two more weeks went by until Whitley met Miner again, at the latter's home, where they whiled away several hours talking about counterfeiting. Miner guaranteed that he was finally ready to get Whitley the plates, after which he would quit the coney business forever.

A few days later, when the mail arrived at Whitley's Bleecker Street headquarters, there was an envelope with two items inside: a claim check for a trunk stored at a New Jersey warehouse and an unsigned letter explaining how to get there. Sure enough, when Whitley's assistant fetched the trunk for him, Whitley found the National Shoe and Leather Bank note plates inside.[34]

In early November 1870 Whitley triumphantly took the plates to Washington, where he presented them to Secretary Boutwell, along with all the other equipment, fake revenue stamps, and phony bonds that he and his men had confiscated in other cases. The whole mass was to be incinerated in a blast furnace at the Navy Yard, in the southeast quadrant of the city, not far from the Capitol.[35]

By no means did the Secret Service chief intend this fiery spectacle to signal the end of his dealings with Joshua D. Miner. The notion of a master criminal conducting illegal business from an exalted position in Manhattan society, with implicit protection from his political connections, intrigued—and annoyed—the Secret Service chief. Going back at least to the Ashburn case, in which Columbus, Georgia's local elite had gotten lower-class men to do the Ku Klux Klan's dirty work, Whitley reserved his purest contempt not for the rank-and-file offender but for the high-class criminals who often manipulated them from behind a facade of wealth and respectability.

Those fortunate enough to have education and wealth had a special responsibility to society, and yet, as the Secret Service chief would later write, "Cultivated criminals stalk about in church and mart, seemingly exemplary in thought and act but in reality a lie and a cheat." These "hypocritical thieves in the garden of life" were more reprehensible, he observed, than the poor man whose "cravings…for a loaf of bread and the theft of it make him a common thief."[36]

Now that Whitley knew firsthand that Miner was nothing but a well-groomed predator, he was doubly determined to assemble proof of his guilt that would stand up in court. The engraving plates alone would not suffice; Miner could disavow any knowledge of the trunk in which Whitley's man had found them, or the anonymous letter that led to it. The situation called for a large-scale undercover operation, which could only work if Whitley were given complete latitude to offer lower-level counterfeiters immunity from prosecution in exchange for cooperation—and that would have to culminate by capturing Joshua D. Miner himself, red-handed.

The Washington trip provided Whitley cover for a meeting with Secretary Boutwell and Solicitor Banfield, at which he briefed them on Miner's organization, and laid out his plans to penetrate it. This proposition must have struck Banfield as distasteful, and even the more worldly Boutwell as risky. As his pitch to General Meade and Captain Mills in the Ashburn case had shown, however, Whitley had a way of portraying aggressive and unorthodox methods as the only ones with any chance of success. The Secret Service chief was "determined in willpower, peculiarly communicative of the subtle sentiment he entertains, and mentally resolved *to carry his point* in any personal or individual controversy," as a journalist of his acquaintance put it.[37]

Nor could the significance of "Jot" Miner's links to the New York Democratic Party machine, Tammany Hall, fail to impress the Republican partisans who ran the Treasury Department. If Whitley succeeded, it would help fight counterfeiting and embarrass their political enemies at the same time.

Boutwell and Banfield agreed to support him.[38] Whitley

placed Miner under full-time surveillance and meanwhile instructed his men in New York to squeeze every low-level dealer they arrested for any detail that might lead to Miner.

In September 1871 an informant's tip led Whitley's detectives to David Kirkbride, a shover, whom they arrested at the Hudson River Depot, a railroad station at the corner of Liberty Street and West Broadway in Lower Manhattan. Kirkbride was about to depart for Chicago with $5,000 in counterfeit money, neatly wrapped in tinfoil, ready for sale. The Secret Service men took Kirkbride to Whitley's second-floor office at Bleecker Street, where the chief explained to Kirkbride that he was not interested in sending him to prison—or wouldn't be, as long as Kirkbride told him where he had gotten the coney.[39]

Kirkbride gave Whitley the name and address of his supplier, David Keene, and agreed to set up another buy at Keene's house a few nights later, on October 6—under Secret Service surveillance. As Keene went to his backyard to unearth a large metal box containing more tinfoil packages filled with phony bills, Whitley's men sprang from the tall grass where they were hiding and handcuffed him. To save himself from prosecution, Keene told Whitley that he bought the counterfeit from someone who enjoyed direct access to Miner: a veteran of the coney trade known as Harry Cole.

When Secret Service detectives picked up Cole at his house on 84th Street on October 10, he was carrying $2,400 in twenty-dollar National Shoe and Leather Bank notes. For the next three days and nights, Whitley held Cole incommunicado in his office at Bleecker Street, until the old shover finally broke down and admitted that he had trafficked hundreds of thousands of dollars' worth of counterfeit notes from Miner since 1863. He knew Miner well and could identify his engraver, too, though he knew that member of Miner's ring only by sight, not by name.

Cole's sunken eyes and emaciation told of chronic illness, and exhaustion from his life of crime.[40] He had previously done time at the state penitentiary in Albany, New York, and was in no shape to repeat the experience. He was ready to deal, and Whitley was, too. He told Cole that the government would waive his $10,000 bail, allow him back out on the street, and guarantee him immunity from prosecution. The federal government would even help arrange a state pardon for him from New York, which would restore his civil rights, including, under the law of the time, his right to testify in court.

All Whitley asked in return was that Cole help the Secret Service set up a sting operation against Miner, be a witness against him at trial—and surrender the deed to his house in Manhattan, as a guarantee that he wouldn't double-cross the detectives. Whitley sent word to the federal prosecutor and magistrate for New York, who came down to Bleecker Street and assured Cole that they, too, endorsed the deal. Cole agreed.

Shortly after seven in the evening on October 25, 1871, a steady rain poured on the Boulevard, as the wide extension of Broadway on the Upper West Side of Manhattan was then called. Flickering gaslights glowed dimly, forming illuminated spheres in the mist. Most sensible people stayed indoors, except for three or four laborers straggling home with their picks and shovels—and two more elegantly attired men, protected by umbrellas, who exited a brownstone mansion on 67th Street, proceeded south along the Boulevard for five blocks, and then paused.

One of the pair, dressed in a fine broadcloth suit, and sporting dark muttonchop whiskers, crossed the Boulevard toward the grassy median strip, where yet a third individual stood. As the man with muttonchop whiskers huddled with him under an umbrella, the figure handed over a bundle wrapped in brown paper—and immediately fled.

The man with muttonchop whiskers returned to his original

companion, who accepted the brown-paper package, offering in return a similar-sized bundle he had been carrying in his coat pocket.

Suddenly, one of the construction laborers dashed straight at the two men, throwing himself on the one with muttonchop whiskers, knocking him off his feet and attempting to pin him to the ground. The target of the apparent assault shouted, "Thieves! Robbery! Help!" Despite his modest size, no more than five and a half feet tall, he fought back ferociously, punching, kicking, and biting—his assailant howled as the teeth sank into his hand.

Another laborer in blue overalls joined the fray, rushing to assist the first upon hearing his screams. This one got a grip on the muttonchopped man's neck, forcing him facedown into the muddy street and binding his arms behind his back with iron handcuffs. Panting and sweating from the struggle, the attackers dragged their captive, covered in wet grime, to a waiting horse-drawn carriage, and rode off with him downtown.

A half dozen miles later, the carriage pulled up in front of a nondescript brick building at 52 Bleecker Street. The two laborers hustled their prisoner up the stairs to a second-floor office—where Hiram C. Whitley stood waiting with a look of satisfaction on his face.

The assailants who had subdued the gentleman on the New York streets that night were not construction laborers, and they were not robbers or kidnappers. They were Secret Service detectives. Their prisoner, now bleeding profusely from a punch in the mouth administered by one of the disguised Secret Service men during the struggle, was Joshua D. Miner.

Everything had gone just as Whitley planned. Harry Cole had arranged to rendezvous with an unsuspecting Miner, and to pay the counterfeiting magnate $1,500 in marked bills—supplied to him discreetly by Whitley in a saloon near the Bleecker Street headquarters—for two- and ten-dollar bill engraving plates, as undercover Secret Service agents watched, and then, at a prearranged signal from Cole, pounced. The Secret Service had caught

Miner in the act of selling the counterfeit engraving plates: the force had him, as detectives liked to say, "dead to rights."

When Miner arrived at Bleecker Street, his expensive clothes soaked and caked in mud, his wrists pinched by handcuffs, and his four front false teeth missing, he presented a pathetic picture indeed.

"Sorry you got into this scrape," Whitley mocked.

"I got into it through trying to help a friend," Miner muttered.[41]

Miner's arrest electrified New York. Whitley reveled in the conquest, summoning members of the press to Bleecker Street, where he held court surrounded by piles of captured bills, along with confiscated plates and printing presses. He explained to the reporters that the mysterious figure across the Boulevard who had handed Miner the package of engraving plates, and then fled, was none other than Thomas Ballard, the counterfeiting boss's master engraver. Whitley's men had followed Ballard and taken him into custody, too. He led them the next morning to a safe house at 256 Rivington Street, where they discovered an astonishing factory for making the same "fiber paper" used in genuine currency.[42] Ballard refused to cooperate—and promptly escaped from jail, probably because Miner's minions bribed his guards. Still, to Whitley, what mattered most was that Ballard's equipment had been confiscated and that his boss, Miner, remained in government custody.

"We have reached the bottom of this business," Whitley crowed. "We have got the plates now of every issue of counterfeit known to the Treasury Department."[43]

The papers splashed Whitley's dramatic assertions across their front pages, extolling the methodical way his Secret Service had dismantled Miner's previously impermeable organization. By this time, Whitley had begun calling himself "Colonel," based on his brief provisional appointment to that rank, not "Major," his previous title. Military résumé inflation was not uncommon; American men of the era were judged by what they had done, or claimed to have done, during the Civil War. "Colonel Whitley and his detectives may well feel proud of their captures," the *New York Dispatch* opined. "These are by all odds the most important arrests ever made in the history of the Secret Service Division."[44]

Crime boss Joshua D. Miner fought furiously when Secret Service detectives caught him in the act of selling counterfeit engraving plates on the streets of New York. (*From Thirty Years a Detective by Allan Pinkerton*)

What remained, however, was to convict Miner, in a trial that the government intended to hold quickly so that Miner would have as little time as possible to bribe or intimidate potential witnesses or jurors. Whitley himself reported offers of up to $20,000 if he would somehow give up the case; he refused.[45] A mere five weeks passed between November 2, 1871, the day when Miner posted $30,000 bond and left the Ludlow Street Jail, and December 11, 1871, when his trial opened at the high-ceilinged United States court on Chambers Street in Lower Manhattan.

New Yorkers flocked to watch proceedings that would determine the fate of a man previously known as one of their town's wealthiest and most influential citizens. "The case excited a good deal of interest on account of the respectable position previously occupied by Miner," the *New York Herald* reported.[46] Among those who packed the dimly lit court were Secret Service detectives who had worked the case. They expected Miner's conviction and wanted to savor every minute leading up to that result.

Prosecuting the case for the United States was Edwards Pierrepont, an eminent Republican lawyer and leader of anti-Tammany political forces in New York. He had stepped down as the city's federal prosecutor in 1870, but was filling in for his successor, who had recently experienced a death in the family. Whitley had urged Pierrepont to substitute, to avoid any delay.[47]

Pierrepont's opening argument to the jury took up an hour on the first day of the trial. He cast Joshua D. Miner's crimes as anything but victimless, and the defendant as anything but the Robin Hood of much local lore. The harm from fake money, Pierrepont explained, "was done to the community, falling upon the more moderate and humbler classes of society." Meanwhile, the beneficiaries tended to be wealthy and privileged, because counterfeiting "required great skill and capacity and a great deal of money. No poor man could manufacture counterfeit money." What's more, Pierrepont noted, anticipating defense objections to the government's bargains with low-ranking criminals, the only way to tackle such powerful, adroit, and secretive offenders was to offer underlings immunity from prosecution in return for their testimony. This strategy, he told the jury, had been personally approved by the top officials of the Treasury Department.[48]

With that, Pierrepont called Harry Cole to the witness stand, and, over the next two days, led Hiram C. Whitley's coerced informant through the story of his years-long involvement with "Jot" Miner, culminating in their rendezvous that rainy night on the Boulevard. William Kennoch, the first of Whitley's undercover men to tackle Miner, followed Cole, on the third day of the trial. Kennoch confirmed that he searched Cole prior to his departure for the meeting with Miner and found nothing on him except the $1,500 Whitley had given him to pay Miner.

This was important: it anticipated what was likely to be the defense's main argument: that Cole had not received the plates from Miner but had brought them to help the Secret Service's duplicitous detectives stage a put-up job against Miner. Kennoch acknowledged that Miner did not have the $1,500 when he returned to Bleecker Street after the sting. He explained that Miner threw the cash away in a desperate attempt to get rid of evidence as he fought with the Secret Service men. Kennoch testified he and a colleague later returned to the scene and crawled around by lantern light until they recovered the bills Miner had scattered.[49]

On December 14, Hiram C. Whitley testified. Under Pierrepont's guidance, he recounted every detail of his steady assembly of a case against Miner, from the arrest of Bill Gurney to the tense negotiations with Harry Cole. Pierrepont dramatically presented him with a stack of special fiber paper for making currency, and Whitley confirmed that he and his agents had discovered it in Thomas Ballard's workshop. He swore that his arrangement with Cole to set up Miner was not a put-up job, but a well-designed tactic that served "the ends of justice," and enjoyed the approval of the government's top lawyers, just as Pierrepont had said in his opening statement.[50]

Whitley spoke serenely, almost triumphantly, betraying not the slightest doubt that Miner was guilty, and that the jury would agree. Matters were not quite so simple, however, as he was about to discover, once Miner's lawyers began their cross-examination. The Secret Service had infiltrated "Jot" Miner's operation, but the wily counterfeiter had managed to infiltrate the Secret Service, too.

Abraham Beatty served in a New York regiment during the Civil War, and eventually became the pilot of the small steamboat Union General Ambrose Burnside used as a floating headquarters during campaigns in the Virginia Tidewater.[51] In September 1865 Beatty had a brush with the law on Long Island: he attacked and beat a man who, in Beatty's estimation, had been paying too much attention to Beatty's girlfriend. The man died, but a court convicted Beatty only of assault, not murder: two expert witnesses, doctors paid by Beatty, testified that the wounds he inflicted could not have been fatal. He paid a fine and went free.

That blot on Beatty's record did not damage his good relationship with the police in New York, for whom he had briefly worked after leaving the United States Army; and, in early 1870, a high-ranking inspector recommended him to Hiram C. Whitley at the Secret Service. Beatty quickly became one of Whitley's favorite assistants, initially specializing in tracking tobacco and wine smugglers before graduating to the division's most sensitive anti-counterfeiting missions. It was Beatty who posed as "Jake Buck" and set up the arrest of Bill Gurney; and it was Beatty whom Whitley sent to retrieve Joshua D. Miner's trunk full of engraving plates.

THREE UNITED STATES DETECTIVES,
(WHOSE PORTRAITS ARE GIVEN IN THIS WORK,)
DISGUISED FOR AN EXPEDITION.
WHO ARE THEY?

Among many talents, Whitley was a master of disguise. In the arrest of counterfeiter Bill Gurney, he posed as a clergyman (center), accompanied by Secret Service detectives Abraham Beatty (left) and Michael G. Bauer (right). (*Memoirs of the United States Secret Service*)

Like Whitley's other employees at the Bleecker Street office, Beatty earned extra income by claiming a share of negotiated settlements the government routinely reached with the various smugglers and traffickers they caught in possession of contraband. Secret Service men would take guilty parties to the United States attorney, who offered to drop the charges against them in exchange for a "fine," plus forfeiture of the captured cigars, wine, or jewelry. Up to half of the proceeds would go to the detectives, a reward known as a moiety. Until abolished by a new federal statute in late 1872, moieties were a perfectly legal, if uniquely American, practice, instituted by the First Congress, and considered necessary to encourage collection of desperately needed tax revenue and custom fees.[52]

Whitley himself received moieties on top of his $3,000 annual salary. He devoted much of 1871, in fact, to a highly public, if thoroughly tawdry, court dispute over the moiety on a particularly lucrative illicit shipment of diamonds.[53] Whitley's innovation was to require his detectives to split their moieties with him. He kept some of the money in a "special fund" for official purposes, such as supplying cash for sting operations, and pocketed the rest.[54] Neither a smoker nor a drinker, he allowed his detectives—as well as New York's policemen and journalists— to dip into a hoard of confiscated Cuban cigars and European wine in the back room of his headquarters. The best smokes were set aside for Solicitor Banfield, and shipped to him at the Treasury Department in Washington.[55]

None of this was strictly by the book; contraband was supposed to be turned over to the United States Marshals for auction. Whitley assured his men that, as he told one detective, "the government doesn't care about this sort of thing; all it wants to do is stop the frauds."[56]

These arrangements ultimately caused a falling-out between Whitley and Beatty in April 1871. Whitley caught Beatty taking much more than his share of a confiscated shipment of wine: ninety out of three hundred bottles, instead of three or four. Even more irksome to Whitley, Beatty subtracted the bottles before the United States attorney had settled with the smuggler, reducing the potential value of the seized merchandise, upon which their moieties depended. Whitley fired Beatty, claiming publicly that it was because Beatty had stolen the wine, black-mailed merchants, and concealed his criminal record.

Six months later, when the Secret Service arrested Joshua D. Miner, Abraham Beatty was still stewing over Whitley's treatment of him. With revenge on his mind, he approached Miner's lawyers and offered to provide them inside information on Whitley's methods, as well as to dig up any new dirt they might require.

Miner's lawyers listened eagerly as Beatty described how Whitley had schemed to profit from Miner's surrender of the trunk full of engraving plates. According to him, self-enrichment had motivated the Secret Service chief's pursuit of Miner all along; Whitley assumed the National Shoe and Leather Bank would pay a handsome reward to whoever took the counterfeits of its notes off the street. And, Beatty said, Whitley concocted a plan to make sure they did.

Though recovering the plates had been a simple matter of retrieving the items from storage in New Jersey, Whitley planted a story in the *New York Herald* portraying it as the result of arduous surveillance conducted over nearly two weeks.[57] Next, he took Beatty to the National Shoe and Leather Bank, boasted to the management that this was the man who had conducted the undercover work, and informed them it was "customary" for banks to provide a cash bonus for such heroism. Prior to doing so, Whitley had told Beatty he expected half of whatever the bank decided to give Beatty.

Beatty also served up sordid details of his former colleagues' backgrounds. He told Miner's defense team that William Kennoch, the first Secret Service man to tackle the counterfeiter on the Boulevard, had been a crew member on illegal slave ships prior to the Civil War, and on cigar-smuggling vessels more recently. Kennoch started working for the Secret Service only after the division captured him and blackmailed him into serving as an infiltrator among his former criminal associates.[58]

Beatty traveled to Boston, paid by Miner's lawyers, to gather evidence of Whitley's checkered business career in that city, quickly learning about his feud with R. M. Campbell before the Civil War, and the brief stint as a pawnbroker after the Civil War, which ended in Whitley's being stripped of his license.

Armed with this information, Miner's defense lawyer, William S. Fullerton—a brilliant former state court judge whose client list included shipping and railroad magnate Cornelius Vanderbilt and "Boss" Tweed himself—set out to thwart the prosecution.

First, Fullerton cross-examined William Kennoch, forcing the detective to acknowledge that he had been arrested in 1858 as a crew member of a slave ship, and that his Secret Service career began when Ichabod C. Nettleship caught him with forty-eight hundred bootleg cigars but dropped the charges in return for his turning informant. And yes, Kennoch had done some jail time for his part in a brawl, though he insisted he had only been "protecting my mother from an assault."[59]

This was a mere warm-up for the attack Fullerton launched on Hiram C. Whitley after the Secret Service chief finished his direct testimony. Miner's lawyer confronted Whitley with the embarrassing fact that the prosecution had introduced into evidence only the serial numbers of the $1,500 in legitimate bills Harry Cole paid Joshua D. Miner, not the actual cash. What happened to the money? Fullerton demanded. Whitley admitted he spent it. "I used the money because it was mine and I had a right to it," he snapped.

Fullerton presented Whitley a copy of a newspaper containing his concocted story about a supposed Secret Service surveillance operation to capture the twenty-dollar engraving plates, the one he had planted to support his scheme to talk the National Shoe and Leather Bank into giving Abraham Beatty—and

Whitley—a reward. Whitley claimed he did not recall telling the reporter that false story.

Fullerton insisted, "Will you swear you did not give such information?"

"I will not," Whitley admitted. "Well, I remember that I promised Miner to cover it up in the papers, and I may have given the story a little different from what the real facts were."

"Then you told an untruth," Miner's lawyer parried.

"I would not call it an untruth," Whitley muttered.

Fullerton demanded to know if it was true that he had told the cashier of the National Shoe and Leather Bank that Beatty deserved a reward.

"I do not remember that," the Secret Service chief replied, claiming that he had heard later that Beatty did receive a bonus from the bank, and that he admonished him not to accept it.

Fullerton took Whitley back to the 1867 revocation of his pawnbroking license in Boston. "There was some investigation in reference to a watch," Whitley conceded. "I was not there at the time."

Hadn't he also swindled a man out of an apothecary shop in Boston? the lawyer asked. "I forget what the charge was," the Secret Service chief responded.

What about R. M. Campbell? Didn't that businessman fire Whitley for stealing from his restaurant back in the 1850s? "No, sir, never," Whitley snapped.

The grueling review of Whitley's past went on for hours, over the course of two days. For the finale, Fullerton dredged up the darkest chapter of all: the day in January 1859, when twenty-six-year-old Hiram C. Whitley had helped waylay the abolitionist John Doy and his party of freedom-seeking African Americans outside Lawrence, Kansas.

How, exactly, Fullerton learned the details of that duplicitous deed was unclear. Whitley's role, while not widely known, was not a secret, either. The case made the news in 1859, and press accounts described Whitley's subsequent confrontation with the abolitionists in Lawrence; John Doy, too, had published a memoir in which he mentioned Whitley's pointing a gun at him.

Hadn't the Secret Service chief been charged with crimes for his part in the Doy ambush? Fullerton asked.

Stunned at having this long-ago treachery thrown back in his face, Whitley lied. "I was in the service of the marshal there," he asserted, "and assisted in the capture of fugitive slaves. I was not charged with cruel treatment of the slaves."[60]

He made no mention of his conspiring with the Missouri-based slave catchers for weeks prior to the ambush, much less of the fact that two of the people he helped to kidnap were not slaves at all, but free men of color.

With that burst of denial, Whitley stepped down.

The prosecution quickly fired back, producing several Ohio officials to testify to Miner's record as a convicted counterfeiter in that state. Yet Fullerton had made his point. The jury, twelve men drawn mostly from the ranks of Manhattan's shopkeepers and small-time merchants, had already seen and heard plenty to make them wonder whose record was more disreputable: the defendant, or the lawman who had investigated him.

"This whole case is surrounded by fraud, imposture, and falsehood," Fullerton's assistant told the jury when Whitley and the other prosecution witnesses had finished testifying.[61] Then the defense began trying to conjure reasonable doubt through the testimony of Joshua D. Miner's friends and relatives. Some of them swore, falsely, that they had witnessed Harry Cole drop and pick up a package—by implication, the engraving plates—prior to meeting Miner on the night of October 25, 1871. Others, including a parade of pompous Tammany Hall worthies, testified to the defendant's good character.

Edwards Pierrepont's closing argument for the prosecution reminded the jury of how difficult it was to prove a case of counterfeiting, and that the government therefore had little realistic

alternative to using "peculiar, though not dishonorable means...
to get such proof." The defense's denunciation of Whitley had
been "unfair," given the detectives' undeniable "success in capturing Miner and fixing his guilt upon him."[62]

Yet there was no getting around the fact that the case could
hinge on the credibility of the government's witnesses, led by
Whitley, and his informant, Harry Cole. And the man presid-
ing over the trial, Judge Charles Linnaeus Benedict, thought the
jury had every reason to doubt them. A Republican former state
assemblyman who had been appointed to the federal bench by
President Lincoln in 1865, Benedict was no friend of Tammany
Hall, or of Joshua D. Miner. He was, however, an old-fashioned
gentleman, the son of a college professor born and educated in
stern, puritanical Vermont.[63]

On the trial's twelfth and final day, December 26, 1871, Benedict instructed the jury on the law, pointing out that they could
convict Miner if, and only if, the government had convinced
them of his guilt beyond a reasonable doubt. In making that determination, the judge said, they should consider not only the
evidence against Miner, but what sort of people procured and
presented it.

Harry Cole, he emphasized, was a known criminal who
helped ensnare Joshua D. Miner in return for Whitley's promise of leniency. Cole could be believed—if others corroborated
his testimony.[64] The only corroboration, however, came from
detectives. As for them, Judge Benedict told the jurors,

I but repeat what has often been said—that as a class their
evidence is always to be scrutinized and accepted with caution. I do not say that detectives never tell the truth upon
the stand. I do not say that they always misstate upon the
stand. What I do say is that, from their occupation, from
their calling, and living a life of deceit, constantly engaged
in the manufacture of this and that and the other story,

their statements on the witness stand are not entitled to the same weight as that of ordinary witnesses of good character taken from the mass of the community.[65]

Whitley, watching the proceedings with his detectives, could hardly believe his ears. The judge was practically urging the jury to acquit Miner based on what he saw as the dubious character of the government's investigators. The Secret Service chief was perfectly aware that he had been less than candid under cross-examination. To him, however, that had nothing to do with the matter at hand, which was that Joshua D. Miner had been caught red-handed selling counterfeit engraving plates, months after promising Whitley he would have nothing more to do with the coney trade. What were white lies Whitley might have told to cover his own youthful indiscretions compared to an entire defense composed of perjury?

Whitley continued to believe a conviction was coming even after the jurors, who retired to deliberate at 3:00 p.m., twice returned to the courtroom—at 4:40 p.m. and again at five minutes before midnight—to say they were deadlocked. Each time, Judge Benedict instructed them to keep trying for a unanimous verdict. At five minutes before one o'clock in the morning of December 27, they finally informed the court that they had reached one.

Joshua D. Miner nervously stroked his chin as the twelve men filed back into the court, looking "fearfully solemn," in the words of one journalist.

"Gentlemen, what say you?" the bailiff asked. "Is the prisoner at the bar guilty or not guilty?"

"Not guilty," the jury foreman responded—whereupon Miner's tense face spread into a grin and his friends erupted in applause. Judge Benedict pounded his gavel for silence. In disbelief, the prosecution asked to poll the jury. All twelve men concurred in the verdict. Within minutes, the counterfeiter was celebrating with champagne and lobsters at the Jockey Club uptown, accompanied by his lawyers—and several members of the jury.[66]

Whitley and his detectives, by contrast, lingered in the court-room, staring blankly around them in utter shock.

Joshua D. Miner had escaped justice, despite the effort Whitley and his team poured into the case. In the process, Whitley's rep-utation, and that of the Secret Service, had taken a hit. The trial was Whitley's first appearance as Secret Service chief in a public forum, though he, and his men, had starred in the many news-paper accounts of the Secret Service's exploits he served up to reporters—along with contraband cigars. New York knew little of his past. Now William S. Fullerton's cross-examination had recast the master detective as a liar and kidnapper of freedom-seeking slaves and their white allies.

That Miner's legal team did this with the aid of Beatty, Whit-ley's former employee, made the outcome doubly galling. Pos-sibly the only thing that might have stung Whitley more was the exultation Miner's acquittal caused among his old foes in Columbus, Georgia. In that town, the editor of the *Daily Sun* greeted the news with an article trumpeting Judge Benedict's instructions to the jury, and crowing about Whitley's defeat: "Columbus has every reason to detest him and rejoice at the detection of his villainies."

Whitley pasted a clipping of the *Daily Sun* piece in the scrap-book he kept at Bleecker Street and scrawled an angry rejoinder across it in pencil: "I arrested this man in 1868 for murdering Geo. W. Ashburn. They were Ku Klux."[67]

The most pressing practical issue, though, was the possible impact on the Secret Service, if federal courts started to adopt the view of him and his detectives expressed in Judge Benedict's skeptical jury instructions.

Prior to the Miner case, only one federal judge had told ju-rors to discount sworn testimony from detectives. In Whitley's old haunt, New Orleans, Judge Edward Henry Durell—a trans-planted New Englander who had worked with Union forces during the war—gave such instructions so frequently that Whit-ley had informed Solicitor Banfield in the fall of 1871 that he saw no point in continuing operations against counterfeiting in New Orleans.[68]

Judge Durell's position was regrettable but tolerable, Whitley believed, given the relatively small scale of the counterfeiting business in the Deep South. However, if Durell's interpretation "were to be confirmed by the other U.S. judges throughout the country," he noted, "there would be an end to the detection of counterfeiters." The Secret Service "would be paralyzed."[69]

Now that hypothetical prospect seemed real; Judge Benedict, who handled most federal criminal cases in New York, the hub of counterfeiting in the United States, had echoed Durell's view. After Miner's trial, Whitley learned from seven of the jurors that they believed Miner guilty, but voted to acquit because of the judge's instructions.[70]

The Secret Service chief decided to fight back—swiftly, and in the same bold, argumentative manner with which he had coun-tered all of his previous antagonists, from R. M. Campbell in Cambridge to the pro-Klan newspapers in Georgia. He decided to send his own message to the future federal jurors of America.

As December 1871 gave way to January 1872, and a bitter winter cold wave enveloped the northeastern United States, Hiram C. Whitley sat down at his desk to compose an open letter, titled "To the People." Salted with quotations from legal authorities, lyrics of Puritan hymns, and a full measure of Whit-ley's abundant sarcasm, the document ran to some five thousand words. The Secret Service chief ordered it printed as a pam-phlet and distributed to newspapers across the country. Over the last half of January, many papers republished it, either en-tirely or in part.[71]

It was an extraordinary direct appeal from a government official who owed his position neither to his fellow citizens' votes nor to the votes of their representatives in Congress. Possibly for the first time in American history, an unelected federal bureaucrat openly advocated the undercover surveillance of civilians in peacetime, in frank defiance of the contrary views of a federal judge. Whitley declared that Judge Benedict's views "should forever be denied a place in jurisprudence." Undercover stalking of criminals, he insisted, was a noble calling, practiced by honorable men, who bore no bias against any individual, and whose "salary is in no manner contingent on the number of convictions secured."

His detectives deserved comparison not with the criminals they pursued, Whitley wrote, but with the most skilled and humanitarian of professionals: "the detective…dissects society as the surgeon dissects his subject." Accordingly, their testimony was perfectly credible, as was the testimony of counterfeiters whom detectives entrap and induce to turn against former partners in crime, Whitley argued. Having burned their bridges with their erstwhile confederates, such witnesses had little alternative to "sincerity" on the witness stand. They were "far more worthy of belief than the perjured friends of the culprit."

Whitley acknowledged "many honorable people do not fully approve" of what he and his men do, "from the simple fact that they do not fully understand it." The best answer to such well-meaning critics was that his methods worked. "The system of using one counterfeiter against another has created greater distrust, and caused more alarm among them as a class than the untiring labor of the most skilled detectives," Whitley argued.

Obviously, infiltrating counterfeiting gangs involved lying and deception, as Judge Benedict had said, but, Whitley asked, "Is this a wrong done to the criminal, or a right done to society?" There was no alternative. "When fish bite at naked hooks, when nanny goats are adepts at catching weasels and expert rogues turn fools," Whitley sneered, "counterfeiters can be caught without deception and the betrayal of mutual confidence."

It was Whitley at his most articulate, logical, and pragmatic—aggressive, to be sure, but not sanctimonious. The *Boston Times* found Whitley's arguments "plausible," and praised the results the Secret Service had achieved against the coney traffic so far. The *Pittsburgh Chronicle* agreed with Whitley's main argument that the damage counterfeiting did to the public "would turn the balance in favor of employing detectives."[72]

Joshua D. Miner, however, thought that Whitley protested too much. The counterfeiter, recalling how the detective squirmed under cross-examination at his trial, decided to press the attack.

At the very time Whitley published his open letter, a Senate committee was on an extended visit to New York for hearings on allegations that officials at the gigantic New York Custom House had steered warehousing contracts to a crony of President Grant. The scandal had no direct connection to Whitley or the Secret Service, but Miner and his Tammany Hall lawyers took advantage of the situation to stage a further attack on their nemesis: they persuaded Democrats on the committee to call Abraham C. Beatty as a witness.

On February 6, 1872, Beatty sat before the committee and regaled the senators with his tale of alleged corruption at Whitley's Secret Service, from the manipulation of moieties to the hoarding and distribution of contraband cigars. Miner's lawyers had not called Beatty as a witness in the trial, probably to avoid cross-examination about his checkered past, so this was the first time he had testified personally in public. The New York newspapers splashed his allegations across their front pages.

Whitley, enraged, wrote Solicitor Banfield in Washington, assuring him Beatty's "tissue of falsehoods," was a story "only equaled perhaps by the famed legends of the Arabian Nights or of the Baron Munchausen." His testimony, Whitley assured his boss, was part of Miner's attempt at "breaking me down in the estimation of the government and the people." The whole business might even be the prelude to an attempt on his life, Whitley wrote.[73]

Whitley demanded an opportunity to respond, and the committee gave it to him. His daylong testimony on February 8 represented the first time the chief of the Secret Service had faced Congress. The morning session consisted of mostly friendly questioning from Republican senators, who gave Whitley a platform to deny everything they had heard from Beatty—"certainly the most unmitigated scoundrel I ever met," Whitley called him. He made an equally sweeping condemnation of the jury's verdict in favor of Joshua D. Miner. It was the result, he said, of "rank perjury; I know it."[74]

Whitley was confident and persuasive on that point, but when the committee resumed the hearing after a dinner break, Democratic Senator Eugene Casserly of California had consulted with Miner and his lawyers, who occupied seats near the front of the committee's makeshift auditorium—a grim basement storeroom in the opulent Fifth Avenue Hotel. Facing questions from Senator Casserly scripted by Miner's team, Whitley "seemed very anxious to exculpate himself," and "spoke so rapidly as to be hardly understood," a journalist noted.[75] He repeatedly claimed lapses of memory about his dealings with Beatty. Senator Casserly confronted Whitley about his Boston pawnbroker license, about the contraband cigars stockpiled at Bleecker Street—and about his time in Kansas before the Civil War.

"Were you ever engaged during that period…in catching runaway Negro slaves?" Casserly asked.

"I went, sir, by request of an officer, and aided him in the execution of the fugitive-slave law," Whitley responded, adding that he had gone along "at the suggestion of a friend," and "never received a cent for it."

"Now do you think an amateur hunter of runaway Negro

slaves is more respectable than an official hunter of them?'" Casserly sneered.

"Yes, sir," Whitley insisted, as Miner's friends hooted with derision.[76] "I did this in a legal manner, and...did no wrong against the law or anything else." He claimed, preposterously, that the captured African Americans had voluntarily returned with him and the rest of the posse to Missouri. "They saw their master and they were tickled to death."

Senator Casserly ridiculed this obvious falsehood. "Then it was a philanthropic pursuit you were engaged in, was it?"

Toward the end of the long evening, Senator Casserly tried to get the Secret Service chief to admit that, given Miner's acquittal, the deal Whitley struck with Harry Cole had "resulted in nothing," except for enabling that known counterfeiter to go free.

To this, Whitley did have a convincing answer: despite the acquittal—based on perjury, he hastened to repeat—his investigation had resulted in the capture of Miner's counterfeiting plates, presses, and money-fabricating matériel, including Thomas Ballard's ersatz fiber paper. None of that would have been achieved unless Cole had cooperated.

"It was a very valuable transaction to the Government, according to my judgment," he said. "It broke up a very extensive gang of counterfeiters of which Miner was the head."

Miner and his friends were not laughing now. Whitley was right. Miner's counterfeiting organization could not easily recover from its thorough exposure in court. Neither would Miner's reputation as a legitimate businessman; acquitted or not, undisputed evidence at his trial established that he agreed to meet with known criminals like Bill Gurney and Harry Cole. The erstwhile Tammany big shot could not readily explain that. He had his freedom, but was "far from coming out of the ordeal with clean hands or with an untarnished name," the *New York Sunday Dispatch* opined.[77] In fact, there were still separate indictments pending against him, though it was unclear when or if he would face trial on those charges.

Every fiber of Whitley's contentious being told him to keep on talking—to litigate, in the court of public opinion, against both Miner's attempted character assassination and Judge Benedict's more legalistic, but no less damaging, criticism. His open letter was still circulating, in pamphlet form, and it was winning him a few converts.

Whitley decided to play his ultimate card: the Secret Service's confidential dossiers.

Squirreled away at Bleecker Street were a half dozen out-of-court statements from "Jot" Miner's former neighbors in Steuben County, detailing his youthful criminal activities, and those of his family. These raw investigative files described counterfeiting and horse-stealing by the Miners going back to the 1840s; a former judge had told Whitley's detectives that Miner was hauled into his court in 1854 on a charge of bastardy by the unwed mother of his now eighteen-year-old daughter. Such allegations could not be introduced at Miner's trial, but would certainly taint perceptions of the contractor once they did enter the public domain.

Whitley cleverly understood that they would be most damaging to his enemies if they appeared to come from someone else's mouth. He approached an old acquaintance, Massachusetts journalist George P. Burnham—a former United States Army mess hall boss, Republican Party spoilsman, and poultry breeder—whose previous published book *History of the Hen Fever*, recounted the speculative mania in exotic chicken breeds that swept the United States in the 1850s.[78] Whitley asked Burnham to be the credited author of a book, derived from the Secret Service's records, that would present the division and its men in the best possible light, and their underworld opponents in the worst.

The 436-page result, *Memoirs of the United States Secret Service*, appeared within weeks of Whitley's testimony before the committee. The epigraph, a quotation from a French monarchist journalist who fled that country's Revolution in 1789, Antoine Rivarol, set the tone: "Wrong is wrong. No fallacy can hide it, no subterfuge cover it so shrewdly but that the All-seeing Eye will discover it and punish it." This French allusion was in keeping with the book's contention that the Secret Service arose because "it was...deemed advisable that our National Government should inaugurate an elaborate plan of detection—similar to that supported advantageously in European countries." The first chapter, a twenty-nine-page biography of Whitley, praised him for combining "a Fouché's power of organization and combination, with the executive capacity of a Vidocq."[79] He had put these gifts to work on behalf of the federal government in the Ashburn case—which had "previously baffled all predecessors"—and in his more recent battle against the counterfeiters. His fight against crime had inevitably prompted a "stealthy attack" from "vilifiers," but Whitley possessed the "true moral courage" to withstand it.

Yes, Whitley had helped in the capture of "certain fugitives he encountered or followed up" in Kansas before the war, but that was a youthful indiscretion, attributable to his lack of "the training that was needed for one to cope with the prejudices of the people he found there." As much as Whitley now "regretted" this "mistaken course," it reflected his otherwise admirable zeal about "the supremacy of the law," and the law, at that time, included the Fugitive Slave Act. Like many others at the time, he "honestly then believed that he was following the *right* in lending his assistance to the government," *Memoirs* noted.

It was a self-serving account, a blatant attempt at limiting the damage he sustained during the Miner trial and the committee hearing. It was also as close as Whitley would ever come to apologizing for his treachery toward John Doy. If anyone still held that against him, *Memoirs* offered a final argument: nowadays Whitley enjoyed the "unlimited confidence" of the Grant ad-

ministration, from President Grant, Secretary Boutwell, and Solicitor Banfield on down. If he was good and honorable enough
for stalwart Republicans and antislavery men such as these, he
should be good and honorable enough for anyone.

The same applied to the men who worked for Whitley, who
must be "honest, temperate, morally upright, and of good general standing in the community." *Memoirs* presented laudatory
biographies of selected detectives: Ichabod C. Nettleship, Abner
B. Newcomb, Thomas Lonergan, Charles Anchisi. Through
detailed recitation of their educational, business, and military
credentials—accompanied by handsome "accurate portraits"—
these chapters sought to persuade the public that Judge Benedict's
mistrust of undercover operatives was biased and out-of-date:
"It can hardly be fairly said of men such as these...that they are
not worthy of being believed, on oath."[80]

Memoirs contrasted the detectives' qualities with those of the
counterfeiters whose evil deeds the book described in lavish detail. The criminals' likenesses appeared in *Memoirs*, too: Whitley
wanted to be sure that people everywhere knew not only the
damning contents of the Secret Service's files about these men,
but could also recognize their faces.

The portraits were drawn by professional illustrators from
photographs Whitley had ordered taken of suspected counterfeiters while in custody, and which he hung like trophies on
the walls of his Bleecker Street office. This "rogues' gallery,"
much commented-upon by visiting journalists, was no mere
publicity ploy.[81] It represented the first systematic use of photography as an identification tool by a federal agency. With
this innovation, Whitley kept pace with police departments in
London, Paris, and Berlin that adopted photographic technology in the 1870s.[82]

The book's dramatic final chapter laid out, almost verbatim,
everything the Secret Service had on "the autocrat of American
coney men," Joshua D. Miner, including that previously secret

affidavit about his out-of-wedlock child. Miner had escaped formal punishment for counterfeiting, due to Judge Benedict's words, *Memoirs* acknowledged. Nor would Joshua D. Miner face trial on the charges still pending against him after his 1871 acquittal. Judge Benedict ruled that out as a form of double jeopardy.[83]

Still, on what Whitley considered the key long-term issue—whether the courts would accept his detectives' testimony—his view, not Judge Benedict's, would ultimately prevail. Whether due to Whitley's advocacy or other factors, more and more federal judges concluded that detectives could indeed be trusted. One judge in New Jersey instructed a Trenton grand jury in 1873 that "there had been too much disposition on the part of the press and public to find fault with" the Secret Service. A few years after the Miner trial, even Judge Benedict would change his tune, telling a detective he "would be pleased to have any and all members of the Secret Service...give any information that would throw light on any case."[84]

Meanwhile, the publication of all the dirt the Secret Service had on Joshua D. Miner, accompanied by an accurate portrait of him, took a toll on the erstwhile Tammany contractor's reputation and the licit businesses that depended on it. Public exposure also meant that he was "effectually reduced to impotence in crime," as *Memoirs* put it, echoing Whitley's argument at the Senate hearing. Miner never returned to counterfeiting prior to his death in 1886.

Hiram C. Whitley had managed to get the last word against his nemesis, the so-called "autocrat of coney men." The Secret Service chief could devote attention to other missions, including the highly innovative—and highly risky—investigation in which he and the Secret Service had been covertly engaged simultaneously with their pursuit of Joshua D. Miner.

As a publisher's note in *Memoirs* explained, that special assignment would be the subject of a forthcoming second book, also based on government files: the "intensely thrilling records of the doings of the United States Secret Service division in shadowing, hunting down, and arresting many noted members of 'The Ku Klux Klan.'"[85]

5

"The government secret agents were everywhere upon their track."

Hiram C. Whitley had interpreted the denouement of the George W. Ashburn case optimistically. The Ku Klux Klan conspirators escaped conviction in July 1868, but the detective saw a consolation prize in the state legislature's ratification of the Fourteenth Amendment and Georgia's reinstatement to the Union under a Republican governor and Republican-drafted constitution. Such reforms, Whitley believed, could not give Ashburn justice, but they might serve his cause: the "equality of the oppressed race."

Subsequent events undercut that hope. As soon as United States Army authority in Georgia lapsed, the state's white supremacist Democrats set about overturning the new Reconstruction political order. By September 1868 they had engineered the expulsion of twenty-eight African American lawmakers, all Republicans, from the state legislature on the spurious grounds that the state's new constitution did not specifically allow black men to serve. Republicans, most of them black, staged a protest march; when they reached the town of Camilla on September 19, 1868, an armed white mob opened fire, killing twelve.[1]

The Klan replicated these tactics across the South, and the terror continued for the next three years.[2] In October 1868 an Arkansas Klan leader murdered a white Republican congressman; that same year the South Carolina Klan assassinated three black members of the state legislature. Late in 1869, a mob in North Carolina shot at the home of freedman Dan Blue, a witness against several Klansmen in an arson case, wounding him and killing his pregnant wife and five children. In 1870, armed whites attacked a political rally of two thousand mostly black Republicans in Eutaw, Alabama, leaving two dead and fifty-four injured. In March 1871, the Klan massacred thirty African Americans in Meridian, Mississippi.

At a time when state legislators still selected United States senators, and Southern and border states combined controlled roughly half of the electoral college, Republican leaders realized that the violence against their supporters in the South posed a political threat as well as a moral one. The Ku Klux Klan—numbering tens of thousands of sworn members across the southeastern United States, and enjoying the informal support of many times that number in the white population—constituted the Democratic party's terrorist wing.[3] Unchecked, it could stamp out black voting, thus enabling Democrats to take control of state governments in the former Confederacy, followed, possibly, by control of the federal government.

The Republicans managed to win Congress and the White House in 1868, and to hold on to Congress in 1870. As 1871 began, however, the Democrats held at least one branch of state government in Georgia, Alabama, Virginia, Tennessee, and North Carolina. This boded ill for Republicans in the upcoming 1872 contest, when the presidency and Congress would again be at stake.

An editorial in the pro-Republican *Harper's Weekly* summarized the party's predicament, and the country's:[4]

If our political system really be one which forbids the government to protect its own citizens when voting for its officers, and which requires the country to look on passively while mobs controlling various State authorities harry those voters, it will certainly be necessary to reconsider some of our raptures over the infinite superiority of the American to all other possible systems of government.

As *Harper's* implied, the federal government had been slow to respond, even with Republicans in charge of the White House and Congress. Sensitive, as a former general, to accusations of "military despotism," President Grant hesitated to intervene in the South for what could easily be portrayed as partisan purposes. There was also reluctance in Washington to admit that Reconstruction might not be working as planned, and—still—a strong presumption that law and order was a state responsibility, not a federal one. As late as February 11, 1871, Grant's attorney general instructed a Department of Justice official in Alabama that the states are "the regular and usual protectors of person and property."[5]

The most important constitutional authority for a federal crackdown on the Klan—the Fifteenth Amendment, which banned racial discrimination in voting rights, and empowered Congress to enforce that prohibition—did not take effect until February 3, 1870. Not until May 31, 1870, did Congress make it a federal crime to "go in disguise upon the highway" and attack those who exercised the right to vote or other civil rights.[6] Another month and a half went by before Congress created the Department of Justice, headed by the attorney general, and empowered it to enforce that statute.

Republican governments in Tennessee, Arkansas, Mississippi, and the Carolinas, meanwhile, tried to take on the Klan using state authority and resources. North Carolina's campaign was among the most aggressive.[7] In 1869, a year before Congress enacted its voting-rights enforcement law, the Tar Heel state legislature had already adopted a similar measure. Next, Republican Governor William Woods Holden secured legal authority and funding to beef up the state militia and recruit two dozen detectives.[8] After the murder of one of these detectives—who doubled as a Republican state legislator—in Caswell County on May 21, 1870, Governor Holden dispatched three hundred militia troops to the area. They arrested one hundred Klansmen.

Governor Holden's crackdown failed, though. Planning to try the Klan detainees before a state militia commission, he revoked their right to ask state courts for writs of habeas corpus. A federal district judge, noting that the legislature had denied the governor this power, ordered the Klansmen released. The uproar over Holden's supposed dictatorial methods demoralized Republicans and buoyed Democrats; the latter won the legislature in North Carolina's August 4, 1870, election. The new majority, led by well-known Klansmen, abolished the anti-Klan detective force and militia, and impeached Holden.

Other Southern states, too, proved unable to curb the Klan. Vivid atrocity reports poured in to Congress and the executive branch in Washington. In his annual message to Congress on December 5, 1870, President Grant alluded to "violence and intimidation" in recent elections; eleven days later, the Senate asked President Grant for a full report. He responded in January with two volumes documenting the rampant terror in North Carolina and other states.[9]

On March 10, 1871, President Grant ordered the United States Army's 7th Cavalry to South Carolina, at the request of that state's Republican governor; the troops arrived sixteen days later. In the meantime, the president declared he would give South Carolina's Klan twenty days "to disperse and retire peaceably to their respective abodes," or else he would order the cavalry into action. On March 23, he visited the Capitol and asked Congress for new laws to "secure life, liberty, and property, and the enforcement of law, in all parts of the United States."[10]

In the House, Representative Benjamin Butler of Massachusetts, Hiram C. Whitley's old boss in New Orleans, recounted the Klan's whipping of a Northern-born white superintendent of African American schools in Mississippi. The attack left the victim's nightshirt soaked in blood. Why, Butler demanded, could the federal government use its forces lawfully to protect a United States citizen attacked by enemies abroad, but not "on our own soil, under his own rooftree, and covered by our own flag?"[11]

The resulting Ku Klux Klan Act of April 20, 1871, strengthened the previous year's law by allowing President Grant to suspend habeas corpus where he determined Klan violence could not otherwise be controlled; by requiring jurors in federal Klan trials to swear they were not members of the organization; and by authorizing federal troops to assist United States Marshals in arresting Klan suspects. Also, Congress empaneled a joint committee, bipartisan but chaired by a Republican, to investigate—and publicize—the truth behind the atrocity reports.

As of May 1871, the basic elements of Washington's anti-Klan strategy were in place. It essentially replicated, at the federal level, the state-level measures that North Carolina and others had already tried: tougher laws, armed force, selective suspension of habeas corpus. There was, however, one exception: the federal government had not committed to a role for covert action—for detectives.

In all of American history, there had never been a federal undercover operation to investigate civilians for alleged criminal violations of the constitutional rights of fellow citizens, much less whites' violations of African Americans' rights. Novel as the idea might be, it had become a practical necessity. If Klansmen were to be put on trial in federal courts, as Congress and the Grant administration envisioned, the government would have to infiltrate the conspiracy and gather evidence to use against its members.

That, at least, was the view of a small but influential group of Southern Republicans, who feared for their political futures, and their lives—and those of their African American fellow citizens. The group's leader in Congress was North Carolina Senator John Pool. A pre–Civil War opponent of secession, Senator Pool's close alliance with Governor Holden began in the 1864 North Carolina "peace movement," which unsuccessfully advocated a unilateral state exit from the Confederate military effort. After the Civil War, Pool became a Republican and, in the Senate, drafted the key enforcement provision of the 1870 federal anti-Klan law—modeling it on his home state's legislation.[12]

In early 1871, Pool began quietly seeking money and legal authority for a team of federal detectives to penetrate the Klan. He proposed it to the Republican Senate Appropriations Committee chairman, Cornelius Cole of California, but Senator Cole doubted its propriety. At Pool's insistence, however, Cole agreed to consult President Grant's attorney general, Amos Tappan Akerman.[13]

As Pool knew, the attorney general would sympathize with his idea. Akerman, too, was a Southern Republican, the only one in President Grant's cabinet, and a strong advocate of equal civil and political rights.[14] Born in Portsmouth, New Hampshire, in 1821, Akerman graduated Dartmouth in 1842, then wandered various states, North and South, before settling in Georgia, where he taught school while receiving legal training. Throughout the 1850s, he practiced law; he also farmed and held slaves, but opposed secession until the firing on Fort Sumter. At that point, the Union's failure to protect its Southern loyalists gave Akerman no alternative but to collaborate with the Confederacy.

New Hampshire–born Amos T. Akerman hoped to save freedom in his adopted home state of Georgia by crushing the Ku Klux Klan. He recruited Hiram C. Whitley and the Secret Service to that cause. (*National Archives*)

Or so he would rationalize after the war, when he repented his brief Confederate military service (in the rear echelons), became a Republican, and urged white Georgians to accept Reconstruction. Akerman believed, as he would later write, that "there would be strife as long as one part of this free people were denied rights which the other part enjoyed." Akerman served with George W. Ashburn in Georgia's constitutional convention, and ran for presidential elector on the Republican ticket in 1868, in return for which President Grant appointed him Georgia's United States Attorney in 1869. (Congress passed a special law making him eligible, despite his Confederate past.) In June 1870, the president promoted him to attorney general at the urging of Representative Butler, who had met Akerman while the latter lobbied for his state in Washington.

In July 1870, his first month in office, Akerman instructed Department of Justice lawyers in the South to prosecute every alleged violation of the federal anti-Klan criminal laws that came to their attention. "That any large portion of our people should be so ensavaged as to perpetuate or excuse such actions is the darkest blot on Southern character in this age," he would confide to his diary.[15] Yet he grew frustrated with the difficulty of securing indictments and convictions. In a January 23, 1871, letter to Senator Cole, the attorney general explained that the federal government needed detectives to overcome these problems. "In some parts of the country, the sufferers by the crimes punishable in these [anti-Klan] acts are, for the most part, poor and ignorant men," he wrote, "who do not know how to put the law in motion, or who have some well-grounded apprehension of danger to themselves from the attempt to enforce it."[16]

Senator Pool's proposed legislative language was "vague," Akerman conceded. As written, it would provide funds for "the detection and prosecution of crimes against the United States, to be expended under the direction of the attorney general."[17] However, these phrases could only refer to violations of the federal anti-Klan law, since, except for a relative handful of offenses—tax evasion, interference with the mails, and the like—there were hardly any other "crimes against the United States" at the time.

What the attorney general did not tell Cole, perhaps because he thought it went without saying, was the real reason for the indirect statutory language: political caution. A clear statement might arouse potential opponents of the bill, or tip off the Klan.

Persuaded by the attorney general's argument, Cole inserted funding authority for Pool's plan into a must-pass appropriations bill, which President Grant signed on March 3, 1871.

Four weeks later, Pool forwarded the Department of Justice a request for a federal detective from Tod R. Caldwell, the Republican acting governor of North Carolina, who had replaced the impeached William Woods Holden. Klan leaders "can be ferreted out if proper measures are taken to do so," Caldwell asserted. "In order to accomplish this, I think it necessary that some discreet person should be sent...as a detective. I have no authority to appoint such an officer nor any funds to defray his expenses. Cannot the president do so?"[18]

Caldwell wanted a detective sent from New York or Washington "at once." Time was of the essence because the same Democratic North Carolina legislature that had impeached Holden had also called a referendum for August 3, 1871, on whether to hold a new state constitutional convention. Democrats hoped to win through Klan intimidation, then use the convention to gut the civil and political rights established in the constitution drafted in 1868 under the Reconstruction Acts.[19] Pool scribbled at the bottom of Caldwell's letter: "I hope the Attorney General will be able to act on his suggestions promptly." When Akerman responded, accurately, that the new authority to fund detectives did not take effect until July 1, 1871, Pool went back to his colleagues on Capitol Hill, who were about to vote on the Ku Klux Klan Act, and got them to make the money available immediately.[20]

Still, Attorney General Akerman hesitated to take the momentous step of deploying detectives without a clear order from the president. Thus far, Pool, Akerman, and their allies had proceeded stealthily, so stealthily that it was not entirely clear President Grant grasped the full meaning of the measure he had signed. It was one thing to gain the authority and funding that way, and quite another to use them without informing him.

There were risks in approaching Grant directly, the main one being he would say no. Having Akerman float the idea at a cabinet meeting might elicit the president's support, or trigger objections from Grant's other advisers. The more people who knew about the plan, the more likely it would leak. Possibly

Senator Pool could approach the president, but that, too, posed questions of discretion and plausible deniability.

Finally, Pool, Akerman, and other advocates decided to sound out the president indirectly, through a third party, whom they could disavow if he met with rejection, or if his mission became public. Getting presidential approval for an undercover operation, in short, required an undercover operation.

On June 7, 1871, Congress's new Joint Select Committee to Inquire into the Condition of Affairs in the Late Insurrectionary States—the "Ku Klux Committee"—heard testimony from North Carolina witnesses that Senator John Pool had invited to Capitol Hill.

Joseph Goodman Hester, a deputy United States Marshal based in Raleigh, told the panel of his forays into North Carolina's Klan strongholds over the previous six months. He had executed arrest warrants on six men in Moore County wanted for whipping two black Republicans, and forcing a white man to burn down a school he had built for black children; seized another half dozen men in Caswell County for assaulting a politically active freedman, Essic Harris; and, with help from United States Army troops, rounded up thirty perpetrators of a mob attack in Cleveland County on a sixty-year-old white Republican, Aaron Biggerstaff, and his family. Klansmen, Hester reported, would tell their victims that "they are not human beings, that they come from the boneyards at Richmond, that they have been seven years in the boneyards, and have come for vengeance."[21]

Chilling as it was, Hester's testimony was not original. Several others recounted the same incidents to the committee that day.

His appearance seems to have been a cover for the true purpose of his trip north: Pool recruited him to take North Carolina's plea for federal detectives to President Grant, in the discreet form of a letter signed not by Attorney General Akerman, or any

North Carolina Republican, but by Pool's political ally, Republican Senator John Scott of Pennsylvania, the Ku Klux Committee chairman.

After testifying, Hester boarded a northbound train with the ultimate destination of West Point, New York. Grant was attending his son Fred's graduation from the United States Military Academy, and he had agreed to receive a messenger from Senator Scott there.

The son of a Methodist minister, Hester's roots lay in "respectable" North Carolina Piedmont society.[22] Otherwise, though, the thirty-year-old was an unlikely emissary to the president of the United States. He left home in 1855, at the age of fourteen, purportedly fleeing because he killed one of his father's colts and tried to shoot his brother. Still in his teens, he fought with the United States Army against the Seminoles in Florida, then, in 1856, joined the United States Navy. Left ashore in Rio de Janeiro after contracting yellow fever, he recovered and worked on railroads in Brazil and Argentina. Hester volunteered for a belligerent faction when civil conflict erupted in Buenos Aires; escaped a prisoner of war camp; and found his way to England on a British merchant bark. The ship sailed into an Atlantic hurricane, whereupon Hester took the wheel and piloted it safely home.

In 1862, Hester quit the crew of a British merchant ship in Gibraltar and signed on to the Confederate frigate *Sumter*. While the *Sumter* was still at anchor, he sneaked into the captain's cabin and shot the sleeping man in the head. Some suspected he did so because the officer had caught him stealing; others, because Hester coveted command himself. Hester contended he had acted to thwart the captain's defection to a Union vessel. The British jailed Hester at Bermuda, then handed him to Confederate authorities, who not only declined to press charges but hired him to smuggle goods through the Union naval blockade of the

South. In December 1864 the United States Navy captured and burned Hester's ship, but released him, reportedly in return for a promise to spy for the Union.

Back in North Carolina after the war, Hester came up with a scheme to raffle off former property of bankrupt planters, as well as silverware he bought on credit in New York. The plan fell apart when the New York creditors charged Hester with fraud. Former owners of his burned-up blockade-runner tried to sue him. Hester settled these disputes out of court but, as 1870 ended, he was bankrupt.

The United States Marshal for North Carolina approached Hester at a Raleigh boardinghouse and offered to make him a deputy. Hester agreed and became a Republican. He needed work, and believed, as he later put it, that "the Ku Klux or Democratic Party [was] murdering innocent citizens on account of their loyalty to the government."

Impressed with the results Hester produced as a deputy marshal, North Carolina Republicans abandoned their request for a New York– or Washington-based detective, and planned instead to recommend that the federal government deploy Hester to infiltrate the Klan if President Grant gave Attorney General Akerman the go-ahead.

On June 9, 1871, Grant's staff ushered Hester in to West Point's guest quarters.[23] The six-footer with light blue eyes and a brown beard handed the president Senator Scott's letter. Grant opened it and read:

> Mr. Hester, of North Carolina, will bear this to you & explain fully the service, which he believes may be rendered to the country. We are satisfied of the character & competency of Mr. Hester, & respectfully recommend that such directions in the premises be given to the Attorney General as to make him feel authorized in the matter, at once. The Attorney General hesitates for want of instructions,

& Mr. Hester is sent at my instance to communicate with you. There is an appropriation of $50,000, made at the last Session, to aid in prosecuting offenses against the criminal laws of the United States. This matter should be put into operation without delay, in order to insure success, & secrecy is indispensible [*sic*]. For this reason, I have deemed it best to send Mr. Hester in person.

Grant listened as Hester provided a grassroots report on Klan violence in North Carolina, and explained the need for undercover work. His story fit all too well with the information the president had already compiled and sent to Congress in January, and with subsequent pleas for assistance he had received from the state's officials and other Klan victims. The proposed $50,000 cost was the same amount the Republican government of Mississippi budgeted for its state anti-Klan detective unit in 1870, which had since been disbanded.[24] The expenditure seemed especially modest relative to the political stakes: in addition to the impending August 3 state referendum, North Carolina, with one of the South's largest concentrations of white Republican sympathizers, would be crucial to Grant's reelection campaign in 1872.

The president saw no reason to say no. He reached for a pen and scrawled a note on the reverse side of the letter: "Respectfully referred to the Atty. Gn. who will please carry out the desires of the writer," he wrote, signing it, "U.S. Grant." Hester carried the document back to the Department of Justice in Washington.

A few days later, on June 15, President Grant instructed an aide to send Attorney General Akerman another message: the president had been thinking about the question of where to send detectives since his meeting with Joseph G. Hester, and he had decided not to limit their use to the Carolinas. They should be sent to Alabama, as well.

★ ★ ★

In New York, Hiram C. Whitley remained unaware that Washington contemplated a covert operation against the Ku Klux Klan.

Through the first half of 1871, Whitley focused on the same kinds of crimes that had occupied him and his detectives since he became Secret Service chief in May 1869. He could claim real progress, especially since mid-1870, when Solicitor Banfield had approved his reorganization plan, and Congress had increased his funding. In March 1871, Whitley told the *New York Herald* that the Secret Service had made eight hundred total arrests between May 1869 and the end of February 1871. Of that number, he said, slightly over half involved accused counterfeiters of currency or federal excise tax stamps, including one hundred twenty-nine deemed manufacturers or wholesalers. The majority had been convicted at trial or pled guilty.[25]

His men had seized half a million dollars' worth of counterfeit currency, as well as many engraving plates used for manufacturing false bills in every conceivable denomination. For good measure, the Secret Service cracked down on black-market cigars, confiscating four hundred thousand untaxed stogies, shutting down sixty clandestine factories for producing them, and seizing two steamships caught smuggling tobacco into the port of New York.

And, having secured the backing of top officials in the Treasury Department, Whitley was hard at work on his undercover pursuit of Joshua D. Miner.

With his trusted subordinates in charge of branch offices from Boston to San Francisco to New Orleans, Whitley could plausibly boast, as he did to the *New York Herald*, that the Secret Service was "national in character" and "permeate[d] the entire country." Based on what Whitley told him, the *New York Herald*'s reporter noted that the division's "officers are selected with special reference to their honesty and integrity and their

peculiar fitness and adaptability to the duties required of them."
The Secret Service had risen to "the leading detective organization of the country, within whose ranks it is nothing less than an
honor to be enrolled." William S. Fullerton's cross-examination
in the Miner trial, and Abraham Beatty's embarrassing accusations, still lay months in the future.

Another important change at the Secret Service had occurred
in 1870: as of July of that year, Whitley no longer worked exclusively for the Treasury Department. July 1870 was the month
Congress created the Department of Justice—in the process
granting the attorney general shared authority with the secretary of the Treasury over Whitley's direct boss, the solicitor of
the Treasury. By extension, this meant that the Secret Service
chief answered to Amos T. Akerman, and that the latter could
employ his detective force, "national in character" as it was, to
assist the coming crackdown on the Klan.

In addition to the legal and bureaucratic advantages, there was
another reason Akerman would entrust this assignment to the
Secret Service: having been one of George W. Ashburn's Republican colleagues in Georgia, he knew Hiram C. Whitley's
record. He remembered that the Secret Service chief was one
of the very few men in the federal government with experience
investigating the Klan.

With presidential approval for the detective mission secured,
Akerman summoned Whitley to Washington on June 19, 1871,
to let him in on what were still highly secret plans. As he me-
morialized his conversation with Whitley in a subsequent letter,
the attorney general explained the appropriation to investigate
"crimes against the United States," and his authority to allocate it. "On account of your expertness in the detective system,"
Akerman flattered Whitley, "I desire your assistance in effect-
ing the end of this appropriation." Akerman added that he had
"reason to believe" that Congress meant "certain sorts of crimes
which are reported to be more frequent in the Southern states

than elsewhere"—Klan terrorism.[26] In Akerman's view, the Secret Service's role would be to give federal prosecutors in Klan cases the same sort of specialized investigative support that they got from internal revenue officers in internal revenue cases, or from post office agents in postal cases.

He staked Whitley to an initial $20,000 and asked him to recruit capable and trustworthy people to head south, "and as soon as you have made any important discoveries you will report to the attorney general the ascertained facts of each case together with the names of witnesses."

Once again, the federal government was relying on a pre–Civil War slave-hunter to fight its undercover battles with the Ku Klux Klan, though it was unclear whether Akerman knew what Whitley had done in Kansas. (The attorney general surely knew about the Secret Service chief's treatment of the black detainees in Fort Pulaski.)

This was ironic, but not necessarily inconsistent. Before the Civil War, Congress enacted the Fugitive Slave Act, pursuant to Article IV, Section 2 of the Constitution: the act provided that slaves fleeing to Free States be returned to slaveholders in slave states. When he ambushed the Doy party, Whitley purported to be following that body of law. After the Civil War, the Thirteenth, Fourteenth, and Fifteenth Amendments, in conjunction with new civil rights statutes, tilted federal law in the opposite direction: enforcement power that had previously been brought to bear against those who helped smuggle African Americans to freedom in the North would now be used against those who terrorized black people and their white allies in the South. As Republican Representative James F. Wilson of Iowa said on the floor of the House while speaking in favor of the 1866 Civil Rights Act, pre–Civil War legal reasoning "uttered in behalf of slavery...is perfectly applicable to this case."[27]

The federal authorities had switched sides; and, thanks to fate, political connections, and his own knack for clandestine operations, so, too, had Hiram C. Whitley. Surprised as he was to receive the Klan assignment even in the midst of his complex pursuit of the counterfeiter Joshua D. Miner, Whitley unhesitatingly assured Akerman that he would get the job done. He wrote back to the attorney general, promising to carry out his instructions "to the best of my ability," and to spend government funds wisely. "You will receive my reports in due course of time, showing the progress of any operations," he added.[28]

For Whitley, it was a chance to expand the Secret Service's jurisdiction beyond what he could have anticipated when he took the job in 1869. Whitley would not be on the front lines, conducting interrogations or staking out suspects in disguise. His role would be that of spymaster, organizer, and supervisor of what amounted to a domestic anti-terrorism unit within the Secret Service. Still, he must have relished a rematch with the Klan conspiracy that had so viciously attacked his reputation in 1868, not to mention gotten away with Ashburn's murder.

Within two weeks of receiving Akerman's orders, Whitley had already sent three men to the South. Whitley imposed strict compartmentalization on them, telling each that he was going on a special mission to "ascertain if a certain condition of affairs said to exist in a certain locality, did so exist," but not revealing that others had been sent to different regions with the same task.[29] This would ensure the credibility of the information they gathered and protect the security of the overall operation if anyone were captured or discovered. Whitley was so effective in this regard that two Secret Service members would eventually infiltrate the same Klan den, each believing the other to be an actual member.[30]

Whitley devoted special attention to each detective's "stall," Secret Service slang for an assumed identity. His men could travel as laborers searching for seasonal work, tradesmen casting about for good business locations, even newspaper reporters—whatever it took to make local populations believe that the detectives were actually sympathetic to the Klan.

The ideal "stall," in Whitley's view, was itinerant black marketeer. As Whitley well knew from his time smashing stills in Virginia, Southerners despised federal excise taxes on alcohol and tobacco, almost as much as the abolition of.slavery. This created a natural overlap between illicit trafficking in these substances and support for the Ku Klux Klan. When first spreading their conspiracy from Tennessee to the surrounding states, in fact, Klan recruiters had sometimes posed as bootleg alcohol and tobacco peddlers.

Joseph G. Hester would infiltrate the crucial state of North Carolina. As the first Southerner to work with the Secret Service during Whitley's tenure, he knew the customs, speech, and dress; the Secret Service chief would not have to teach him, as he did some others.

For Whitley, there was just one problem: Hester had not been recruited by the Secret Service chief but by the attorney general, at the behest of the North Carolina politicians whom Whitley barely knew and to whom Hester enjoyed independent access. Akerman had issued Hester $1,000 for expenses, on June 10, 1871, along with a Department of Justice commission "to operate in North Carolina and country contiguous thereto."[31] This was the day after Hester met President Grant, and nine days before Akerman conferred with Whitley for the first time. Hester knew more about the government's plans because he had been in on them long before Whitley.

Whitley was agreeable to absorbing Hester into the Secret Service, but not unless he had clear authority and control over him, with the North Carolinian to receive his pay and expense money through Whitley and reporting to Bleecker Street, not the Department of Justice. Akerman agreed. As soon as his June 19, 1871, meeting with the attorney general ended, Whitley went to the telegraph office and wired his first order to Hester, who had meanwhile returned to North Carolina: "I have just arrived here [in Washington] from New York and consulted with the attorney general in regard to matters in the South," Whitley wrote. "Highly important business requires your presence here."[32] Hester had to come meet the Secret Service chief in Washington immediately.

Hester did not actually receive Whitley's message until June 29, by which time he was already traveling through the Tar Heel state, conducting new investigations.[33] In response, he telegraphed not Whitley but the Department of Justice, telling a senior official that Whitley was demanding that he interrupt his work to return north. "Must I come?" Hester pleaded. The department's answer was yes; Hester dutifully trekked back to Washington.

Whitley then put off seeing him for a week, claiming the press of other business, before telling Hester to travel to New York. He finally received Hester at the Secret Service's Bleecker Street headquarters on July 7, 1871, having forced him to expend much valuable time in what Hester surely understood was at least partly an effort to show who was boss.

There was nevertheless a certain logic to Whitley's request that he and Hester meet face-to-face, and take each other's measure, before the Secret Service started paying the North Carolinian's expenses—and accepting responsibility for his actions. Over the course of hours, the two discussed the violent events Hester had witnessed in the South, and Hester listened to Whitley's "ideas and plans of operation against the Ku Klux," as Hester later wrote.

The similarity of the paths these two former teenage runaways had followed through life must have occurred to both federal lawmen, and perhaps helped them establish mutual understanding. Like Whitley, Hester had changed sides once or twice during America's great sectional conflict of the previous two decades; now, they had definitively thrown in their lots with the federal government, and their commitment to this new mission, for the United States against the Ku Klux Klan, would have to be unconditional.

Satisfied that his new detective was a man he could rely on, and having devised a good "stall" for him, Whitley ordered Hester back to North Carolina. A few weeks later, Akerman could reassure a prominent member of Congress impatient with the government's efforts against the Klan that there was "more quiet work going on in the way of unearthing them than the public has any suspicion of."[34]

No one in the Moore County, North Carolina, hamlet of Swann's Station considered it unusual to see a pair of denim-clad strangers driving a wagon into town at noon on a hot day in early August 1871.[35] The travelers introduced themselves as merchants, with tobacco for sale—cheap, because they had not paid federal excise tax on it.

A local approached the visitors. "What's the news?" he asked.

"What kind of news do you want to hear?" the wagon driver replied.

The local immediately recognized these passwords of the Ku Klux Klan.

"Convention news," the local man replied.

With that, he approached one of the peddlers and extended his hand. The visitor took it, and gave a firm shake, having first folded his right index finger into his right palm to form the Klan grip.

The rituals complete, the newcomers could be taken into their fellow Klansman's confidence. He introduced them to the Moore County den, and they spent hours together over the next two days, regaling one another with stories of recent raids. The Moore County Klansmen spoke freely of murders and beatings they had administered against local Republicans, white and black; they told these tales partly because they knew they were among friends, and partly to compete with the apparent boss of the peddlers, who called himself Goodwin. He boasted of astonishingly violent deeds; he even claimed complicity in the May 21, 1870, murder of a state detective that had triggered then-Governor Holden's ill-fated crackdown on Klan counties.

Perhaps it was also a desire to impress Goodwin that caused the Moore County den to let him in on their plan for the night of August 10: they were going to don Klan disguises, mount their horses, and take John A. Campbell from his home to a carefully chosen spot in the poplar forest. Then they would hang Campbell from a tree limb.

Campbell was thirty-five years old, married, with four children. He sold liquor by the glass to help support his family, since a disability that caused him to walk with a limp limited his capacity for other work. He also traded in cotton purchased from black farmers who grew it on land rented from whites, even though white planters, falsely, complained the African Americans stole it from them. The Klan had condemned him for other reasons, however: Campbell had been a Union man who helped the United States Army during the Civil War and had joined the Moore County Republican Party afterward. He hosted meetings for its members, black and white, at his little dram shop. On two previous nights in 1871, the Klan had punished Campbell by whipping him with tree branches. They admonished him to cease his Republican activities each time. In spite of those warnings, he had persisted.

In late July the den decided enough was enough. They intended to kill Campbell on the night of August 3, just after that day's state referendum, but a United States Army patrol unexpectedly passed through Moore County, so they postponed the murder a week. Meanwhile, the Klan had acquired a fresh reason to hate Campbell and the Republicans: the referendum failed, with Moore County voting "no" by a 41-vote margin out of 1,719 cast.[36]

Goodwin and his tobacco-peddling companion not only approved the murder, they asked to join in. The Moore County den promptly assented.

A day before the raid, Goodwin helped the gang fetch their costumes from a hiding place under a neighbor's porch. The next evening, August 10, just before the group headed out in their black cambric robes and high, conical black hoods, Goodwin urged everyone to test-fire his gun, then gave each man fresh gunpowder to reload.

Then the nine Klansmen dragged Campbell out of bed, commandeered his wagon, and drove him to the poplar forest. They encircled him, their faces obscured by the hoods, which were ghoulishly adorned with bull's horns and emblazoned with white crosses and three white letters—"K.K.K." They looped a noose around his neck and ordered him to his knees. Goodwin began to read a list of the offenses for which the Ku Klux Klan had condemned Campbell.

Yet when the reading of Campbell's death sentence ended, and the moment to execute it arrived, Goodwin did not pull the noose tighter around the Republican's neck. Instead, he cried out—and the Klansmen heard the sound of booted feet crashing toward them through the underbrush. A squad of federal soldiers, answering Goodwin's signal, emerged into the clearing.

The stunned Klansmen reached for their firearms. Perhaps they could still shoot their way out of the trap Goodwin had laid for them. When they pulled the triggers, though, nothing happened. Goodwin had reloaded their guns with black sand.

Goodwin removed his hood and helped the soldiers handcuff his prisoners and bind them together with the rope the Klan had been using on John A. Campbell. Then Goodwin turned to the group and revealed his true identity: United States detective Joseph G. Hester.

Hester had not come to Moore County expecting to break up a plot against John A. Campbell. The timing of his first operation as a Secret Service detective rather suggests that he was there to engage in clandestine monitoring of the August 3 referendum, alongside the United States Army troops whose surprise visit temporarily aborted the Klan's attack on Campbell. Prior to setting out, Hester had spent a few days at a safe house in Fayetteville, North Carolina, refreshing his knowledge of Klan passwords and secret grips in discreet conversations with defectors from the organization.

When he learned the Klan's plan, Hester and his fellow "tobacco peddler"—actually an assistant he had hired with Secret Service funds—faced a choice between warning Campbell, which would blow their cover, and letting the Klan kill him. Hester's solution was to get a secret message to the Army, which was still nearby, then rely on the troops to appear at his signal, all while keeping up the pretense that he and his assistant were looking forward to hanging Campbell. It was a tremendous gamble. Under the circumstances, however, Hester considered it the only chance for all of them—Hester, his assistant, and Campbell—to survive.

Hester had heard members of the Moore County den say something that raised the stakes even higher: this group was responsible for a notorious spate of violence earlier in 1871, near the boundary between Moore and Chatham counties.[37] The rampage began in April, when the Klan attacked Frances Gilmore, a twenty-year-old African American mother of two: they stripped her, beat her with a board, slashed her with a knife, and burned her pubic hair with a match. A few nights later, thirty disguised men burst into the house of a sixty-year-old white woman, Sally Gilmore—no relation—who was known for letting African American men hold political meetings at her home. A black man who was there at the time, Murchison McLean, tried to flee, but two Klansmen caught him and shot him at point-blank range; he died the next day.

The rest of the mob beat the two remaining African American men at the Gilmore house unconscious with clubs and switches, then dumped the victims in the mud outside. Next, they stripped Gilmore's teenage son and daughter and forced them to dance, as Klansmen lashed them with a cowhide whip. The attackers administered similar cruelties to the naked bodies of Sally Gilmore and a female houseguest.

"Let's make the old she-radical dance now!" a Klansman cried.

"We can do better than that," another said. "We can lick the damned nigger-loving blood out of her."

When Hester, his assistant, and the squad of federal troops sprang their trap on the night of August 10, therefore, they were not only taking John A. Campbell's tormentors into custody, but also arresting a half dozen of those who had thus far escaped accountability for the atrocities against the two Gilmore families and Murchison McLean.

The Secret Service men loaded the captive Klansmen onto wagons and drove them eight miles north to the railroad depot at Sanford, North Carolina, where they all boarded the next train to Raleigh. Arriving at the state capital on August 11, Hester asked five of the soldiers to put on captured Klan regalia, then paraded them up Fayetteville Street, the city's main commercial thoroughfare, with the actual Klansmen walking ahead, in handcuffs. Hester led the procession, a pistol hanging from his belt, along with the cowhide whip the Klan had used on the Gilmores.

Raleigh "was thrown into the wildest state of excitement," a Republican newspaper reported.[38] Hundreds flocked to Fayetteville Street. Klansmen on parade was an all-too-familiar phenomenon, after dark; but to see the white terrorists being herded through town in the middle of the day, by federal officers, was astonishing and—especially for African Americans in the throng—a rare moment of triumph. Black spectators jeered at Hester's prisoners as he led them to the United States commissioner's office, in a rented house a block from the North Carolina state capitol. The detective presented them to be arraigned, then committed to jail. He submitted the cowhide whip and Klan disguises as evidence.

Most in the crowd did not realize that the figures in robes were not actual Klansmen, but that hardly diminished the spectacle's impact.

Just as the Democratic papers in Georgia had blamed "Negroes" or his fellow "radicals" for killing George W. Ashburn, North Carolina's white supremacist press insisted that there was no Klan, and no Klan terrorism, only personal quarrels that might be violent, but had nothing to do with politics or race. "I do not believe there is any such organization," lawyer and Democratic politician Plato Durham, a North Carolina Klan chieftain, lied, under oath, to the Ku Klux Committee in Washington a week before Hester made his arrests.[39]

Hester's parade debunked the myths. A pro-Republican newspaper reported it under the headline ARRIVAL OF KU KLUX IN OUR MIDST, WITH THEIR DISGUISES! THEY ARE OF THE GENUINE BRAND! THE TRUTH ESTABLISHED. "Who now will have the effrontery to stand up and deny the existence of an organized band of Ku Klux in North Carolina?" the accompanying article asked.[40]

Hester cleverly spread the message using the latest technology. At Watson's Photograph Studio in Raleigh, he and eight other men posed in the Klan costumes, reenacting the attempted hanging of John A. Campbell, who had accompanied Hester to Raleigh.[41] Hester delivered the black-and-white photograph to the acting governor, Tod R. Caldwell, who forwarded it to the War Department in Washington. The September 9, 1871, front page of the *National Republican* carried a woodcut reproduction of the image, accompanied by a detailed account of Hester's operation, supplied by Senator John Pool. Eventually, the image would be reprinted and distributed on thousands of handbills across the country.[42]

Whitley's top detective in North Carolina, Joseph G. Hester, used photography to prove that the Ku Klux Klan was no mere Republican myth and that he had captured Klansmen in the act of attempting to murder John A. Campbell. (*Courtesy of The Abraham Lincoln Foundation of The Union League of Philadelphia*)

The pro-Klan North Carolina press mounted a furious counterattack. The *Raleigh Sentinel* published a letter purportedly from the father of one of Hester's detainees. It claimed, accurately, that Hester had dressed impostors in the Klan costumes, but added, falsely, that the detective had brought the robes with him to Moore County, then tricked the man's son and others into wearing them so he could stage an unwarranted arrest. Klan apologists smeared Sally Gilmore as the "keeper of a bawdy house for negroes," and John A. Campbell as a man of "low, base character," whipped not for his politics but for being cruel to his wife and selling bootleg liquor.[43]

What a *Sentinel* editorialist most reviled was the "Horried Sight" [*sic*] of "six white men brought forty miles for whipping Sally Gilmore and her negro paramours," then paraded by "a United States marshal with pistol and cowhide at his side, marching front of the prisoners, with negroes in kuklux [*sic*] dress following in the rear, yelling and roaring like savages."[44]

The pistol and cowhide were the accoutrements of antebellum slave patrollers and plantation overseers, to be wielded exclusively by whites against blacks; this made Hester's display of them especially intolerable to the *Sentinel*. It warned the state's Republican officials: "You must not suppose that the white blood of the State will submit to such indignities from unprincipled officer-holders and ignorant negroes."

If there was any ambiguity as to what this implied, the *Sentinel*'s sister publication, the *Fayetteville Eagle*, cleared it up in an editorial:[45]

Hester and other suspicious characters are prowling around in the country as secret detectives, really secret agents of Radical officers to keep up political hate and strife for profit to that party and its leaders. We hope our citizens will shoot down, on sight, any strangers caught in mischief while prowling stealthily around our homes. A legitimate and well-meaning government employee should be respected and assisted; but an assassin and incendiary, and a bare-faced tool for low-lived treachery and oppression, should not be allowed to carry out his nefarious purposes.

Yet there was a note of desperation in these threats. Hester's face and physical description remained unknown to most people in North Carolina; he had not been foolish enough to allow a photograph. This helped him dupe the Moore County Klan, and on at least one subsequent occasion, Klan sympathizers bent on murder seized someone they believed to be Hester, only to discover that they had captured the wrong man.[46]

Fearful of federal prosecution, sincerely repentant, or both, Klansmen began to confess their crimes and name their coconspirators. One "puker"—as the Klan called those who violated their oaths of secrecy—was nineteen-year-old William Washington Wicker. Hester had detained Wicker in Moore County and charged him with murdering Murchison McLean.[47] After eleven days in a Raleigh jail, he decided to risk Klan retribution rather than take the fall for that crime. Wicker went before the United States commissioner and swore out the first of what would eventually be two affidavits in which he recounted his career in the Moore County Klan, identified the murderers of Murchison McLean, and described not only the invasion of Sally Gilmore's home, but also a separate April attack, as well as the plot to assassinate John A. Campbell. He named every member of the Moore County den.

Wicker confirmed the Klan regalia Hester displayed in Raleigh was genuine—the same costumes, made by the Klansmen's wives, that Wicker and others had worn during all their attacks. The cowhide was the one they had used to whip Sally Gilmore and many others.

Two weeks after Wicker confessed, Jesse Bryan of Moore County told Hester he wanted to make a statement, too.[48] He recounted Wicker's initiation ceremony, during which Klansmen held a knife to Wicker's throat and a gun to his chest, as he swore to keep the Klan's secrets. Bryan also vividly described the attack on Sally Gilmore's house, confirming that the cowhide Hester wore in Raleigh was the one with which Klansmen had slashed Gilmore's naked flesh. He corroborated Wicker's account of Murchison McLean's murder. Bryan admitted he had taken his oath to the Klan freely. However, he now said, "when I saw the full meaning of the obligation revealed at Sally Gilmore's,

I was convinced it was wrong, was willing to abandon it, and did abandon the organization."

With these affidavits in hand, a biracial federal grand jury in Raleigh quickly indicted a dozen Moore County Klansmen for the attack on Sally Gilmore.

In a letter to Attorney General Akerman, Hiram C. Whitley had called the "reticence" of the Klan's victims the "greatest obstacle" his detectives faced. The situation was all too reminiscent of the one Whitley had encountered in Columbus, Georgia, three years earlier: "Those who have escaped with life have had a seal put upon their lips which they dare not break upon pain of death, and the dead have nothing but their mangled corpses to tell the story of their wrongs," Whitley wrote.[49]

Yet after Hester arrested Klan insiders, paraded them humiliatingly through Raleigh, and turned them into witnesses for the prosecution, Klan victims in North Carolina started to overcome their fear of testifying. In early September 1871 word reached the Secret Service man in Raleigh that twenty-year-old Sarah Jane Ferguson of Chatham County was willing to tell him about her family's ordeal at the hands of the Klan.[50]

Everyone in their little community on the western edge of Chatham County knew Sarah Ferguson's father, Dennis Ferguson, had opposed secession, but was nevertheless drafted into the Confederate Army, and died as a Union prisoner of war at Elmira, New York. His widow, Catherine, still adhered to Dennis's Unionist principles and taught them to Sarah and her three younger brothers. Sarah freely talked Republican politics with her African American neighbors.

The Chatham County Ku Klux Klan warned the Fergusons to cease Republican activities or leave the county. The family paid no attention.

Shortly before midnight on November 10, 1870, Sarah Ferguson heard a sound like the shuffling of horses' hooves on the frozen ground outside her family's home. The next thing she knew, the front door flew open, and a man in bizarre black robes stood before her. "Have you ever seen a Ku Klux?" he asked. "I never have," Sarah replied, "and I never wish to, without it looks better than you."

To this defiance, the intruder's response was to usher in a mob of similarly dressed men, who dragged Sarah Ferguson's brothers outside. They gave each boy fifty lashes, using a switch cut from a nearby sweet gum tree. Trying to protect them, Sarah knocked off one assailant's mask, and recognized him as a neighbor, Dick Taylor. He cocked his pistol and threatened to kill her if she ever reported him to authorities.

Taylor informed the Fergusons they had ten days to leave the area—or die. Not only did the Fergusons stay; they also told their neighbors about the beatings, which were impossible to conceal anyway, given the marks on the bodies of the three Ferguson brothers. No one supported the family; local authorities took no action.

At ten o'clock on the rainy night of December 11, 1870, the Klan stormed back to the Ferguson home, cursing Sarah and her mother for naming them publicly. They stripped forty-year-old Catherine Ferguson, threw her on the floor, and administered one hundred lashes, leaving "many ugly wounds and bruises," as Sarah later put it. Two of the brothers, and a visitor, Eli Phillips, were also stripped and given two hundred lashes each, or so it seemed to Sarah; she lost count.

Sarah was the last to be flogged, pinned facedown and naked on muddy ground outside her house. Five men took turns giving her thirty lashes each, beating her until the branches had already snapped and frayed, and all that remained were the butt ends, tightly gripped in their fists.

For the next month, as winter deepened, the Fergusons hid in nearby woods. "We suffered a great deal with cold and hunger," Sarah later said. When the family recovered enough to travel, they left behind belongings they had not already sold for food, and moved to the Chatham County Quaker community known as Snow Camp. By some miracle, they were all still alive.

Joseph G. Hester interviewed Sarah Ferguson at Snow Camp, then persuaded her to come with him to Raleigh on September 8, 1871, and make a complaint to the United States commissioner. "I have given a plain statement of the facts as they occurred," she testified, "more terrible, however, in reality than can possibly be depicted." Hester and his assistant took arrest warrants to Chatham County and rounded up the five men Sarah Ferguson identified as her attackers.

The *Raleigh Sentinel* dismissed the violence against the Fergusons as punishment for a woman who "like Sally [Gilmore], keeps an evil house." With the aid of some of Raleigh's wealthiest white citizens, the Klansmen made bail.[51]

On September 20, 1871, three members of the Chatham County Klan tracked Catherine and Sarah Ferguson down at the remote mountain hut where they had been hiding since giving testimony in Raleigh. The Klansmen declared that, this time, they would administer a beating the women would not survive, but, in the middle of the attack, Ferguson recognized one masked man by his voice, and shouted his name. A neighbor had also seen and recognized two of the men earlier that night; apparently worried that they might be discovered, the attackers fled.

The next day, Sarah and Catherine Ferguson returned to Raleigh and made yet another affidavit. Astonished at the Klan's savagery, but awed by the women's stamina, Hester managed to bring two of the suspects in; the commissioner ordered them jailed without bond.

The Secret Service provided the Fergusons a secure place to stay in the city, protected and paid for by the federal government. Their nightmare, at last, was over.

By the fall of 1871, "the fright among the Ku Klux and their friends in the state is becoming terrible, and…as an organization the Ku Klux is rapidly collapsing," as federal officials arriving in Washington from North Carolina told the *New York Times*.[52] That was a slight overstatement, but in a letter to President Grant, Attorney General Akerman confirmed privately that "there is now some abatement in their activity."[53]

Approximately sixteen hundred Klansmen, of an estimated forty thousand in the state, had been arrested during 1871, and roughly eleven hundred indicted. Some three hundred of the defendants were indicted based on facts Joseph G. Hester of the Secret Service had gathered.[54]

Hester reveled in his success. Toward the end of 1871, he again marched Klan captives through Raleigh, and mockingly displayed a human skull on which they had laid their hands to swear the Klan's oath of silence. His prisoners then broke that oath by confessing to a federal commissioner.[55] Hester bought advertising space in the *Carolina Era* to taunt the Klan. "Hunters for wolves set their traps near the dens and put such bait there as they usually bite at," the Secret Service man wrote, "and when one or more of them are entrapped, the others usually begin to howl."[56]

Calhoun County, Alabama, in the northeastern corner of that state, had been the scene of a spectacular Klan mass murder on the night of June 11, 1870. A mob of robed and hooded Klansmen hanged William Luke, a Canadian who taught school for black children, and who had supplied firearms for self-defense to black men. The same night, after a brawl broke out in town between blacks and whites, the Klan shot or hanged five African American men.[57]

No one had been punished for those heinous offenses as of July 1871, when two itinerant bootleg liquor salesmen arrived in the Calhoun County hamlet of Cross Plains and set up shop. They spoke convincingly of their support for the Ku Klux Klan, into whose ranks both were quickly inducted. No one suspected they were Louis Del'Omo and George W. Carter of the Secret Service, much less that the capital for their enterprise came from the man who had instructed them to set it up as a "stall," Hiram C. Whitley.[58]

At first, Del'Omo and Carter witnessed little new Klan activity. As their initial report to Whitley noted, the Alabama Klan was keeping a low profile lest it provoke the president to send troops as he had done in South Carolina in March. Also, a subcommittee of the congressional Ku Klux panel traveled to Huntsville, Alabama, for an on-scene hearing and the Klan was "anxious to convince the committee that there are no Ku Klux in the state," the detectives reported.[59]

After the committee left, the detectives informed Whitley, dens once again "originated raids and issued warnings to such of the citizens—white and colored—as they pleased." In due course, the Calhoun County Klan's leaders informed Del'Omo and Carter that they were planning to punish William F. Fletcher, another white Canadian in their area whom they deemed guilty of agitating the black population. Del'Omo and Carter would be expected to take part in the "amusement," as the Klan's leaders called it.

The Secret Service men drafted an anonymous note warning Fletcher of what was about to happen, but could not find a moment in which to deliver it without blowing their cover. With no federal soldiers close at hand, they had no chance to summon military aid as Joseph G. Hester had done when faced with a similar dilemma in North Carolina.

Del'Omo, the senior of the two Secret Service men, was under subpoena to testify in a Florida Klan case. He had therefore been concocting a plausible excuse to leave town even before the Klan ordered him to participate in the planned crime. He could still get away without taking part in the assault on Fletcher.

For Carter suddenly to beg off, however, would arouse too

much suspicion. There was no choice, Del'Omo instructed Carter: he had to stay in Cross Plains, go along on the attack against the Canadian, and take notes of everything he saw and heard.

On the night of November 23, 1871, a Klansman came to Carter at his hotel and showed him how to trim his bedsheet into a robe. Two others appeared later and provided Carter a high conical hat, white gloves, white stockings to wear over his boots, and black face paint. The four men—three Klan members and an undercover Secret Service detective—then found Fletcher at a grocery store, put guns to his head, blindfolded him, and led him to a patch of woods on the northern edge of Cross Plains. There, they removed his coat and tied him face-first to a tree.

"Say your prayers, you don't have but a short time to live," a Klansman told Fletcher.

The Canadian begged for mercy, but his captors responded with ridicule; then two of the men began beating him with rods on his bare back and legs until he lost consciousness.

Prior to joining the Secret Service in 1871, George W. Carter skippered a barge in New York harbor, and worked as a federal revenue officer in Brooklyn.[60] Little in his experience prepared the thirty-one-year-old for this moment, but it was obvious that the slightest hesitation could cost him his life. He held Fletcher's coat and counted, out loud, the blows on the Canadian's body, which continued long after his flesh was a bloody pulp, and his attackers' robes were thoroughly splashed with blood.

The flogging over, Fletcher slumped against the tree. Minutes ticked by. Then, surprisingly, he stirred. A Klansman asked if he had a last request.

"Write to my mother, Mrs. William Fletcher, Hamilton, Ontario, and say how I died," the Canadian murmured. He added, "Is there no chance to live?"

The Klansmen considered the matter. If Fletcher agreed to leave Alabama within the next three hours, and never return, they told him, they would not kill him. Fletcher accepted; his captors took him at gunpoint to the railroad leading out of Cross Plains. Carter last saw him staggering down the tracks, with Klansmen threatening to shoot if he so much as turned to look back.

Now the Calhoun County Klan drew Carter deeper into their confidence, and their plots. Immediately after the flogging of William Fletcher, one of the men who had wielded the rods came to see the undercover Secret Service man in his hotel, and reminisced, in detail, about the murder of William Luke and the five African American companions at Cross Plains. Another member of the den revealed that Nathan Bedford Forrest, the former Confederate cavalry general, had personally organized the Klan in a nearby town, and had come to Cross Plains after Luke's murder to help the Klansmen who committed it avoid prosecution.

A third Klansman told Carter he had just returned from Montgomery, Alabama, the state capital, where he had denied to a federal grand jury that he had any information about the Klan. He had committed perjury, he told Carter, "although I know every one of them and have rode with them many a time."

Carter also found out what happened to those who did not put their oaths to the Klan above any oath to tell the truth in court: the Calhoun County Klan had recently murdered a former member who had dared to testify against them in the William Luke murder case.

Still, by the third week of December 1871, the Calhoun County Klan was beginning to feel pressure from federal law enforcement once again. Members confided to Carter they were considering fleeing to Texas, lest they be arrested on one of the indictments a federal grand jury in Montgomery had just managed to issue. One Klansman became so anxious that he decided to sell his 50 percent stake in an illegal whiskey distillery, in case he had to leave the state. He stunned Carter by asking him to buy it.

Carter "hardly knew what to do for a moment," as he later reported to Whitley. It was one thing to spend government funds on an illegal still as a front for his detective work but quite another to sink taxpayer money into an illegal enterprise so as to facilitate the escape of someone the government was likely to indict. Until now, the more Carter became enmeshed in the Klan's criminal network, the better for his mission. Buying into the distillery might make it too hard to extricate himself from Calhoun County when the time to do so inevitably came.

Carter felt he could not say no, any more than he could have refused to go along with the beating of William F. Fletcher. He paid the man twenty dollars of the agreed-upon $275 price in cash, and promised the rest in whiskey. As soon as he got a moment to himself, the detective realized the time had come to wind up his covert operation and began planning his escape to Montgomery.

There, he met with federal authorities, and, over the course of two days, told them everything he had found out in Calhoun County: new details of the Luke murder; the identities, and admitted crimes, of dozens of Klansmen; the names of people willing to testify against them; and the ugly details of the William Fletcher beating.

Based on Carter's information, the federal grand jury indicted sixty-seven Alabama Klansmen for their parts in whippings and murders, and seventy for illicit distilling.[61] The United States Attorney in Montgomery, John A. Minnis, considered the Secret Service infiltration of Calhoun County the government's biggest success against the Klan in Alabama. Carter's work contributed to the fact that, after the Carolinas, Alabama became the Southern state in which the most Klansmen eventually faced arrest, trial, and incarceration. Ten Alabamians ended up imprisoned, including two who received the maximum penalty for conspiracy under the Ku Klux Klan Act, ten years.

George W. Carter "deserves the commendations of his superiors, and of the government," Minnis wrote Whitley, "and I am truly thankful for the aid you have afforded."[62]

The Secret Service's Klan hunt forced Hiram C. Whitley to split his time between the long-distance supervision of that mission and direct management of his undercover operations in New York against counterfeiting kingpin Joshua D. Miner. His meetings with Attorney General Akerman and Joseph G. Hester in June and July, followed by the recruitment of detectives for the anti-Klan mission, and Whitley's perusal of their reports in August and September, probably accounted at least partly for the fact that the Secret Service's sting operation on Miner could not take place until late October 1871.

As he studied the messages flowing in from Hester, Del'Omo, Carter, and others across the South, what most impressed the Secret Service chief was how greatly the federal government had underestimated the Ku Klux Klan, and might still be doing so. Whitley, who had dealt with the Klan in its early days, was amazed at its metastasis since then.

On September 29, 1871, the Secret Service chief distilled his analysis into his first update—seventy-three handwritten legal pages—for the attorney general.[63] There was no question, he wrote, that the federal government faced a widespread conspiracy "inimical to the laws of the United States, formidable in numbers, in many instances well armed, and determined to accomplish its illegal purposes even to the sacrifice of life." The conspiracy enjoyed overwhelming support from the white population, of all social classes, in every state where the Secret Service had operated. It was sophisticated, using hand signals and whistles to "guide and direct the movements of the members without the aid of the human voice."

All of these factors made Whitley's detectives' work "of the most arduous and hazardous nature," but, for all that, doubly necessary. Where the general public supports law and order, the Secret Service chief wrote, investigating crime "is a comparatively easy task…but in localities where the masses are defective, where the local police are governed by the popular prejudice, and where every stranger is looked upon with suspicion, all routine methods of detection become useless and must be superseded by entirely new and original modes of procedure."

Whitley's account of his German-born detective Michael G. Bauer's ingenious operations in York County, South Carolina, illustrated his point.[64] The Klan's strength in the South Carolina Piedmont had prompted President Grant to deploy the United States Army's 7th Cavalry in March 1871, and with that unit still camped in white tents on the edge of Yorkville, the York County seat, the Congressional Ku Klux Klan Committee dispatched a subcommittee to the area in mid-July, to take testimony from witnesses unable or unwilling to come to Washington.

Unbeknownst either to the committee or to the commander of the cavalry unit, Major Lewis Merrill, Bauer had also come to York County, posing as the representative of a German emigration agency in the market for homesteads. Bauer found that Klan violence had indeed decreased since federal troops arrived—but that this was a tactical retreat. The Klan planned to exploit the lull by sending witnesses to tell the Ku Klux subcommittee that the peace proved the Klan had been a myth all along. As soon as the cavalry left, Bauer reported, the Klan would go back on the attack, with black members of the community who testified to the subcommittee as their first targets.

The informant who unwittingly supplied this intelligence to Bauer ran a livery stable in Spartanburg, South Carolina, near the hotel where the subcommittee stayed while visiting. His words confirmed what Bauer had heard on the moonless night of July 19, 1871, as he listened in from the bushes on the edge of an outdoor Ku Klux Klan meeting. The assembly, and its location, were secret, but some local Klansmen had told Bauer about it after he got them drunk. Bauer also heard the Klan consider—and reject—the idea of ambushing the Ku Klux committee on its way out of town and stealing its records.

Many had speculated that the reduction in violence by the South Carolina Klan was a ruse, but Bauer's report constituted the first hard intelligence from human sources. As Whitley recounted this and other findings, his tone was businesslike—but tinged by an unmistakable note of outrage. It was as if the Klan's deception and barbarism, documented in chilling firsthand detail by his own trusted operatives, triggered an attack of conscience like the one Whitley experienced listening to a Louisiana slave describe an overseer's barbarous abuse in 1863. As in that case, Whitley believed the only remedy lay in asserting federal authority, backed by the United States Army.

"The time for vigorous and prompt action has arrived," he wrote Akerman, insisting that "many arrests can be made, provided sufficient [military] force is at hand to support the U.S. marshals." He proposed secret interrogation centers in the South—similar in concept to the one he had previously improvised at Fort Pulaski—where detectives could question suspects and witnesses. Secret Service men "could even be arrested themselves with other suspected parties, a fact that would the more establish their status" with the Ku Klux Klan, thus facilitating their spying. The government should try just about anything that would further the goal of "crushing out the Ku Klux organization and bringing the violators of the laws to speedy justice."

Whitley's report reached Washington in early October 1871, just as President Grant and his advisers weighed their next steps against the Klan. The pivotal question was whether to follow up the deployment of troops in South Carolina by suspending habeas corpus in all or part of that state, as provided for in the April 20, 1871, Ku Klux Klan Act. This would not be martial law, though the press often used that term; it entailed no military commissions such as the one General George Meade empaneled in Atlanta in 1868. Still, the measure would facilitate mass arrests of Klansmen against whom the government already had evidence of criminal wrongdoing, and whom it could then detain pending trial in civilian federal court.

Habeas corpus—the "Great Writ"—represented a fundamental protection of civil liberty in the Anglo-American legal tradition. Any curtailment was bound to be controversial. Certain of President Grant's advisers, notably Secretary of State Hamilton Fish, fretted the crackdown on the Klan might be both constitutionally dubious and politically counterproductive. This was in character for Secretary Fish, the scion of a wealthy New York Dutch family, and a former United States senator. Since his days as a moderate antislavery leader of the pre–Civil War Whig Party, Fish's instinct had been to try to conciliate the South rather than risk national disunity. That had proved impossible in the 1850s, but might still be feasible in the very different climate after the Confederacy's defeat.

Attorney General Akerman spoke for those who believed that, to the contrary, stamping out the Klan was the only hope to salvage national cohesion, the new post–Civil War political order and, last but not least, the Republican Party's future. Whitley's September 29 report, along with similar information from Major Merrill, helped Akerman make this argument to the president. If it was true that the recent lull in Klan violence was merely tactical, as Michael G. Bauer had reported, President Grant could not possibly relent.

On October 12, 1871, the president sided with his attorney general, issuing a proclamation that gave the Ku Klux Klan in nine counties of the South Carolina Piedmont until October 17 to disperse, and to surrender their arms and disguises—or face the suspension of habeas corpus. When, predictably, the Klan refused, President Grant followed through; on October 19, mass arrests, carried out by United States Marshals with the assistance of the 7th Cavalry, began.

President Grant's decision hit the South Carolina Klan hard. By the end of 1871, nearly five hundred of its members had been detained on federal charges. A hundred had fled the state; hundreds more turned themselves in to the 7th Cavalry, often confessing in return for leniency. Of the two hundred twenty South Carolina Klansmen ultimately indicted, fifty-four pled guilty when federal court convened at Columbia, South Carolina, in late November 1871. Another five went to trial; juries made up of both blacks and whites convicted them. The last guilty verdict came when the court's fall–winter term ended on January 2, 1872.[65]

To Whitley, the obvious lesson of the Klan's retreat in the Carolinas and Alabama was that the crackdown was working, and should be extended. He set his sights on Georgia. The government's campaign could not truly be considered a success until it rid that strategic state, the largest in the Deep South, of the organization that had murdered George W. Ashburn in 1868, and many others since.

So far, however, federal enforcement efforts had hardly touched Georgia, as Secret Service reports from the state confirmed. In the last week of September 1871 Whitley sent Ichabod C. Nettleship, his right-hand man, to Atlanta. His ostensible purpose was to check on federal anti-fraud cases; Nettleship's probable real mission, though, was to provide Whitley an update on Klan terrorism. Klan victims and federal officials told Nettleship of a recent surge in violence, and Nettleship relayed the news to Whitley in an October 2 telegram.[66] Nettleship found the situation so urgent that, acting on his own authority, he ordered Secret Service detective Judson Knight to transfer from North Carolina to Georgia immediately.

Whitley had recruited Knight just two months earlier, specifically for the anti-Klan mission. As former chief of scouts for General George Meade's Army of the Potomac during the Civil War, Knight was the rare politically reliable Union man with experience operating undercover in the South. Knight's record of working closely with enslaved African Americans behind rebel lines made him especially well suited for a job that would involve obtaining testimony from the Klan's black victims.[67]

Soon Knight was in Macon, Georgia, posing as a correspondent for a pro-Klan newspaper. There, he made contact with Henry Lowther, a forty-year-old black Republican who farmed a plot of land in Wilkinson County, about one hundred ten miles southeast of Atlanta, and whose body still showed the terrible scars of a harrowing ordeal at the hands of the Klan.[68]

Lowther told Knight that on August 27, 1871, Klansmen had shot and killed Wilkinson County's white Republican sheriff, and drowned his African American common-law wife, the mother of their five children. Then, on the night of September 2, the Klan came for Lowther, accusing him of plotting an armed uprising of black men, and sleeping with a white woman. They locked him in jail until 2:00 a.m. on September 4, when one hundred eighty Klansmen appeared on horseback outside Lowther's window. Some entered his cell, tied him up with a rope, and led him to a swamp two miles away. There, a hooded Klansman told Lowther he could either be lynched or "altered"—castrated. Lowther soon found himself writhing and screaming in pain under a knife wielded by the town's physician, a former Confederate Army surgeon.

Nearly naked and covered in blood, Lowther staggered out of the swamp and eventually reached the nearby settlement of Irvinton, begging for aid. No white person would help him. He collapsed, unconscious, on the ground, awakening shortly before dawn to find, at last, a black woman who was willing to take him in. Later that day, he received a visit from the doctor, who seemed mainly concerned with denying that he had been in the swamp the night before, and warning Lowther not to say otherwise.

From Macon, Judson Knight took Henry Lowther to Atlanta, where he placed him under federal protection and had him swear out a criminal complaint before the United States commissioner. To Knight's amazement, however, the United States Attorney in Atlanta, John D. Pope, who seemed thoroughly intimidated by the Klan, refused to convene a grand jury in Lowther's case, ostensibly because the alleged crime had occurred in the southern portion of the state, and he was responsible only for the northern.[69] Pope's position did not change even after Secret Service detectives received a confession from a repentant member of the Klan in Wilkinson County, who identified all of the participants in the grotesque assault on Lowther, including the doctor who castrated him.

Judson Knight poured out his frustration in a letter to Whitley. "Unless they go into this thing here in the same shape they have in South Carolina," he wrote, "there will be no good results arrived at and it is a shame that such a state of things should be allowed to exist in the United States as does exist right here in Georgia today." If the government did not get tough soon, Knight added, "I don't want to stay in the business."[70]

Whitley agreed with his detective and lobbied for a more aggressive policy. On October 12, the same day President Grant issued his proclamation threatening a suspension of habeas corpus in South Carolina, Whitley wrote Attorney General Akerman, urging him to ask the president to send a company of cavalry to Georgia.[71] The Klan was out of control in that state, and both Whitley and the attorney general knew this was partly because of United States Attorney John D. Pope. However, the United States Marshal for Georgia, whom Whitley had assigned to hand-carry this letter to Akerman, was committed to the anti-Klan struggle. If backed by cavalry, he would carry out mass arrests based on testimony and intelligence accumulated by Whitley's detectives.

On October 16 Whitley sent Akerman Judson Knight's report on the shocking atrocity against Henry Lowther. He did so knowing that the attorney general raised Ku Klux Klan terrorism at every cabinet meeting, often supporting his arguments with facts drawn from Secret Service reports. The attorney general's persistence had paid off in President Grant's decision to suspend habeas corpus in South Carolina. Perhaps the explosive facts of Lowther's case would galvanize the president into taking similar action in Georgia.

What Whitley failed to anticipate was that the attorney general's influence in Grant administration circles had already peaked, and was about to decline, rapidly. By the fall of 1871, Washington's ever-changing political winds were shifting yet again. Twelve months earlier, in the wake of a violence-marred election campaign, President Grant had faced a clamor for the administration and Congress to do something—anything—about the Klan violence. Now, more voices were heard suggesting that the Klan's retreat in the Carolinas and Alabama meant that the president had gone far enough, and could safely relax federal pressure against the conspiracy. Some even maintained that the apparent peace in South Carolina proved the threat might have been exaggerated in the first place.

If Democrats were the only ones making these arguments, President Grant could have safely ignored them, but Republicans were saying similar things, too. In addition to Secretary of State Fish, whose misgivings were well-known, Representative James A. Garfield of Ohio fretted that the Ku Klux Klan Act threatened to "abolish the state Governments."[72] A new faction in the president's party, the "Liberal Republicans," contended more broadly that Reconstruction was distracting from other important issues, such as federal corruption; the government should reconsider its commitment to Southern blacks, they contended, and try instead to address those grievances of Southern whites, such as the exclusion of ex-rebels from office-holding, that had purportedly provoked the rise of the Ku Klux Klan.

During a November 24, 1871, cabinet meeting, Akerman read from Judson Knight's report, apparently hoping that it would help persuade his colleagues and President Grant to support the same kind of vigorous federal action against the Klan in Georgia that he had recently authorized in South Carolina. It did not work. Secretary of State Hamilton Fish fairly rolled his eyes at the attorney general's dramatic appeal. In his diary, Fish sneered that Akerman was obsessed with the Klan, and had taken discussion of Lowther's castration into "terribly minute and tedious details. It has got to be a bore to listen twice a week to this same thing."[73] At the next cabinet meeting, on December 1, 1871, the attorney general followed up by proposing Whitley's idea of sending more troops for Georgia, albeit without naming the Secret Service chief, and presenting the deployment as a way to protect the Republican governor from potential violence. President Grant rejected the proposal, agreeing with Fish that the threat to the governor was too hypothetical.[74]

Grant's annual message to Congress on December 4, 1871, confirmed the White House's new, more cautious, posture. The president unequivocally condemned Klan violence as he had always done and sincerely believed. However, instead of announcing that he would suspend habeas corpus in additional Southern states, or send more troops to Georgia, as Whitley and Akerman wanted, the president implied that he had intended the suspension in South Carolina as an exceptional measure, which he had carried out only with "reluctance." Contrary to the wishes of many pro-Reconstruction Republicans, including a majority of the Ku Klux Committee, he also declined to request reauthorization of the soon-to-expire Ku Klux Klan Act provision that empowered him to suspend habeas. The president did, however, voice sympathy for an amnesty that would permit all but a few former Confederate soldiers and officials to hold federal office again.[75]

Akerman lamented the changing political climate in a letter to a Georgia friend, writing that "[t]he feeling here is that the Southern republicans must cease to look for special support to congressional action."[76] On December 13, 1871, he resigned, at President Grant's request. Why Grant ousted Akerman at that moment, neither man ever fully explained. Newspapers cited pressure from influential Republican railroad barons, hostile to Akerman because he had disallowed subsidies for them. The timing of Akerman's departure, however—nineteen days after he had antagonized Secretary of State Fish by recounting the Klan atrocity against Henry Lowther; twelve days after the president rejected Akerman's request for troops in Georgia; and nine days after the president presented his conciliatory annual message—suggested to anxious Southern Republicans that the attorney general's aggressive policy on the Klan had fallen out of favor.

For Hiram C. Whitley, Amos T. Akerman's ouster meant that he had suddenly lost the strongest supporter in the cabinet of Whitley's preferred hard-line policy toward the Klan, which was, after all, the basis for the Secret Service's mission in the South. Never one to concede even the smallest point in an argument, however, Whitley refused to surrender on this vital question for both his detectives and for the country.

The Secret Service chief lobbied even harder in favor of the crackdown, seeking to sway Akerman's successor as attorney general, former Senator George H. Williams of Oregon. In his January 15, 1872, report to the Department of Justice, his first of Williams's tenure, Whitley told his new boss that the Klan was impervious to anything short of what he called "vigorous measures." The contrast between the government's success in the Carolinas and Alabama, and its failure in Georgia, proved the point, in his view. Whitley conceded that "proclamations of martial law and the suspension of the habeas corpus are measures that should not be resorted to until all others have failed," but, he insisted, "the milder mode of dealing with the organization in question has not been attended with results that can be considered in any manner satisfactory or effectual."[77]

At the time, Whitley was also waging a defense of his men's integrity against Judge Benedict's jury instructions in the Joshua D. Miner trial. To that campaign in the press, Whitley added advocacy for its role in the battle against the Klan—which had previously been kept secret. He fed news of his men's operations to the Washington newspapers, though not specific operational details, in return for favorable coverage. "The secret service division [*sic*] of the Department of Justice is entitled to much credit for its efforts during the last six or eight months in ferreting out the Kuklux and protecting the revenue," an editorial in the *Washington Chronicle*, a Republican mouthpiece, declared.

> Colonel Whitley, the chief, has shown himself the very man for the place he fills. There is much work yet for this division to do. Colonel Whitley is ably sustained by his subordinates. This branch of the service, one of the most indispensable to the Government in the present condition of things in the Southern States, should be liberally sustained by the Congress.[78]

There was at least a reason to hope the new attorney general would see things Whitley's way. Though a man of the West, with less at stake, personally, in the struggle against the Klan than Southern Republicans like Akerman, George H. Williams was a partisan, pro-Reconstruction Republican. In the Senate, he sponsored the 1867 law that empowered General George Meade to hold the military trial for George W. Ashburn's killers in Georgia. "If those who commit or countenance...atrocious crimes expect any favors from me," Williams assured Senator

John Pool of North Carolina in a Dec. 30, 1871, letter, "they are doomed to signal and bitter disappointment."[79] He urged John D. Pope, the federal prosecutor in Georgia, to show more "diligence and earnestness." Taking the hint, Pope resigned, in favor of a close Akerman associate.[80] During Williams's first year in office, convictions in Klan cases increased, from one hundred twenty-eight in 1871 to four hundred fifty-six in 1872.[81]

Williams achieved this mostly by working through the backlog of indictments left over from 1871, however. As 1872 wore on, it became clear that he sympathized with those in Washington who believed that the previous year's use of troops, detectives and mass arrests was an emergency policy that had accomplished the Grant administration's main goal, which was to stop the violence—not necessarily to punish every offender—and that the crackdown could safely be scaled back.[82]

The attorney general imposed new spending restrictions on the Secret Service. Whitley, backed by Pool and other North Carolina Republicans, had told the attorney general in February that a pay raise for Joseph G. Hester was in order. It certainly seemed to be: in the entire detective force, the Secret Service chief wrote, no other man "has been more effective in their operations" than Hester, who had been "somewhat destructive to the organized bands of armed and disguised men committing outrages in the State of North Carolina." A pay hike for this daring detective would serve not only to reward him, but to demonstrate, in a small but significant way, the federal government's resolve. The attorney general, however, responded that Hester already made eight dollars per day, plus expenses—three dollars more than other Secret Service detectives got. He rejected the raise.[83]

A few weeks later, Whitley asked Williams to release $5,000 of his appropriated funds. Williams approved only $1,500.[84] Williams said this was necessary for government economy. Whitley had not yet spent all of the March 3, 1871, special appropriation from Congress, and his new boss seemed to think he should stretch his leftover funds. Congress did not make a fresh $50,000 available to the Secret Service until the next fiscal year began on July 1, 1872.

Whitley had little choice but to demand that his detectives squeeze every penny. When George W. Carter proposed setting up a dry goods store as his cover in Mississippi, Whitley rejected it as "both impracticable and too expensive."[85] He urged Carter's assistant to "get up another stall for him, such as peddling tobacco or something else that can be purchased there and may answer your purposes just as well." Later, Whitley reprimanded Michael G. Bauer for submitting an expense report that was "altogether exorbitant and not in proportion to the results produced."[86]

There was a certain logic to the new attorney general's approach. Even Amos T. Akerman, by the end of his tenure, favored selective prosecution of only the most aggravated Klan crimes, because the federal courts were swamped, and the Department of Justice was spending beyond its 1871–1872 budget.[87] The violence, meanwhile, had indeed abated—markedly. In the first half of 1872, the Secret Service heard from an informant in North Carolina that a Klan insider in that state considered the organization "very nearly destroyed." In two South Carolina counties where President Grant had suspended habeas corpus, the Klan seemed to be "entirely suppressed," according to another Secret Service source. A detective's report from Mississippi called the K.K.K. "very bold in their expressions though quiet in their actions."[88] Whitley himself wrote that the restoration of peace had "inspired the negroes with a sense of security" across the South.[89]

Whitley, though, kept arguing for a hard line. He simply did not believe terrorists would remain quiescent absent sustained government pressure, and he interpreted the information from the field to confirm this suspicion. The "spirit of Ku Kluxism still exists among the disaffected portion of the community," he wrote to Williams. There were indications in several states that some Klan dens that had supposedly been crushed were reorganizing as "Farmer's Clubs." From his men in Mississippi, he learned that white supremacists in that state expected President Grant to lose his reelection bid, in part because of the rise of the anti-Grant Liberal Republicans. When that happened, "they say, they will get the Ku Klux laws suspended and have things their own way," the report to Whitley noted.[90] On April 8, 1872, a *New York Times* headline warned: THE KUKLUX WAITING FOR THE ASCENDANCY OF THE DEMOCRATS. The accompanying story suggested the Klan was just playing possum; the article's only named source was Hiram C. Whitley.

By the end of June 1872, however, Whitley still had received no clear guidance from the attorney general as to how he expected the Secret Service to deal with this situation, or even how long he wanted the detectives to continue in the field. All Whitley had to go on was a brief recent conversation with a subordinate of the attorney general, who told him to leave his men in place.[91]

Finally, Whitley dropped Williams a stronger hint. In early July he wrote to the attorney general, reminding him of the "almost entire cessation" of violence in the South that the Secret Service helped achieve, predicting that it might continue for another two months. During that lull, his men could continue working in the South for "only a small expenditure of money," just as Williams wanted. Consequently, Whitley wrote, he had "not in absence of further orders withdrawn the men and await[ed] your instructions."

The problem, he noted ominously, was that the peace could not last. An election was coming up in November, and "judging from information received at this office, they"—the Klan—"may become very active during the months of September and October...requiring more extended operations to prevent election frauds and afford full protection to all classes of citizens in the exercise of the elective franchise."

Elliptically but unmistakably, Whitley was confronting Williams with a choice: he could provide Whitley clear orders, and sufficient funding, to support detectives in the South through the election, or else Whitley would "withdraw the men"—right in the middle of the Republican campaign.

That campaign had kicked off just three weeks earlier, on June 6, 1872, with the Republican National Convention's nomination of President Grant to run for a second term. His opponent would be the newspaper publisher Horace Greeley, a former abolitionist grown weary of Reconstruction, who was running as the standard-bearer for an odd alliance of Liberal Republicans and Democrats. The experts forecast a close race.

If Whitley's detectives had to pull out, Klan attacks on Republicans in the South resumed, and the party's electoral fortunes suffered, the attorney general might have to explain why he had risked letting the Secret Service mission lapse even after Whitley had advised him, in a letter (of which the wily detective undoubtedly preserved a copy), that he could maintain it at relatively modest cost.

Williams got the message. He consented to Whitley's terms. He, too, had a price, though. For the highly partisan attorney general, it was only common sense that, as long as Whitley's men were going to be down South, they should operate not only as law enforcement investigators but also as the eyes and ears of the Republican campaign.

The Secret Service chief agreed, telling the attorney general that he would concentrate detectives "at various points where elections are on the eve of taking place." He sent a new directive to detectives in Alabama, Georgia, and Mississippi, requesting "special reports," not on crime, but on the general political situation in these states, including the "feeling amongst, and the plans of, the opponents of the government, etc., etc., so far as you can judge from what you see and hear."[92] This contradicted his testimony to the Custom House investigation committee hearing just a few months earlier, in which he swore that he had "never received any instructions to look after any particular political clique, or anything of the kind, and I would not do it."[93]

To Whitley, though, inconsistency was a small price to pay for the larger goal of keeping the Klan under Secret Service surveillance. Nor did he genuinely object to using his position for partisan Republican interests. During his dickering with Williams, Whitley was already preparing to publish excerpts from his Ku Klux Klan files as a Republican Party campaign document.

The resulting 144-page anti-Klan tract, titled *The Nation's Peril*, was the sequel to *Memoirs of the United States Secret Service* advertised in a publisher's note in that volume. Like *Memoirs*, *The Nation's Peril* showed that Whitley knew how to exploit confidential information for propaganda purposes, without exposing operational secrets. The text alluded to the book's reliance on information from "officers of the United States Secret Service," but identified none of them. Whitley had personally redacted their names, with a pencil, when he selected atrocity reports for inclusion in the publication. *The Nation's Peril* identified no author on its cover, though the first chapter was credited to "Justin Knight," supposedly a Northerner who had witnessed Klan violence while living in South Carolina. Only those who read the legal boilerplate inside the front cover noticed that E. A. Ireland owned the copyright; and even they could not guess that this was the name of a Secret Service detective then working in Mississippi.

Though Whitley's hand in the book's production remained hidden, its political message could not have been clearer.[94] It began by detailing the Klan's internal rituals, oaths, and codes, simultaneously holding the organization up to ridicule, and demonstrating to its members the demoralizing fact that the Secret Service had infiltrated their ranks. Then came case studies of

Klan atrocities—"thrilling stories of outrage and crime," the text called them—calculated to arouse indignation among the voting public: Henry Lowther's castration in Georgia; William Fletcher's whipping in Alabama; Murchison McLean's murder, and Sarah Ferguson's ordeal, in North Carolina.

As a political manifesto, *The Nation's Peril* had the advantage of being grounded in the truth. Indeed, its facts, about both the Klan's internal workings and its atrocities, were not new. Some had appeared in the press, others in the Ku Klux committee's twelve volumes of published testimony. Whitley's book, though, offered a portable, novelistic digest, cloaked in the authority of secret government intelligence. It concluded with a paean to the Republican Party and President Grant, to whom "the people turn instinctively as the standard-bearer in the coming political contest."[95]

The Nation's Peril exemplified the Republican campaign theme of "waving the bloody shirt," a reference to Representative Benjamin Butler's famous 1871 speech describing the Mississippi Klan attack that left the superintendent of an African American school drenched in his own blood. Atrocity stories energized the party's pro-Reconstruction base.

Yet the Republicans simultaneously pushed a more conciliatory theme, to counter opponents' charges that the Klan crackdown had gone too far. Liberal Republican and Democratic papers in New York, Greeley's home state, with thirty-five electoral votes of the one hundred eighty-four then needed to win, harped on the supposed unfairness and cruelty of incarcerating Klan "political prisoners." The *New York World* depicted the convicts as victims of "hordes of detectives" sent to the South to fabricate charges against them.[96] Parallels were drawn between the Bastille, or Siberia, and the Albany Penitentiary in New York's capital, where the federal government housed Klan convicts from the South. The *New York Sun* said Klansmen had been "sentenced to rot to death," and implicitly likened their journey north from South Carolina, "stowed away between decks" of a federally chartered ship, to slave ship voyages from Africa to the United States.[97]

These insinuations were preposterous, and the Klansmen richly deserved their prison sentences, but the Republicans felt defensive. The party's 1872 platform boasted equally of quelling the Klan and of passing an amnesty law for former Confederates. "Congress and the President have only fulfilled an imperative duty in their measures for the suppression of violent and treasonable organizations," the platform said. "We heartily approve the action of Congress in extending amnesty to those lately in rebellion, and rejoice in the growth of peace and fraternal feeling throughout the land."[98]

"Influential Republicans" thought that additional leniency might further defuse agitation against the president's anti-Klan policy, the *Washington Daily Critic* reported.[99] A general pardon for Klansmen, Republican Jacob R. Davis of Washington wrote the president, would be a political "ten strike," because it would "give the lie to assertions…that the President is opposed to the South." Another member of the party suggested pardons would drive the "final nail in the liberal coffin."[100]

Such sentiments not only reflected contemporary political calculations. They also tapped a long-standing American belief that pardons could help to pacify political uprisings. In fact, the pardon had been included among the president's constitutional powers with that very purpose in mind. Alexander Hamilton argued in *The Federalist Papers* that "in seasons of insurrection or rebellion, there are often critical moments, when a well-timed offer of pardon to the insurgents or rebels may restore the tranquillity of the commonwealth."[101] If you thought of the Ku Klux Klan both as a political insurrection and as a criminal conspiracy—and it was not far-fetched to do so—Hamilton's logic could apply.

No less a "radical" Republican than Gerrit Smith came to

believe certain Klan prisoners deserved clemency from the president. A wealthy abolitionist, Smith had served in Congress before the Civil War, and secretly funded John Brown's attack on Harpers Ferry in 1859. After the war, Smith bankrolled Republican campaigns; he gave a nominating speech for Grant at the party's June 1872 National Convention. A couple of weeks later, Smith condemned the Klan, and supported the federal campaign to stamp it out, in a speech to a Republican rally at Peterboro, New York. "Let President Grant withdraw his repressing hand for even a week," Smith said, "and the flames of hell would again burst."[102]

Shortly after the speech, however, Smith got a letter from his old friend Horace Greeley, who was now the president's opponent in his reelection campaign. Greeley reminded him that, in 1867, the two had helped bail former Confederate President Jefferson Davis out of a Union military prison, to promote reconciliation with the South. Greeley asked Smith to investigate the plight of the Klan prisoners at Albany, in the same spirit.

After visiting the penitentiary on July 8, 1872, Smith concluded that three Klan convicts did indeed deserve clemency, due to age or illness, and wrote President Grant a letter the next day telling him so.[103]

Grant was not eager to comply. It was awfully soon to be pardoning Southern recalcitrants duly convicted and punished for political violence against defenseless civilians, the overwhelming majority of whom were targeted for supporting the president's party. The latest group of Klan felons, twenty-three South Carolinians facing sentences of up to ten years, had just arrived at the Albany Penitentiary.[104]

Pardons might help Republicans politically in New York but hurt them in the South, as Greeley undoubtedly understood, even if Smith did not. North Carolina would hold its 1872 election for seven Congressional seats, the state legislature, and the governorship on August 1, several months earlier than the rest of the country. (North Carolina's presidential election would take place along with the other states' in November.) This would be the first voting in the South since the crackdown on the Klan had restored at least apparent calm and security. Leniency toward white supremacist terrorists at such a moment, Grant feared, might embolden the Klan and demoralize his Southern Republican supporters.

The president let almost two weeks elapse before answering Smith. When he finally responded on July 22, 1872, he gently explained political reality: "Any pardon now, before the North Carolina election, would be misinterpreted," he wrote.[105] He would take up the pardons later.

As soon as the voting ended in North Carolina, and it became clear that the Republicans had held their own—winning the governorship and retaking a seat in the United States House of Representatives they had lost in the violence-marred 1870 election—President Grant kept his word to Smith. He asked Attorney General Williams to dispatch a "discreet officer" to assess Klansmen at the Albany Penitentiary, and recommend which, if any, might deserve some executive clemency.[106]

Williams thought he knew just the man for the job.

Perched atop a green hill overlooking New York's capital city, with fourteen-foot whitewashed brick walls and crenellated guard towers, the Albany Penitentiary resembled nothing so much as a medieval fortress. Actually, it was a modern facility, well lit and salubrious. The five hundred or so male inmates, black and white, manufactured shoes for sale in the surrounding community, to rehabilitate themselves through labor while helping finance the prison. For years, the federal government had been sending the District of Columbia's offenders to this model institution, along with violators of federal criminal law from the various states, most recently Klansmen from the Carolinas and Alabama.

On the morning of August 7, 1872, the penitentiary's heavy iron doors swung open, and a wiry figure with intense blue eyes and a trim brown goatee stepped briskly inside. After he and the warden exchanged pleasantries, the visitor, accompanied by an assistant, took a seat at a table in the prison's spacious reception room.

Then Hiram C. Whitley instructed a guard to send in the first of the Ku Klux Klan conspirators scheduled to meet him.[107]

Penitentiary rules forbade conversation among inmates. Still, the authorities could not cut off the prison grapevine. The Klansmen had found out that Whitley was coming to see them on a mission from the attorney general. What's more, they had learned that the Secret Service chief, the very man who had helped put them in prison, was there to help decide who among them, if anyone, could get out.

Attorney General Williams picked Whitley because of his familiarity with the Klan and the government's operations against it in the South. A master interrogator, he could be relied on to probe the prisoners thoroughly, and to recommend leniency only for those who clearly deserved it. Whitley's assessment "would be more impartial and just, than that of a person unaccustomed to dealing with hard cases," the *National Republican* reported.[108] Whitley's "line of duty, it was thought, required him to deal justly with all classes, while he could not be easily deceived," the *New York Herald*'s Washington correspondent echoed.[109]

Whitley was far from inclined to empty all of the penitentiary cells his men had worked so hard, and so recently, to populate. He knew too many of the details of the Klansmen's crimes, and after meeting them face-to-face he still felt that, "on the whole they have got off pretty lightly," as he told a reporter. A ten-year sentence for complicity in murder, he said, was "certainly not too heavy."[110] Whitley quickly ruled out pardoning one man for whom Gerrit Smith had recommended clemency due to advanced age: sixty-three-year-old Samuel G. Brown, a boss of the York County, South Carolina, Klan. Serving a five-year sentence, Brown showed no remorse to Whitley but protested his innocence and complained he did not get a fair trial. Whitley glared at him and called him a liar. "Brown himself was with the Ku Klux on several of its raids and had been justice of the peace for some years in his district," Whitley later explained. "I could find no palliation in his case...he certainly should have known better."

Whitley also met twenty-seven-year-old Confederate Army veteran and newspaper editor Randolph A. Shotwell from Rutherfordton, North Carolina. He was serving six years for masterminding a June 11, 1870, Klan assault on Republican state legislator James M. Justice. The federal trial of Shotwell and ten other Klansmen at Raleigh in September 1871 was the first of its kind that the Grant administration mounted under the new anti-Klan laws. Spectators, white and black, packed the state Senate chamber to see it. Shotwell scorned the racially mixed federal jury that eventually convicted him, and defiantly denounced the charges as "ridiculously false," when given the chance to address the judge before sentencing.[111]

Still unrepentant in Albany, where he chafed at having to cobble shoes beside an African American inmate, Shotwell assumed the Secret Service chief's mission of mercy was a trap, a ruse to wring intelligence from unsuspecting lower-ranking Klansmen. He scowled at Whitley and minced words with him. When Whitley asked him why he was in prison, Shotwell claimed that he and his fellow Klansmen had acted to defend themselves and their families against the horrors of "Negro rule," in accordance with "Nature's law of self-preservation." The prisoner's sarcasm, and his lack of contrition, quickly exhausted Whitley's patience.

"Oh, very well," Whitley snapped, "I haven't got time to argue. Send the next man!"

"Good morning, Mr. Whitley," Shotwell said as he headed

for the door, demonstrating his defiance—and that Whitley had failed to keep his identity a secret.

Whitley seems nevertheless to have believed the remaining three dozen prisoners he met that day did not know his identity or his mission, and that they were "frank and communicative" with him, as he later put it, despite a similarity in their stories that Whitley himself found "singular." To a man, they professed to have joined the organization out of fear, or because they were told its purpose was benign: "to put down meanness in the country." And now they expressed remorse, as well as anger at Klan leaders who had absconded when federal troops and marshals arrived, leaving their underlings to face arrest.

This aroused the Secret Service chief's instinctive sympathy for humbler offenders who had become entangled in the conspiracies concocted by the socially higher-ranking. In interviews with the press after his visit, he described these prisoners as "white trash," who had often joined the Klan out of blind deference to their local leaders. For them, in contrast to Brown or Shotwell, Whitley found "greater latitude for doubt of moral responsibility."

In his August 9, 1872, report to the attorney general, scrawled by hand over eight pages, Whitley recommended pardon for only one of the three prisoners Gerrit Smith had named: David Collins, an illiterate sixty-three-year-old from South Carolina. However, based on his interviews in Albany, he listed twenty-one other men, none of whom Smith had mentioned, as pardon candidates—almost a third of the sixty-four incarcerated Klan convicts.[112]

It was far more leniency than he would have recommended if left entirely to his own devices, but far less than the Grant critics who advocated a blanket pardon had expected. The *New York Herald* expressed dismay that Whitley was not more supportive of clemency. The paper urged the president to "be more liberal than the judgment of his chief detective."[113]

President Grant rejected the *Herald*'s advice. After he reviewed Whitley's report with Attorney General Williams at the White House on August 15, 1872, the president agreed to pardon only four Klansmen: David Collins; William Teal, a twenty-six-year-old accomplice of Shotwell's from North Carolina, who was terminally ill; and two additional low-ranking convicts who were of relatively advanced age, and had made what Whitley thought were sincere expressions of remorse. The president reserved judgment on the remaining eighteen men.[114]

Even this limited grant of clemency was too much for the Republicans in North Carolina, however. They were alarmed for the very reason the president had anticipated when he balked at Gerrit Smith's request prior to the North Carolina vote: they feared violent white supremacists would not take the pardons as a federal peace gesture to be reciprocated, but as a display of federal weakness to be exploited. When Grant announced his decision publicly on August 22, 1872, North Carolina Republicans bombarded Attorney General Williams with letters pointing out, as the *Chicago Post* reported, that at least two of the four men "were most ferocious and cruel in their treatment of colored men and were at the head of the Ku Klux organization in their districts."[115]

Williams blamed Whitley for the uproar. The Secret Service chief had given an interview about his trip to Albany, along with a summary of his report, to the *New York Herald*, on August 13, and the paper published it the next day—before the attorney general had a chance to present the report to the president. The coverage of what was supposed to have been a confidential mission to Albany gave pardon opponents a head start rallying public opinion.

It was never resolved whether Whitley went to the press intending to claim credit for the pardons, sabotage them, or somehow—in the detective's byzantine way—both. When Williams questioned him about it, the Secret Service chief calmly denied any indiscretion.[116]

What was clear was that the Southern Republicans' reaction forced the president to take a different tack yet again. Less than a week after Grant issued his initial offer of four pardons, Williams retracted them, citing the need for a "separate investigation" of all the "shocking barbarities," for which the Albany prisoners had been convicted. In addition, he said, Democrats in the South had reacted to the possible pardons in a vindictive spirit; many pro-Klan newspapers claimed, Williams noted, "that the sole object of the President's generous offer was to influence votes." The Southern press was also spreading the notion that Grant meant to let future Klan violence go "unwhipped of justice."[117] The administration could not allow either impression to take hold.

There would be no pardons for the Klan before the presidential election on November 5, 1872. There still were none as of President Grant's annual message to Congress on December 2, in which he seemed to dangle executive clemency as a reward for continued peace in the South: "I am disposed, as far as my sense of justice will permit, to give to these [pardon] applications a favorable consideration," he wrote, "but any action thereon is not to be construed as indicating any change in my determination to enforce with vigor such acts so long as the conspiracies and combinations therein named disturb the peace of the country."[118]

By this time, of course, the president had been reelected handily, carrying thirty-one out of thirty-seven states. The issue of clemency for the Klan was, in the end, not as decisive as it had seemed to Republican politicos who fretted over it in the heat of the campaign. What mattered more was the forced retreat of white supremacist terrorism across the South: the 1872 presidential elections were the most peaceful and orderly of any during Reconstruction. The stability impressed voters in the North; in the South, security enabled Republican voters, including hundreds of thousands of black men, to cast ballots. President Grant won eight of eleven former Confederate states, including those—the Carolinas and Alabama—where the federal campaign against the Klan had been most active. Georgia, where that campaign never gained traction, was one of the few states that Greeley carried.

The Grant administration crackdown on the Klan had mostly achieved its short-term political goal: to save the Southern states, and, potentially, the federal government, from recapture by white supremacist Democrats. Grant himself deserved the most credit. He made the tough decisions: to throw his power and prestige behind the Ku Klux Klan Act, and, later, to suspend habeas corpus in South Carolina. Also indispensable were Attorney General Akerman's personal commitment, and the United States Army's help in rounding up Klan suspects, especially in South Carolina, where 7th Cavalry commander Major Lewis Merrill acted with a zeal comparable to Akerman's. Jurors, judges, and prosecution witnesses all defied death threats to bring a small but symbolically significant number of Klansmen to justice in federal courts.

Hiram C. Whitley was one of the heroes, too, though an unlikely one. Brought in relatively late to the anti-Klan struggle, he had improvised an unprecedented peacetime covert operation, maintained control over it via lines of communication stretching from New York to Mississippi, and done so without sacrificing his investigation of Joshua D. Miner's counterfeiting ring in New York. Whitley had to cope with the vagaries of Washington politics, which abruptly cost the anti-Klan mission's strongest supporter in the Grant administration, Amos T. Akerman, his job, obliging the Secret Service chief to cajole Akerman's budget-conscious successor to keep his detectives on duty during the crucial final months of the campaign. Then Whitley had to help the new attorney general and President

Grant manage pressures for what could have been excessive leniency toward the Klan.

Unlike Akerman, Whitley was no moralist. And unlike Joseph G. Hester, his role was not the daring one of an actual infiltrator in the field. His contribution was strategic and tactical insight, just as it had been in the Ashburn case, and just as Amos T. Akerman had expected when he turned to Whitley for help. Whitley's expertise in disguise, infiltration, and compartmentalization enabled him to get the most out of his tight budget, and the efforts of no more than a dozen detectives in the South. He ordered them to pursue cases where there was a high probability of successful prosecution, rather "than attempt numerous cases that might in the end have to be abandoned for want of funds," as he explained to Akerman.[119]

Whitley also possessed a keen and highly modern grasp of psychological warfare, worthy of the ruthless French detectives whom he admired and professed to emulate. His exploitation of his files for propaganda purposes in *The Nation's Peril* showed that. Secret Service surveillance sowed suspicion, betrayal, and demoralization in Klan ranks, well beyond the direct impact of arrests and indictments. Whitley boasted of "the dread inspired in the Ku Klux orders by a belief that the government secret agents were everywhere upon their track."[120] An indication that he was right was the surge of commentary in the pro-Klan newspapers of the South, complaining about the presence of government "spies." The angry articles themselves paid Whitley a backhanded compliment.

Conversely, Whitley concluded, the Klan terrorists' erstwhile victims gained confidence from "the knowledge…that the Government is well informed of all movements having for their object the intimidation of voters of any class, and also, that it has its agents among the people, working silently but effectually in ferreting out violators of the laws and bringing the perpetrators to justice."[121] Though actual convictions proved difficult to achieve, given the limited capacity of the federal courts, the Secret Service had helped shift the balance of terror to the government's advantage, and to the advantage of the people, black and white, whom the government had pledged to protect.

During the summer of 1872, Whitley had evinced skepticism as to whether that shift was permanent or merely temporary. He suspected the Klan's retreat was merely tactical, and urged the attorney general to keep his detectives in the field. After President Grant swept to reelection, buoyed by heavy turnout of African Americans in the South, Whitley modified his view. "The effect of the presidential election appears to have been little less than miraculous among the people of the South generally," he exulted to Attorney General Williams in a year-end report to Washington. "Judging from all the evidence that has thus far reached me," he remarked, "there remains but little of the Ku Klux Klan as a distinctive order."[122]

In late November Whitley concluded that it would, indeed, be safe to begin reducing the Secret Service's presence in the South. He carried out the attorney general's orders to dismiss all but two of the detectives he had hired to investigate the Klan. He notified the chief clerk of the Department of Justice that he was "winding up our Ku Klux reports," and informed him that he would soon need to file away the "mass of information" his detectives had accumulated.[123]

A Klan comeback, which Whitley had considered all too likely earlier in the year, he now rated "barely possible." If it did occur, Whitley promised Williams, he would be on hand, as chief of the Secret Service, to "investigate the circumstances and bring the guilty parties to trial and punishment."[124]

The coming months would determine the accuracy of both predictions.

6

"I am radically opposed to any organized system of espionage."

Hiram C. Whitley had not been the most devoted of family men since he married Catherine Bates in 1856. His work—whatever it was—always came first. Catherine followed her husband to Kansas and Louisiana before the Civil War; thereafter, she settled in Cambridge, Massachusetts, with his mother and hers, contenting herself with visits from her New York–based husband when his duties allowed. The Whitleys had no children, though the precise reason for this was not something they discussed outside the family circle, if at all.

The conclusion of the Secret Service's campaign against the Klan after the 1872 election provided Whitley an opportunity to focus more on his domestic situation than he had probably done for many months, or perhaps made it impossible to neglect it any longer. In the late fall of that year, he and Catherine agreed that they should end their sixteen years of childlessness.

On December 9, 1872, a personal ad appeared in the *New York Herald*: "A gentleman and his wife wish to adopt a female child from two to six years of age. Address with full particulars, K.B., box 127, Herald office."

Though the initials in the return address corresponded to his wife's maiden name—"Katie" Bates—Hiram C. Whitley had written the advertisement. Less than a day later, Lottie N. Luckey of Fishkill, New York, responded, offering the couple her three-year-old daughter, Marie Louise Gladde. "By force of circumstances, I am forced to resort to this plan," she wrote.[1]

By the end of the week, Whitley had custody, paying one hundred dollars for the girl and for the mother's promise "she will never in any manner interfere with or attempt to control" her. Ichabod C. Nettleship witnessed the transaction. Formally, it was not an adoption but an indenture, still legal in New York, and not uncommon. This was a time when the Children's Aid Society resettled some three thousand homeless minors from New York City in the Midwest annually, placing them with farm families on terms not unlike those the Whitleys agreed with Lottie Luckey. The indenture would expire on Marie Louise Gladde's twenty-first birthday. For all practical purposes, however, she was now the Whitleys' child. They renamed her "Kittie Whitley."

The "circumstances" that compelled Lottie Luckey essentially to sell her daughter were not specified, though the official record hinted that she did so because the child was not her husband J. B. Luckey's, as the last name "Gladde" suggested. A Manhattan judge approved the transaction, but only after satisfying himself, in a "private examination" of the mother, that she gave up her child "freely and without fear or compulsion of the husband."[2]

Catherine would have someone besides her aging mother and mother-in-law with whom to pass the time in Cambridge. Hiram C. Whitley would have a proper family to go along with his power and influence.

These were indeed heady times for both the Secret Service and its chief. Congress renewed the division's annual funding on March 3, 1873, and maintained it at a total $175,000. The appropriation included money to investigate counterfeiting, fraud, and any "other crimes against the United States"—the latter being the catchall phrase authorizing the Secret Service to pursue white supremacist terrorists.

Such crimes still did occur. When a wave of attacks by the Ku Klux Klan near Frankfort, Kentucky, made headlines during August 1873, Attorney General Williams ordered Whitley to send detectives to the state. Having promised Williams the previous year that he would be ready for any Klan resurgence, the Secret Service chief took the Kentucky situation as a personal and institutional challenge. "The matter has been placed in my hands by the Hon. Attorney General and I hope to be able to give him more evidence of the skill and ability of the men of this force," he wrote to Michael G. Bauer. Referring to the Klan, he added: "We must show them that the U.S. Secret Service is capable of finding them out and bringing them to justice. This is now a point upon which the eyes of the whole country are turned."[3]

Bauer would lead a three-man team in Kentucky, posing, as usual, as a German interested in buying land for his countrymen in an area, he told the Klansmen he met, "where the negro would be kept down." Whitley instructed his other two detectives to wear homespun suits, not manufactured clothing that might mark them as outsiders. They were to pose as itinerant counterfeiters, and to establish their white supremacist bona fides with the Klan, as Whitley suggested in a letter to his men, by "kicking up a row with some negro."[4]

By October 1, 1873, Whitley's detectives had identified the leaders of the Kentucky Klan, as well as thirty witnesses—Klan victims and defectors from the organization—who were willing to testify against them. Some thirty-nine indictments resulted.[5]

The Secret Service was beginning to look like an American version of the European police agencies Whitley so admired. By mid-1873, it consisted of twenty-nine full-time detectives, plus their respective assistants and informants, based in major United States cities. They specialized as always in investigating counterfeiting, and in recent months Whitley had instructed them to take that battle to previously neglected areas of the South and far West.[6] They also investigated illegal silk imports on the Canadian border and cigar bootlegging in Key West. Whitley hatched a plan to station a detective in Havana, Cuba, though nothing came of it.[7]

A prestigious new weekly magazine, *Appletons' Journal*, sent its correspondent to report on the federal government's fascinating covert crime-fighters and their wily chief. The journalist touted his privileged access to the Secret Service office on the Treasury building's top floor, behind a door marked POSITIVELY NO ADMITTANCE—though the Washington headquarters was, in truth, a bit of a "stall." Whitley and his most trusted subordinates put in their real fifteen-hour workdays, and kept their most sensitive archives, at Bleecker Street in New York. The Treasury building office was more for show, to impress politicians, and the occasional journalist, whom Whitley, visiting the capital, would ostentatiously host. The rooms housed what *Appletons' Journal* called a "museum of crime and cupidity," an exhibition of the most sensational evidence Whitley and his detectives had collected.

There was a scrapbook of fake banknotes; safes filled with confiscated engraving plates; and, on the wall, a placard bearing the portrait, drawn from a photograph, of Thomas Ballard, Joshua D. Miner's henchman, still on the lam: it offered a reward of five thousand dollars. Nearby hung a "most ferocious-looking" suit composed of a bloodred jacket, black muslin pants, and a black leather belt, from which dangled an eighteen-inch dagger in a leather sheath. Completing the outfit was a pointed red cap, embroidered with a black skull and crossbones, and three large letters—K.K.K.—followed by the Latin word for "death," *Mori*.

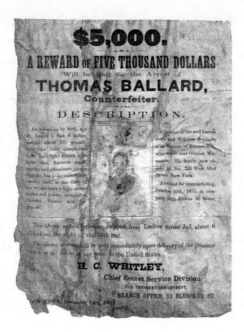

Whitley kept a "wanted" poster with a photograph of Thomas Ballard, Joshua D. Miner's master engraver of counterfeit bills, on the wall of his Washington office. (*Nova Scotia Archives*)

As the journalist toured this gallery, Whitley recounted how he had captured Bill Gurney, the counterfeiter, at the East River ferry landing. He expounded on his crime-fighting philosophy. No serious government could eschew surveillance or deception in all their forms, he lectured, because "desperate cases require desperate remedies."[8]

Now over forty years old, the Secret Service chief was perhaps not quite the same vigorous detective who had chased down Pedro Capdeville on the muddy streets of New Orleans in 1863, or even who wrestled Gurney to the ground on that summer's day in 1870. The incessant and nerve-racking work of the last year or two had taken a toll, to the point where another journalist, in fact, described Whitley as "lank and cadaverous."[9]

Even with gray creeping into his goatee, though, Whitley was as garrulous and as intense as ever. As the captured evidence on display in the Treasury building proved, he could plausibly claim that his methods, modeled on those of Fouché and Vidocq in France, and the Bow Street Runners of England, were working. The *Appletons'* correspondent certainly came away with that impression, just as Whitley undoubtedly intended: "It is with pleasure that we accord to the present efficient chief of our national police...the well-deserved encomium of the Scriptures," the journalist wrote. "Well-done, thou good and faithful servant!"

Others in Washington were not so sure that the results Whitley claimed justified the means by which he obtained them, or, indeed, the means by which the government had created the Secret Service in the first place. The critics, mostly Democrats and anti-Grant Republicans, insisted their objections were not partisan or political, but traditional American civil libertarian concerns about the accumulation of unchecked power in what was, after all, a semiclandestine bureau of the executive branch. *Appletons' Journal* might consider it a compliment to refer to the Secret Service as the "national police." The obvious rejoinder, which opponents made at every opportunity, was to ask whether the Constitution authorized Congress to establish such a force, much less to do so by implication, through an appropriations measure.

The Secret Service's most insistent adversary in Congress was Representative James B. Beck. The Kentucky Democrat had despised Whitley since the Ashburn murder case, when the detective helped to establish the culpability of Beck's friend, Columbus Klan leader William D. Chipley. In speeches on the House floor, Beck and other Democrats alluded to Judge Benedict's jury instructions in the Joshua D. Miner trial, to support their argument that detectives who could not be trusted to testify against counterfeiters could not be relied on to investigate respectable white Southerners.[10] In their dissenting addendum to the Ku Klux Committee's February 1872 report, Beck and another Democrat condemned the use of the Secret Service against the Klan, contending that "such agencies are certainly dangerous in the administration of justice."[11] Later that same year, Beck warned North Carolina that "gangs of spies and informers" led by Whitley and Joseph G. Hester would "flood" the state before its August election.[12]

Throughout Reconstruction, Democrat James Burnie Beck of Kentucky defended white supremacy and opposed federal investigations of Ku Klux Klan violence. (*Library of Congress*)

In February 1873, as the House considered the Department of Justice's appropriation bill, Beck offered an amendment requiring the Secret Service to account publicly for its spending.[13] On its face, the proposal was a reasonable exercise of legislative oversight. Republicans could not view Beck's bill in isolation from his motivations, however. They saw it as payback, even sabotage, anything but a good-faith accountability law.

The chairman of the House Appropriations Committee, Republican Representative James A. Garfield of Ohio, warned his fellow lawmakers that the secretary of the Treasury, George S. Boutwell, had told Garfield he would "lose his means of detection" if Beck's bill passed. The House voted it down.[14]

Whitley's response to this latest round of political pressure was to reassure his nominal supervisors in the executive branch that the Secret Service was, indeed, a professional operation. In May 1873 he composed a "Circular of Instructions" for his detectives, pocket-size and bound in blue leather, and intended to be read not only within the ranks but throughout government circles.

The booklet contained strict new rules for Secret Service spending, a perennial sore point both with Whitley's executive branch supervisors and with Congress. Detectives were to record their movements and their expenses on a daily basis, then report them weekly to Bleecker Street. And, for the first time, Secret Service detectives would have to prove their identity to those with a right to know it, by carrying a numbered metal badge.[15]

Previously, they relied on paper credentials. This nearly led to a disaster in 1872: a man arrived at the Secret Service's San Francisco office claiming to have been appointed to replace the chief operative there, Henry F. Finnegass. He presented a letter purportedly signed by Secretary Boutwell. Finnegass, suspicious, discreetly telegraphed Whitley. Whitley responded that the man was an impostor. Finnegass arrested him; he confessed that he had chemically altered a legitimate but routine letter on Treasury Department stationery.[16]

Whitley's new rulebook also sought to institutionalize the cutting-edge police methods he had borrowed from Europe. The first was the use of photography as a tool of identification. As of mid-1873, many, but not all, of the Secret Service's hundreds of dossiers on counterfeiters and smugglers included photographs. Henceforth, the Circular of Instructions said, detectives would be required to photograph everyone they arrested, and to note the suspect's name, age, and full physical description on the back of each print.[17]

The bulk of the Circular, however, described Whitley's ethical requirements for his men. "He who seeks to make it his vocation should be a man of sincere motives and undoubted integrity," he wrote of detective work. No Secret Service employee should risk conflicts of interest by taking gifts or incurring debt. All must possess "temperate habits," "sound judgment," "large powers of observation," and "knowledge of human nature." They must also respect the rights of the accused: "That which is favorable to the criminal must be stated with fairness, and that which is against him without bias or exaggeration."

Inevitably, though, there were limits to how much transparency Whitley could prescribe, given that the division's mission required its detectives to deceive or, as Whitley referred to it, "assume the criminal role." Whitley's clearest directives related to secrecy, which employees "must observe...in all transactions relating to the business of the service." If it were up to him, the Secret Service chief explained, government undercover agents would be nearly everywhere. "It would be of infinitely greater consequence to the public good," he wrote, "if criminals were so closely followed by the detectives as to inspire them with the fear that, the moment they attempted to commit a crime, that moment they were liable to arrest and punishment."

Nor was Whitley truly inclined to share power over the Secret Service, even if it might be politic to pretend otherwise. Evidence for this was right on the blue leather cover of the Circular of Instructions, where Whitley's name appeared above that of his nominal supervisor, Solicitor Everett C. Banfield—in letters twice as large. Whitley had "prepared" the manual, the text announced, whereas Banfield merely "approved" it.

Whitley's other boss, Attorney General George H. Williams, did not even know of the new rulebook until it had already been printed, at which point Whitley sent a copy to the Department of Justice with a breezy cover letter: "I thought it might be a matter of interest...to have some general idea of our methods of operating."[18]

Despite the professionalism he espoused in the Circular—and demonstrated in fighting counterfeiters and the Klan—Whitley often thought and acted as if he were a law unto himself. He did so with the connivance of high Grant administration officials, who increasingly found it politically and personally useful to have an ethically flexible Secret Service chief and his team available for extracurricular chores.

One such mission was Attorney General Williams's use of Secret Service detectives to gather political intelligence in the South during the 1872 campaign, which yielded a series of reports Whitley passed on to the partisan attorney general. Orville E. Babcock, President Grant's top White House aide, had already used the Secret Service for a political purpose prior to that. The president's top foreign policy priority of his first term was to annex Santo Domingo, as the Dominican Republic was then known. In 1871, when a former American official in Santo Domingo denounced corrupt interests, linked to Babcock, behind the annexation drive, Babcock asked Whitley to stalk the whistleblower at his Rhode Island home, and seize him for extradition to Texas on trumped-up murder charges. Whitley sent Ichabod C. Nettleship to do the job. They only called it off upon learning that Rhode Island courts would not honor the Texas extradition.[19] Later, when Babcock discovered a con man was embarrassing him—and getting rich—by mailing Republican postmasters a phony party fund-raising appeal over Babcock's forged signature, he asked Whitley to handle that case, too. Secret Service detectives covertly staged warrantless searches on the suspected con man's apartment and intercepted his mail, using the information they gathered to track him down and make an arrest.[20]

At about the same time his Circular of Instructions was making its way to operatives around the country, Whitley got a telegram from Attorney General Williams, asking the Secret Service chief to report to Washington immediately.

Whitley boarded the next train from New York to the nation's capital, and he soon found himself being ushered into the attorney general's study at the newly built mansion on Rhode Island Avenue where Williams and his wife, Kate, hosted lavish receptions for the capital's political and diplomatic elite.

There was nothing necessarily unusual about any of this. Whitley had recently carried out a confidential task for the attorney general that arguably fell within his lawful job description: an undercover investigation of corruption by United States Marshals and their deputies. Whitley's detectives had identified one deputy marshal in South Carolina who was riding suspiciously "fine horses," for a man whose official pay did not exceed a few dollars a day.[21] Williams repaid the favor by backing more funding for Whitley's detective force in the March 3, 1873, appropriation bill.

This time, however, the attorney general told Whitley he had a different kind of covert assignment—a personal one. "I need your assistance in a little matter of much concern to my wife and myself," he said.[22]

Everyone in Washington knew Kate Williams as the most beautiful and status-conscious of the cabinet wives, but Whitley knew her better than most. He had first encountered his boss's spouse decades earlier, on the frontier in Kirtland, Ohio, when he was a restless student, and she was the eighteen-year-old bride of a wealthy local miller eight years her senior. In January 1849, less than nine months after her wedding, Kate bore a son.[23] Then she left both husband and child and returned to her family in Keokuk, Iowa. A judge in Keokuk—George H. Williams, the future senator and attorney general—granted her a divorce, on the grounds of infidelity.

Many years later, after his first wife died, George Williams and Kate had renewed acquaintances in Portland, Oregon. In

1867, they married, and she accompanied him to Washington. Unfortunately for the couple, the son Kate Williams left behind in Ohio had grown into a gambler and a thief. To make matters worse, the young man had recently moved to the nation's capital and was living off the proceeds of his crimes—which included blackmailing his mother and stepfather.

Kate Williams's old acquaintance Hiram C. Whitley had repeatedly helped her, and the attorney general, to cover up the crimes of her wayward son, as well as the very fact of his relationship to the couple. When a well-known Baltimore madame came to Washington, demanding the return of the jewelry Kate's son stole from her bordello, Whitley recovered and returned the baubles. Undaunted, the son robbed $27,000 from the attorney general's personal safe and ran off to New York. Again, Whitley tracked him down and forced him to return the cash, except for $1,200 he had spent. And yet the young man kept embarrassing his mother and stepfather by showing up at receptions in their mansion, accompanied by prostitutes.

With his wife at his side, the attorney general explained to Whitley that she was deeply anxious over the situation, and "often wakes at midnight to cry and toss upon her bed." He feared the stress would kill her. Kate Williams then spoke bitterly of her son and said she wished there was a way to send him into exile; she would be equally relieved if he were dead.

The attorney general quashed that suggestion. "Now don't hurt him," Williams said, "or do anything that will disgrace my family, but for God's sake get him out of Washington."

As the attorney general knew, Whitley and the Secret Service had already carried out at least one abduction for the Department of Justice on Williams's watch.

Late in the afternoon of June 4, 1872, a lanky, middle-aged, man with a wispy gray beard strolled along Waterloo Street in London, Ontario. Up ahead, three men loitered around a parked horse-drawn cab. One of the strangers began walking toward the bearded pedestrian—then suddenly accelerated and tackled him. After a furious struggle, the assailant fastened a pair of handcuffs around the bearded man's wrists. He claimed to have an arrest warrant, but when the captive demanded to see it, he was told, curtly, "You'll find out soon enough." The bearded man continued to fight, until his captor forced a chloroform-soaked rag over his mouth, stuffed him into the parked cab, and ordered the driver to take the backstreets to the railroad station.[24]

The next morning, the prisoner awoke to find himself inside a Pullman car at the Detroit, Michigan, railroad station, looking into the light blue eyes of Secret Service man Joseph G. Hester. "You come with me now," Hester barked.

Hester's prisoner called himself "James Simpson." The detective knew him as a fugitive Ku Klux Klan chieftain from South Carolina under federal indictment for murdering an African American state militia officer in 1871. On April 21, 1872, the attorney general obtained a Canadian magistrate's authorization for the local authorities in that country to arrest him and hand him over to a United States officer, as provided for in extradition treaties covering the United States, Canada, and Great Britain.

Based on Hester's success against the Klan in North Carolina, Whitley had tapped him to orchestrate the sensitive international operation. Hester mounted a clandestine hunt for the Klan fugitive, eventually tracking him to the home of another South Carolinian in London, Ontario. Hester recruited one of the Canadian town's law enforcement officials to make the actual capture.

Upon meeting his prisoner in Detroit, Hester showed him a federal warrant for his arrest, then set off with him on the long train ride back to South Carolina. There was only one problem: both the Canadian extradition order and the American arrest warrant identified the Klansman to be taken into custody as James William Avery, but "James Simpson" was, in reality, a different Klan boss, James Rufus Bratton.

Since Bratton had refused to cooperate, insisting that he was "under Canadian law," and using a pseudonym, Hester did not grasp the fact that his Canadian agent had grabbed the wrong fugitive until after he brought Bratton to South Carolina. A federal court there set the prisoner's bail at $12,000, and released him when Klan sympathizers promised to come up with the money.

Bratton promptly violated the bail agreement by returning to Ontario. In theory, this gave the United States a fresh legal reason to arrest and extradite him, but the British and Canadians were angry and embarrassed at the bungled extradition. At Her Majesty's Government's request—and to quiet press critics in the United States—Attorney General Williams dropped the matter, saying he would not enforce a bail bond against Bratton that would not have existed if not for the faulty arrest.[25]

The Canadian official who seized Bratton on Waterloo Street served as a scapegoat for both governments; an Ontario court convicted him of kidnapping. In the United States, Hester paid a milder penalty, in the form of his forced resignation as a deputy United States Marshal. Whitley kept him on as a Secret Service detective through the November 1872 elections, however. Ever fearful of the Klan, North Carolina's Republicans insisted that Whitley retain him.[26]

Hester's manhunt in Canada was a rare failure in his otherwise brilliant federal career. However, it was fundamentally a case of mistaken identity, which meant that better information about his quarry might have prevented it.

Applying this lesson to his new assignment for Whitley, Attorney General Williams gave the Secret Service chief a photograph of his wife's son, whose pale eyes uncannily resembled hers. His name was James Ivins, and his ways were secretive. "It would be somewhat difficult," the attorney general advised

Whitley, "for a stranger to make his acquaintance and obtain his confidence."

Whitley did not try to dissuade his boss, either by reminding him of the admonitions on "sincere motives and undoubted integrity" the Secret Service chief had just issued to his force, or by warning him of the political repercussions should this unlawful operation somehow become public. Nor did Whitley note the contradiction between his boss's previous insistence on budgetary discipline and his willingness, now, to use government resources for this eminently personal purpose.

Instead, Whitley studied James Ivins's handsome face, pondering the intriguing task that the attorney general had just set before him, and thinking, no doubt, that this powerful cabinet member would be indebted to Whitley, and the Secret Service, if they accomplished it.

"I think I have just the man in my employ who can handle the rooster," Whitley said.

Whitley assigned the case to William H. Reed, who had worked with him on the Ashburn murder in 1868, and whom he had recently added to the Secret Service's expanding roster. Whitley had come to admire Reed's imperturbable deadpan and silver tongue. "If ever there was a born confidence man," he later wrote, "he was the one." Reed would be perfect for a job that required overcoming a young gambler's suspicious nature. The Secret Service chief told Reed to take a good look at the photograph of James Ivins, then began laying out his plan for the young "rooster's" bloodless but permanent removal from the nation's capital.

Posing as a counterfeiter from the South, Reed staged a "chance" encounter with Ivins in a billiard parlor on Washington's Pennsylvania Avenue. Within a week, Whitley reported to Attorney General Williams that his detective and James Ivins were living together at the expensive hotel room Williams's blackmail money subsidized.

Soon thereafter, Reed had talked Ivins into traveling with him to New York, supposedly to pursue a counterfeit securities selling scheme. On Broadway, near the Astor Hotel, they happened upon a wealthy Indianan, whom Reed recognized as his old friend "Captain Blake." Reed, Ivins, and the Hoosier spent the afternoon drinking, culminating in a cognac-swilling session at the Merchants' Hotel.

With a confidential wink to Ivins, Reed poured what appeared to be a powdered drug into "Captain Blake's" drink, behind the latter's back. Once "Captain Blake" had drained his glass, and passed out, Reed and Ivins stripped him of his watch, diamond lapel pin, rings, shirt studs, cuff links, and wallet. Then they absconded to a new hideout in Jersey City, New Jersey.

As soon as he heard the hotel-room door shut behind Reed and Ivins, "Blake" rose from his feigned stupor, waited until the two men were well on their way, then headed to Whitley's office on Bleecker Street. "Blake" was William H. Butts, a Secret Service detective, playing his part in Whitley's plot to help the attorney general get rid of his troublesome stepson. Next, Butts went to the *New York Tribune*, where a staffer who owed Whitley a favor printed a convincing-looking article about the robbery and murder of "Captain Blake." Before the poison in his cognac took final effect, the "article" said, the victim had described the killers, two men from Washington, for whom there was now a large reward.

Butts smuggled the bogus clipping to Reed. Reed showed it to Ivins, who panicked. Reed said they should run to Brownsville, Texas, where he had stashed counterfeit bonds; they could live off the proceeds of selling them until it was safe to go back to New York. On their way to Texas, the two men passed through New Orleans, where Whitley had arranged for posters to be hung in the railroad station advertising a $2,000 reward for "Blake's" murderers. If the Secret Service was on their trail, Reed told Ivins, they would have to flee all the way to Mexico.

Reed slipped away from Ivins long enough to telegraph Whitley, informing him that they were en route to Mexico City. Whitley passed the news to the attorney general, who asked him to convey it in person to his wife. Kate Williams laughed and congratulated Whitley on his ruse, and expressed the hope that her son would never show his face in Washington again.

James Ivins followed William H. Reed of the Secret Service all the way to the Mexican city of Veracruz, on the Gulf of Mexico. There, more than two thousand miles away from Washington, Whitley's man abandoned the attorney general's stepson. By the time Ivins figured out that he had been duped, Reed was well on his way to New York.

The troublesome child of Kate Williams's first marriage never bothered his mother or her famous husband again. James Ivins did, however, find his way from Veracruz to California, and gave up his previous illegal ways in favor of real estate speculation and agriculture. By the late 1870s, he owned a thousand-acre dairy farm at Petaluma. When anyone asked what prompted him to move West, he said that he had gone there to seek his fortune after finishing college.[27]

In the latter half of February 1874, Hiram C. Whitley treated himself and his family to a vacation in sunny Jacksonville, Florida. It was a rare and well-earned rest for a man who had driven himself to near-exhaustion on behalf of the federal government for half a decade.

In early March, a telegram to Whitley from Everett C. Banfield, the solicitor of the Treasury, interrupted the Secret Service chief's respite. A chill of fear, and a spasm of anger, ran through him as he read it: Banfield was warning him that a rival detective from Chicago had come to Washington, and was lobbying to replace Whitley as chief of the Secret Service.[28]

It barely seemed possible: Whitley's position had been secure when he left; he would not have ventured so far from home, even for a short interval, otherwise. He felt he had more than earned the Grant administration's full backing, through the discreet and effective performance of both official and unofficial missions.

Even for the most seasoned undercover operator, paranoia can be an occupational hazard; to some extent, it's a job requirement. One of the Secret Service's top detectives described Whitley to a friendly reporter as "circumspect and unfamiliar," with his detectives, a man who kept "his own counsel and impresses the necessity of this on others."[29] And as he pondered Solicitor Banfield's message, Whitley's paranoia mounted. He wired Solicitor Banfield back, asking him to alert his occasional ally Orville E. Babcock at the White House to what was afoot. Then he boarded a northbound train.[30]

As he sped back to Washington in early March 1874, Whitley had every reason to assume Babcock would reciprocate his past services to the administration by protecting him from this rumored new threat to his tenure. Banfield arranged a meeting for Whitley with Babcock; and, sure enough, the latter told the former that he had nothing to fear. Babcock said he had asked President Grant about the matter and had been personally assured there would be no change at the Secret Service.

Relieved, Whitley asked Babcock if there was anything he could do for him in return. A few days later, Babcock informed him that there was.[31]

At that moment, the president's aide found himself embroiled in an annoying little political fight, related not to his White House duties, but to the additional position he held as Superintendent of Public Buildings and Grounds for the city of Washington. In this capacity, Babcock had authority over the Republican-led local government's vast drainage, paving, and park program. The construction beautified and sanitized the capital. It also raised property values, enriching certain Republican-connected landlords and contractors.

Washington's traditional business elite, mainly conservative

Democrats, felt excluded and denounced the program as a waste of their taxes, doubly odious to these erstwhile slaveholders because newly enfranchised African American voters backed the District government. This group lobbied Congress to investigate alleged corruption and cost overruns—targeting Babcock's purported complicity. Congress duly empaneled a select committee, which held its first hearing on March 5, 1874. Democratic newspapers began fanning the flames of scandal.

Babcock wanted Whitley to infiltrate detectives into this nest of critics. To avoid any risk of exposing the White House's involvement, they would not report to Babcock, but to his protégé, the United States Attorney for the District of Columbia, Richard Harrington, who wore two hats as both the chief prosecutor for the city, and its legal representative before the congressional investigative committee.

The request was legally and ethically questionable, as Whitley must have known. It might also have occurred to him that Babcock deliberately started the rumor about a threat to Whitley's job, to maneuver the Secret Service chief into this dubious task.

Whitley also knew, though, that he had executed other murky assignments for Babcock and for Attorney General Williams, without unduly negative consequences. To the contrary, doing the dirty work for powerful figures gave Whitley some leverage over them, and, with it, an added measure of the job security he craved.

Babcock's new proposal seemed especially safe to Whitley since both the president of the United States' right-hand man and the top prosecutor in the city, Richard Harrington, would be in on it. In general, Whitley believed that the ends justified the means, and this mission could be construed to illustrate the maxim: the intended targets were Southern-sympathizing Democratic foes of the Grant administration and Reconstruction who, though less violent than the Ku Klux Klan, basically represented the same social, political, and racial ideology.

The Secret Service chief told Babcock he would get right on it.

By the middle of March, he had delegated Babcock's mission to Ichabod C. Nettleship, who, in turn, assigned two part-time informants to infiltrate Babcock's opponents in the Washington press corps. After a few days, Harrington had heard nothing from them, and Whitley became impatient. Returning to Washington with Nettleship to check on the spies, the Secret Service chief discovered that one had disappeared, while the other had been arrested for selling bootleg cigars.

Whitley told Nettleship to forget about them, as well as the relatively unambitious goal of gathering intelligence on Babcock's journalistic critics. He had a new, more aggressive plan, he explained, which, "if it worked out, would settle the whole thing."[32]

The source for much of the negative press about the public works program was Columbus Alexander, a printer and landowner descended from the English earl whose lands formed the southern half of the national capital's original territory (which had since been restored to Virginia under the name of Alexandria). A pro-Southern slaveholder before the Civil War, Alexander was now obsessed with the idea that one of the city's leading contractors had covered up his corruption by giving the congressional investigating committee false business records. Alexander had let it be known he would not rest until he discovered the real records.[33]

Whitley had no idea whether Alexander's obsession had a basis in fact. But he thought it could be used against him. Suppose, he mused to Nettleship, that the Secret Service arranged to get Alexander the records he so eagerly sought—but under circumstances calculated to destroy his reputation. Specifically, undercover agents posing as government insiders could offer to procure the documents for Alexander, no questions asked, and, if he agreed, frame him for ordering their theft.

A staged burglary of documents planted in United States Attorney Richard Harrington's office safe would be perfect, since anyone would believe that the city's lawyer might have held the "real" records. The Secret Service would recruit safecrackers, and Harrington would be in on the plot, too. When Harrington "discovered" the document theft, Whitley explained, he would drop the charges against the "burglars," in return for their testimony pinning the whole thing on Columbus Alexander. They would then swear to Alexander's guilt in court. It would discredit not only Alexander, but all of Babcock's political foes.

Even for the intellectual author of James Ivins's abduction, this plan was creative, bold, and convoluted. Nettleship thought it might be a bit too convoluted.

"It is a funny job," he told Whitley. "Suppose it don't work. What will become of us?"[34] Nettleship said he wanted no part of a plot that would physically hurt Alexander or anyone else.

Whitley assured Nettleship that the purpose was purely to "throw muck" on Alexander and his political allies. As for the risk the scheme might go awry, it was hardly worth worrying: friends in high places would protect them. Reluctantly, Nettleship agreed to the plan. The chief had never led him astray before.

Whitley had employed both permanent and part-time detectives to infiltrate the Ku Klux Klan in the South. Once the violence ebbed, and the Secret Service's operations wound down, he laid off some of the part-timers. For months thereafter, they found themselves at loose ends. Whitley decided to recruit the key man in his plot to frame Columbus Alexander from this pool of tested but underemployed talent.

Michael Hayes was a New Yorker with a checkered past, who had spent much of his time before and during the Civil War wandering Latin America, from Cuba to Uruguay. This was the sort of thing that small-time criminals sometimes did to escape the law, but there was no proof of wrongdoing by Hayes as of 1871, when Whitley hired him and sent him to Alabama. Hayes, who had learned Southern ways and idioms during his previous travels, used the name "Major Hudson," and worked undercover tending bar in a Tuscaloosa, Alabama, tavern frequented by Klansmen.[35] Since the end of that mission, however, Hayes and his wife had struggled to make ends meet in Manhattan. Hayes earned extra dollars selling Whitley occasional tips on smuggling activity in the port of New York.

On April 5, 1874, a messenger arrived at Hayes's house on Roosevelt Street in New York, bearing the surprising news that the Secret Service chief wanted to see him. At Bleecker Street, Hayes was ushered into Whitley's office, where Whitley rose from behind his desk and crossed the room to shake Hayes's hand. This unusually friendly gesture aroused Hayes's suspicion, but Whitley, in his inimitable manner, persuaded him to go to Washington, where, the Secret Service chief said, Ichabod C. Nettleship would explain a big job to him.

In the nation's capital, Nettleship sounded sympathetic about Hayes's personal problems. Whitley always liked Hayes, Nettleship told him. "It's not our fault you have not got any appointment or steady work," he said. Now Hayes's luck was about to change, precisely because the chief esteemed him so highly. "I have got something for you that will keep you employed while Colonel Whitley has the division," Nettleship confided.

Nettleship laid out the safe burglary plot and Hayes's part in it. Hayes, posing as someone with access to the documents Columbus Alexander wanted, would contact Alexander through an intermediary, to whom Nettleship would soon introduce Hayes. If Alexander took the bait, Hayes would recruit some safecrackers, and introduce one of them to Alexander—as a courier—so that the businessman would recognize him when he came to his house to deliver the documents.

Harrington's part would be crucial. He would be sent a fake

anonymous letter "warning" of an impending theft of documents from his office safe. Citing this letter, he would ask the Washington superintendent of police to join him on a stakeout outside his office on the night of the "burglary." Harrington and the police chief would follow the "burglar" as he left the building, to find out where he took the "stolen" papers. When the "burglar" reached Alexander's house, and Alexander emerged to take the documents, the lawman, unaware of what was really afoot, would make the arrest.

In addition to the Secret Service chief's gratitude, and a permanent place in the division, Hayes would earn $2,000.

The moon was bright, and all was quiet on the streets of Washington as midnight, April 23, 1874, the start time for Whitley's elaborate caper, approached. Harrington, along with Washington's superintendent of police, and his chief detective, crouched behind a billboard at the corner of Fifth Street and Louisiana Avenue, in the heart of the city. They were watching Harrington's office across the street.

Ten minutes went by, then thirty. Things were running behind schedule. It was not until after 1:00 a.m. that a loud explosion shattered the silence: the safe had at last been blown. Neighbors threw open their windows to see what all the commotion was about. Someone emerged from the office carrying a large bag. At Harrington's urging, he and the two police officials followed; yet the man with the bag seemed confused as to where he was going. At one point he paused to ask the men behind him for directions to Columbus Alexander's house.

Whitley's plan was falling apart. By the time the suspected "burglar" reached Alexander's stately mansion at the corner of Tenth and F Streets, the superintendent of police was beginning to suspect some sort of hoax. Then the "burglar" stood in front of the mansion for almost half an hour, furiously ringing the doorbell, while the house remained dark and no one answered. Due to the delays in blowing open the safe, the man had arrived long after Alexander and everyone else in his mansion was sound asleep.

Finally, the police superintendent decided he could wait no longer; he walked across the street to arrest the burglar. There would be no incriminating documents handed to Alexander, no devastating frame-up of Orville E. Babcock's political opponents.

Off the group went to the city jail, a mere five blocks away. Upon their arrival, Whitley's coconspirator Richard Harrington was suddenly overcome by a sensation much different from the feeling of triumph he had expected when the evening began. He turned from his companions and threw up on the sidewalk.

Orville E. Babcock simply shook his head when Hiram C. Whitley came to see him at the White House three days after the botched safe burglary.[36] Babcock was aghast at how far beyond his orders Whitley had gone; the president's secretary never would have approved this outlandish scheme. "I thought you were smarter than that," he scolded the Secret Service chief.

Though initially contained within governmental circles, news of the affair became public in early May. The police superintendent who had arrested the burglar at Columbus Alexander's house filed a report with the city's legislature, in which he suggested the burglary was a setup, somehow intended to smear Alexander, and called for an investigation. This document leaked to the press, prompting Congress to order the committee that was already looking into alleged corruption in the District to probe the safe burglary, as well.

Whitley and his confederates mounted a frenzied cover-up. By the time the congressional committee started closed-door hearings on the case in mid-May, Harrington had arranged for the jailed burglar to swear out an affidavit saying he was indeed working for Alexander. Whitley and Nettleship, meanwhile, had paid Michael Hayes $200 for an affidavit corroborating the burglar's. Then they sent him to Toronto, with the promise of an eight dollars per day stipend until it was safe for him to return to the United States.

Both affidavits reached the committee before Whitley, Nettleship, and Harrington testified. Believing they could not be contradicted by either of the participants in the burglary who were known to the committee, the three falsely, but confidently, swore they were not involved.

Whitley had conceived the entire plot, which meant his lies to the committee would have to be especially brazen. He claimed that he knew "nothing in any way whatever, in the slightest," about the caper before reading about it in the newspapers. He denied having seen Hayes since his work infiltrating the Ku Klux Klan ended almost two years previously. Whitley swore he had no idea where Hayes was now, but vowed that "if you will apply to the Treasury Department for my services, I will do my level best to find him."[37]

Whitley assumed the cover-up would work as long as Michael Hayes followed the rule set forth in the new Secret Service Circular of Instructions: "Employees must observe the utmost secrecy in all transactions relating to the business of the service." What Whitley did not know was that Hayes had already broken it.

While waiting in Washington for his initial April rendezvous with Ichabod C. Nettleship, Hayes used some downtime to visit the Baltimore, Maryland, home of George W. Carter, his old friend from Klan-fighting days in Alabama. This was the same George W. Carter whose brave infiltration of the Calhoun County Klan den had helped break up that branch of the white terrorist organization, earning both Carter and Whitley awestruck praise from a top Department of Justice official.

More recently, though, Carter, like Hayes, had been laid off from the Secret Service. He toiled as a private detective on the railroad between Baltimore and Wheeling, West Virginia, a grim, low-paying job that involved spotting the occasional counterfeiter and breaking up three-card monte games. He resented the Secret Service's refusal to hire him permanently, so much so that he wrote Nettleship calling him a "pot-gutted son of a bitch" for not answering his previous job-seeking letters.

Troubled by the unethical nature of his mission in Washington, and determined to have a friendly witness available in case the safe burglary failed—and Whitley tried to make him the fall guy—Hayes laid out the basic scheme to Carter over the course of an extended drinking session in Baltimore. He had Carter shadow him when he first met Nettleship in Washington, so that there would be a witness to that, as well. Hayes made clear that the goal of the burglary was to smear an innocent party. The only key details he omitted were the name of that party and the location of the safe.

Betraying Hayes's confidence, Carter then tried to shop the story around Washington in April. No one in government or the press was interested in such an implausible tale, especially since it lacked crucial specifics. Not until the news of the bizarre events at Richard Harrington's office broke did Carter put two and two together: this must be the caper that Hayes had described to him, and he was therefore in possession of information that would enable him to get revenge on the Secret Service, the "pot-gutted son of a bitch" Nettleship included.

Carter contacted Columbus Alexander's lawyer, who sent him to the congressional panel investigating the affair. On May 19, 1874, a week after Harrington's appearance, and four days after Whitley and Nettleship testified, Carter went to the committee and revealed everything Hayes had told him, which contradicted the three officials' tales in every important detail.

Whitley still had an ace in the hole: only he knew Michael Hayes was in Toronto. He sent his loyal subordinate, Abner B. Newcomb, to tell the congressional committee that Hayes had told Newcomb the whole safe burglary was George W. Carter's idea. This was remotely plausible, given the latter's admitted hatred of his former employers. Meanwhile, Nettleship went to see Hayes north of the border, with a fresh supply of cash and a revised affidavit for Hayes that would adjust his previous statement to fit the new testimony the committee had heard.

Hayes balked. He felt mistreated, and was beginning to wonder how long he would have to remain in Toronto, living off an allowance away from his wife and family.

On the night of Saturday, June 13, 1874, Ichabod C. Nettleship heard a knock at the front door of his Newark, New Jersey, home, where he and his family were holding a wake for Nettleship's daughter, recently dead of diphtheria.[38]

When Nettleship opened the door, what he saw compounded his grief: Michael Hayes. He had decided to get out of Toronto on his own. And he was in no mood to express sympathy for his erstwhile Secret Service handler.

"In the name of God, what brought you back?" Nettleship demanded.

"I can't live on air and water," Hayes replied angrily.

Nettleship desperately borrowed fifty dollars from the mourners and gave it to Hayes, urging him to go away and lie low in Albany, New York, at least until the congressional committee's scheduled adjournment at the end of June.

Indignant at Nettleship's paltry cash offer, Hayes headed to Washington, determined to unburden himself of the truth once and for all. On June 15, 1874, a mutual friend of Hayes and George W. Carter, who was now assisting Columbus Alexander, escorted Hayes to Capitol Hill. The investigative committee's members were as shocked to see Hayes as Nettleship had been, but they immediately put him under oath and began questioning. Hayes repudiated his previous affidavit, telling lawmakers that he signed it under duress. He confirmed George W. Carter's damning testimony.

Hayes added a devastating new detail: upon arriving in Washington in April, he had sent a telegram to Whitley in New York, asking for help in finding Nettleship. Whitley had responded. These messages, copies of which the committee quickly obtained from telegraph offices in Washington and New York, provided documentary proof of Whitley's guilt.

On June 23, 1874, the committee published all of the testimony, along with a brief report that drew attention to the incriminating discrepancy between Hayes's account of the safe burglary and Whitley's. The committee asked the two cabinet departments with authority over the Secret Service, Justice and Treasury, to investigate the matter further, focusing on the crucial contradiction over the telegram.

Whitley faced potential career destruction and ouster from the detective force that he had only recently taken the liberty of renaming the "U.S. Secret Service" on expensive new official stationery. Irony of ironies, his downfall could be based on the testimony of two men—Hayes and Carter—who were instrumental in his finest moment as chief, the infiltration of the Ku Klux Klan.

Having previously avowed that Secret Service spies could not be taken at their word, the Klan's leading apologist in Congress, Representative James B. Beck of Kentucky, now rejoiced in their revelations. Six years after Hiram C. Whitley pinned the murder of George W. Ashburn on Beck's friend William D. Chipley in Georgia, he thought the detective might be about to get his comeuppance.

On the floor of the House, Beck tried to block publication of the committee's report, on the grounds that it did not condemn the Secret Service chief and his top assistant harshly enough. Whitley and Nettleship should be in the penitentiary, he roared.[39]

At various points throughout his career Hiram C. Whitley had found himself in trouble due to exposure of his secrets. He always reacted the same way: he denied any and all charges, admitted no wrongdoing, and turned the tables on his accusers by leveling charges against them. Now, the Secret Service chief tried the same methods to brazen out the scandal newspapers dubbed "The Washington Safe Burglary Case."

Returning to the congressional investigative committee after Hayes's bombshell, Whitley asserted that he had no recollection of ever reading Hayes's telegram. He had been at a dinner party in Boston when it arrived at Bleecker Street; an aide probably signed Whitley's name on the receipt, per Whitley's standing instructions. It was a normal practice for a busy detective chief who could not possibly attend to all the correspondence that poured into his office each day.

On the same day the committee published its report, June 23, 1874, Whitley wrote to one of the Republican members of the panel, Senator William B. Allison of Iowa, claiming that the telegram receipt was "part of the original plot to implicate me in the job."[40] Hayes and Carter, he wrote, were in on this purported conspiracy, whose true masterminds remained hidden. Whitley was certain, though, that its "sole purpose" was nothing less than "destroying the Secret Service force." All he asked for now, he begged Allison, was a chance to get to the truth. "I am bound to ferret it out," he wrote, "if permitted to do so, if it take a lifetime."

As his frantic tone and increasingly complex narrative implied, Whitley was caught in a very tangled web. He had himself to blame. The safe burglary was, indeed, a "funny job," as Ichabod C. Nettleship had said. No one asked Whitley to try it. He concocted the scheme to curry favor with Orville E. Babcock, hoping to further his own bureaucratic and political interests.

Wise spymasters take care of their former subordinates, lest they become disgruntled and vengefully peddle their skills and knowledge to someone else. Proper handling of such trusted insiders was bound to be difficult for a new undercover organization like the Secret Service, with its limited resources and improvised legal status, and Whitley had not risen to that challenge. Instead, he neglected Michael Hayes and George W. Carter, who had risked their necks for him against the Ku Klux Klan. Now they were getting even. Whitley failed to learn from his experience with Abraham C. Beatty, his former protégé in New York, who had avenged his summary dismissal from the Secret Service by turning against Whitley in the Joshua D. Miner case.

Whitley had also overestimated how much protection his friends in high places would be able to offer. The safe burglary case hit the news just as Attorney General Williams was facing accusations that his wife, Kate, had used Department of Justice funds to buy a fancy new carriage. Given that scandal, and the fact that the safe burglary implicated his subordinates—Whitley and Harrington—Williams had to recuse from the case and appointed an independent prosecutor. Meanwhile, Whitley's allies at the Treasury Department, Secretary William A. Richardson (who replaced George S. Boutwell when Boutwell became a senator in 1873) and Solicitor Everett C. Banfield, had been forced to step down in May due to a contretemps of their own: their recruitment of a private citizen, John B. Sanborn, to collect more than $400,000 in unpaid federal taxes, of which Sanborn was allowed to keep half.

The case of Williams's carriage and the "Sanborn Affair" merged in the public mind with the "salary grab"—Congress's 1873 attempt to vote itself a retroactive pay increase—the safe burglary, and other scandals, to create an impression of an out-of-control government. Certainly, that was the image newspapers affiliated with the Democrats, and with the anti-Grant faction of the Republican Party, promoted. With the 1874 elections approaching, and the economy reeling from a financial panic that began in September 1873, the Grant administration found itself on the political defensive. Voters in the Republican Party's Northern base were losing patience with Washington politicians, and losing interest in what President Grant had done, or might still want to do, to pacify and transform the South under the banner of Reconstruction.

A new secretary of the Treasury, Benjamin H. Bristow, took office in June 1874, vowing to expunge waste and fraud from the department. Reform was a matter of principle for Bristow, a talented Kentucky Unionist lawyer who had risen to the rank of general in the United States Army during the Civil War, supported Reconstruction and the rights of African Americans, and served as Solicitor General of the United States for two years under Attorney General Amos T. Akerman at the Department of Justice.

It was also a matter of ambition. Bristow coveted the Republican presidential nomination in 1876; he hoped to ride the anti-corruption wave to the White House. Leading anti–Grant Republicans encouraged him to think of his new Treasury job as a stepping-stone to higher office. "If you clean out the department, thereby convincing everyone of your capacity and integrity," Supreme Court Justice David Davis wrote Bristow, "I think you stand as good a chance…of being taken up for president as anyone I know."[41]

As solicitor general, Bristow had only minor involvement in the Department of Justice's campaign against the Klan, and little direct knowledge of Whitley's role. Consequently, he had no investment, personal or professional, in the Secret Service and its embattled chief. Whitley tried to ingratiate himself with Bristow, telling him how "happy" he and his detectives were at Bristow's appointment, offering "the congratulations of your humble servant"—and pleading with the new secretary not to fire the Treasury Department official who kept the Secret Service's books and reimbursed detectives for their expenses.[42]

Bristow brushed Whitley off. Nor did Whitley's letter asserting that he was a victim of a conspiracy faze Bristow, when

Senator Allison forwarded it to him at Whitley's request on June 24, 1874.

Bristow was determined to carry out the institutional scrubbing of the Secret Service that neither Congress nor his predecessors at the Treasury Department ever had. He would get to the bottom of the Secret Service's role in the safe burglary, as the congressional committee had recommended. The inquest would go beyond that, too, encompassing the division's history, its finances, its performance—its entire rationale. Bristow said he wanted to know if the present "system" of detectives was indeed the best use of the funds Congress had given his department to fight counterfeiting and other crimes.[43]

Bristow assigned the task to Bluford Wilson, whom President Grant had appointed to take Everett C. Banfield's place as solicitor of the Treasury. Wilson was thirty-three years old, but had only been a lawyer for seven years, having begun legal study after United States Army service in the Civil War. His older brother, James H. Wilson, a well-connected Republican who had been on then-General Grant's staff during the war, helped Bluford Wilson get appointed in 1869 as the United States Attorney for southern Illinois, then recommended him to Bristow in Washington.

For Bristow, Wilson's inexperience was an advantage. He could be counted on to defer to his more seasoned boss. He would be eager to establish his reputation by advancing the cause of reform; and he would be unencumbered by obligations to Washington pols. Upon accepting his new position, Wilson wrote Bristow: "I will strive to the utmost to fill it to the satisfaction of the country, the administration, and my friends."[44] He promptly set out to prove it.

Bluford Wilson devoted July 1874 to his probe, mindful of the need to resolve the matter well before the November midterm elections. Wilson read statute books and Department of

Treasury archives, trying to understand how Whitley's outfit had evolved. He scoured its expense reports, and froze reimbursements upon discovering that Secret Service men were billing hundreds of dollars per month in "incidentals." Ichabod C. Nettleship alone averaged $714.90, four times his regular pay.[45] Wilson wrote United States Marshals and United States Attorneys in the eight cities where the Secret Service maintained branch offices, seeking their views of its effectiveness, and asking if it could be eliminated "without detriment to the public interests."[46]

Wilson traveled to the Bleecker Street office in New York, where he installed himself at Hiram C. Whitley's desk on July 8, 1874, and plowed through his files. Over the next four days, Whitley hovered over the solicitor of the Treasury, pledging his full cooperation, boasting about his accomplishments, and protesting his innocence in the safe burglary. The Secret Service chief escorted Wilson to Boston, to meet witnesses—Whitley's friends—who told him that Whitley had been dining with them on the evening in April when he had supposedly signed for Michael Hayes's telegram in New York.

Whitley exerted all of his formidable powers of persuasion on the earnest new solicitor of the Treasury. For a moment at least, they worked.

From New York, Wilson telegraphed his superiors in Washington, reporting his tentative view that Whitley was not guilty in the safe burglary. Wilson's message was meant to be confidential, but Whitley promptly found out about it and leaked a version to friends in the New York press. The *New York Times* reported that Wilson had decided to exonerate Whitley, having been "perfectly satisfied of the chief's freedom from all knowledge of any connection, in ever so remote a way, with the alleged burglary."[47]

Benjamin H. Bristow was annoyed, if not entirely surprised, to find out from the papers that Wilson had let himself be manipulated. "Bluford is an honest courageous man," he wrote to his brother, James H. Wilson. However, "he has made a mistake in announcing his conclusion in the Secret Service investigation prematurely, and in conferring with some persons with whom he ought not to have conferred, but this is not a matter of surprise, since he was a comparative stranger to people whom he encountered here and in New York."[48]

Wilson's mistake was readily corrected upon his return to Washington. Bristow put him in touch with the newly appointed special prosecutor in the safe burglary case, and with William P. Wood, Whitley's predecessor, now working as a private investigator for Columbus Alexander. Still smarting over his ouster from the Secret Service in 1869, Wood hated Whitley; he had helped Joshua D. Miner dig up dirt on Whitley, and denounced him in a broadside published on January 1, 1872, as "one of the most precious scoundrels who ever went unwhipped of justice."[49]

Wood and the special prosecutor took Wilson to meet Michael Hayes on July 17, 1874; he was not hard to find, having been locked in a jail cell ever since Richard Harrington retaliated for Hayes's testimony to the congressional committee by having him arrested for burglary.[50] Hayes explained the safe burglary and showed the solicitor of the Treasury his diaries and written orders from Whitley.

Realizing that Hayes was a solid witness, and that the Secret Service chief had duped him in New York, Wilson turned decisively against Whitley. With William P. Wood in tow, Wilson went back to New York and offered Whitley forty-eight hours to come clean. Whitley continued to deny everything, and appealed desperately over Wilson's head to Bristow.

"The solicitor has discovered new charges against me," he telegraphed the secretary of the Treasury on July 20, 1874. "They are false and I can disprove them. Shall be in Washington tomorrow."[51]

Bristow paid Whitley no heed. A telegram from Bluford Wilson, warning the secretary that Whitley was "plotting" against them, had reached him first.[52]

Secretary Bristow and Solicitor Wilson believed to a moral certainty that Hiram C. Whitley had abused his power to attempt the political destruction of Columbus Alexander. The Secret Service chief had to go, they concluded.

The question, though, was how best to effectuate his ouster. A federal grand jury was pursuing the case, guided by the special prosecutor Attorney General Williams had appointed. Whitley was almost certain to be indicted. To fire him before the grand jury acted, though, could be seen as improper interference in the criminal case, which Whitley might even exploit to escape punishment. Yet allowing him to stay in office as if all was well would be equally unacceptable.

The solution they hit upon was to call for the abolition of the Secret Service, at least as it was currently constituted, but for reasons unrelated, ostensibly, to the bungled burglary.

Wilson's forty-page handwritten report to Bristow, submitted on July 27, 1874, and quickly leaked to the press, described Wilson's safe burglary inquiry as active but incomplete and, in any case, no substitute for the more definitive work of the grand jury. The solicitor of the Treasury emphasized, however, that he had identified many other irregularities at the Secret Service. The detective force was "not now and never has been expressly authorized by any act of Congress." The dual lines of authority connecting it to the secretary of the Treasury and the attorney general created "confusion in the public business." Placing Secret Service headquarters in New York "served to weaken that sense of direct personal responsibility necessary to perfect discipline and efficiency."

Worst of all, Wilson contended, the Secret Service was just not getting tangible results proportionate to the money it expended. As authority for this accusation, Wilson cited opinions he had received from United States Attorneys and Marshals around the country, the latter of whom assured him that they and their deputies could do the same job cheaper.[53] The time had come, Wilson asserted, for the Secret Service to "be thoroughly reorganized and largely reduced," so that the United States could revert to a decentralized federal law enforcement structure more appropriate to its "free government." This would rely on United States Attorneys and Marshals, as had been the case before the Civil War. Congressional appropriations would be limited to subsidizing rewards for citizens' tips to these officials.

As a final courtesy to Whitley before he submitted this report, Bluford Wilson gave the Secret Service chief twenty-four hours to file a written defense of the detective force he had led for the previous five years.

By now, Whitley boiled with paranoia and fury. Yet he managed to keep his emotions under control as he dictated his point-by-point rebuttal to Wilson. It was as if he knew this might be his final official submission as Secret Service chief, and had determined to go out on a high note.

Whitley's closely reasoned sixteen-page argument for a modern, national detective force did indeed represent the Secret Service chief at his polemical best. It began with a pointed mention of his "detective experience of upward of twelve years in the service of the United States." This experience showed that the division enabled the government to develop "a compact organization which should permeate all parts of the country, and have a responsible central head," and that specialized in truly national crimes: counterfeiting, revenue fraud, and smuggling. Federal marshals, working in their state-level districts, could never match those capabilities.

Proof of this was the central archive of criminal records Whitley's team had assembled, including the photographs and biographies of chronic offenders, which was property of the United States government, and available upon request to all federal officers. Such a database could never have been collected under the reward system—which, Whitley noted, had led to corruption and abuse during William P. Wood's tenure, and would do so again if Wilson insisted on resurrecting it.[54]

These were all excellent points. Whitley might also have noted that gutting the Secret Service would leave the federal government unable to penetrate the Ku Klux Klan, or similar organizations, if and when they staged a comeback in the volatile South. The only United States Attorney who expressed unequivocal support for the Secret Service in response to Bluford Wilson's survey was James R. Beckwith of New Orleans, who had just prosecuted the massacre of more than sixty black men by a white mob at Colfax, Louisiana, in 1873. The Secret Service had helped identify and arrest the suspects, through dangerous undercover work in remote areas.[55]

Whitley concluded his letter to Solicitor Wilson with a defiant plea:

I have labored to render the Secret Service Division of the Treasury Department a compact organization, steady in its purpose of suppressing the crime of counterfeiting, unceasing in the vigilance rendered imperative by its discipline, and which the records show to have been successful in its results.

The solicitor of the Treasury was having none of it. The youthful lawyer countered Whitley's pragmatic arguments with ideological assertions. His trump card was the inveterate American disdain for European-style surveillance and centralized policing. "Upon principle," Bluford Wilson wrote, "I am radically opposed to any organized system of espionage in connection with our free government."

The courts, federal marshals, and United States Attorneys were the only "safe agencies with which to cope with offenders against the United States laws," Wilson insisted. If they were not effective, he insisted, "they should be made so." In any case, they would be preferable to Hiram C. Whitley and his Secret Service, "whose arts and presence are hardly more tolerable to the public than those of the criminals they seek to detect."

Wilson made no comment on the similarity between his views and those voiced by Representative James B. Beck and other white supremacist Democratic foes of the Republican government he served. The convergence was not altogether surprising; the Grant administration's "corruption" had been the joint rallying cry of Democrats and Liberal Republicans in the 1872 election. Whitley's escapades provided an all-too-valid excuse for both to raise it again in 1874.

No one fought more fiercely when cornered than Hiram C. Whitley. He also could tell when he was licked. On September 3, 1874, he submitted his letter of resignation as chief of the Secret Service Division, the job he had held for half a decade and considered preferable to the presidency itself. Secretary Bristow accepted it, effective September 30. Ichabod C. Nettleship, the assistant chief whose warning against the safe burglary Whitley had failed to heed, also stepped down, along with a half dozen of their top detectives.

In interviews with the press, Whitley insisted that he resigned due to ill health. He denied involvement in the safe burglary and declared himself "the victim of as foul a conspiracy as has ever been concocted in this or any other country for the defamation of the character of a public officer." He took a parting shot at Bluford Wilson, describing him, not entirely inaccurately, as "violently prejudiced against the Government system of secret service."[56] It was an exercise in futility. As chief, Whitley had made it his "great aim," as one of his detectives put it, "to lift the Secret Service Division up in respectability and in the confidence of the people," yet now the division faced not only condemnation but extinction.[57]

Whitley's sudden fall, and that of his celebrated force, astonished America. The public's amazement only increased after the grand jury indicted him and Nettleship in October. "Then a whole division, and one that deemed itself impregnably intrenched, by virtue of the confidences it possessed and the work it had performed, was virtually thrust out of the government employ, and its head-quarters removed from New York to the Treasury Department, where, in future, the Secretary could have it under his eye," journalist Henry V. Boynton wrote. "Such an event had never happened before in the history of the government."[58]

Many welcomed it. "The extirpation of that branch of the Treasury service…will *not* grieve the American people," Bluford Wilson's brother, James H. Wilson, wrote to Bristow. "The superiors of those officers have discovered that the secret service [*sic*] was entirely too secret for the interests of the government," the *Philadelphia Inquirer* opined on September 14, 1874. "The system is wrong. It has grown up by degrees, and assumed power after power until it became an inquisition menacing the liberties of citizens and proving an instrument of unmitigated evil." Reminiscent of the secret police in France, "such a department in connection with any American official establishment is contrary to the principles and traditions which we have inherited from our forefathers," the *Inquirer* concluded.[59]

In the end, it would not prove quite as easy to "extirpate" the Secret Service, as James H. Wilson assumed. The division still had friends in high places. One of Washington's most powerful Republicans, Representative Benjamin Butler of Massachusetts, had been a believer in undercover operations since his days directing Hiram C. Whitley's activities in New Orleans. He urged Secretary Bristow not to liquidate the Secret Service precipitously.[60] Now that the 1874 elections were over—the Democrats had swept back into control of the House of Representatives—there was less for the Republicans to gain, politically, from abolishing it anyway, at least in the short term.

What's more, Bristow realized that the post–Civil War United States could not so easily revert to the pre–Civil War status quo in federal law enforcement. Among other things, the country had shifted irreversibly to a national currency, which necessitated a national means of fighting counterfeiting.

Shortly before Christmas 1874, the *New York Evening Post* reported that Bristow had decided against the division's outright abolition. Instead, he would try to reform it.[61] He would retain a streamlined group of newly hired, carefully screened detectives, but also a few holdovers who had proven themselves honest and effective. Bristow would pick a new chief, one who could replicate Whitley's successes without replicating his excesses.

Some crimes really did have national impact; they really could be combated only with the help of specialized personnel, recruited nationally, working undercover, and drawing on a common base of verified information, just as Whitley had always said.

He had lost his power, but he had not lost that argument.

7

"Suspicions come from Heaven."

The Ku Klux Klan arrived in Emporia, Kansas, on March 23, 1906. More than a thousand people—business leaders, farmers, railroad workers—turned out to see the mysterious men in their robes and hoods. Even a few men and women of color joined the audience. These Midwesterners watched, transfixed, as Klansmen captured an African American man who had chased a white girl to the edge of a cliff, where she leaped to her death rather than submit to his lust. Applause erupted when they heard that the Klan had hanged the dark-skinned villain, tied his lifeless body with ropes to the saddle of a galloping horse, and dragged the corpse through the streets.

None of this violence, to be sure, had occurred in real life. The awful events were fictional, acted out on stage at Emporia's thousand-seat opera house. *The Clansman*, Thomas Dixon Jr.'s play presenting his version of Reconstruction in the South, had come to town.[1]

Based on Dixon's bestselling novel, the melodrama demonized African Americans, and glorified the Klan, to a degree that was extreme even for the Jim Crow era. Controversy followed Dixon's show as it played theaters across the United States. Editorialists, politicians, and clergy—white and black—denounced it. Some cities, including Southern towns like Macon and Atlanta in Georgia, banned it. Yet the play's racial, political, and sexual themes, lavish costumes, and live horses prancing across the boards made *The Clansman* a hit. It sold out wherever it did appear, beginning with a September 1905 production in Norfolk, Virginia.[2]

Emporia, a stop along the transcontinental railroad that *The Clansman* cast was riding to engagements in California, proved no exception.

Antislavery emigrants from New England founded the frontier town in the 1850s, and it remained staunchly Republican, with Union veterans among its leading citizens, and a significant African American population.[3] Emporia's Methodist minister sermonized against seeing *The Clansman*, warning that it was "calculated to stir up race strife." Those who attended the performance would be "almost guilty of treason," he preached.[4] The *Emporia Gazette*, under the renowned progressive editor William Allen White, branded Dixon's work "the sort of play that Emporia people ought to avoid."[5]

Nevertheless, Emporia's bookstores sold hundreds of copies of Dixon's novel. At 7:00 a.m. on March 20, 1906, an hour before the box office opened, Emporians lined up in freezing weather to buy seats for the one-night-only March 23 performance, even though the opera house had doubled its usual prices. The prevailing sentiment, it seemed, was that everyone was entitled to make up his or her own mind about *The Clansman*.[6]

To the undoubted dismay of Emporia's religious and journalistic leaders, many who did watch the play seemed receptive to Dixon's message: the Ku Klux Klan had saved the white race during Reconstruction. Women in the audience cried, and men hissed, as an actor portraying a mixed-race Republican politician demanded to marry the play's Southern white heroine. The spectators laughed uproariously as white actors in blackface—the comic relief—stumbled and bumbled with stereotypical hilarity.[7]

There were no such expressions from the Emporia opera house's proprietor, the wealthy citizen who had supplied most of the initial $35,000 cost of the building, and who took in *The Clansman* from his private box near the stage.[8]

The blue-eyed gentleman in his seventies happened to have extensive firsthand experience with the Reconstruction-era Klan, probably as much as anyone else in the United States. His assessment of *The Clansman*, when and if he made it public, would be especially well-informed, and, accordingly, influential.

First, though, Hiram C. Whitley wanted to witness Dixon's show for himself.

Whitley and his family had settled in Emporia roughly three decades earlier, following his forced resignation from the Secret Service. All things considered, Whitley had been fortunate to avoid incarceration.

Whitley's trial, on two counts of conspiring against Columbus Alexander "to cause it to be believed by the people of the United States that he was a corrupt and infamous man," began on October 20, 1874.[9] With a midterm election campaign in full swing, pro-Democratic newspapers trumpeted the alleged abuse of power by the former architect of federal undercover operations against the Ku Klux Klan in the South, and counterfeiters in New York. The Republican press countered that the trial demonstrated the Grant administration's willingness to crack down on wrongdoing, even within its own ranks.

Michael Hayes was the government's star witness, testifying in return for immunity from prosecution. His story received corroboration from a Treasury Department clerk who swore the signature on the receipt for Hayes's now-notorious telegram to Whitley in New York was indeed that of the erstwhile Secret Service chief. Whitley's lawyer called Whitley's friends and former Secret Service detectives to vouch for his version of events: Whitley was in Boston at a dinner party when the telegram supposedly arrived, so the handwriting on the receipt must be that of someone he had delegated to sign for him.

An advertisement for *The Clansman* at the Whitley Opera House. (*Emporia Gazette*)

Whitley did not take the stand, but was otherwise his usual combative self—admitting nothing, denying everything, making wild counteraccusations. Outside court one day, he accosted Columbus Alexander, pointed at a prosecution witness, and shouted, "All that man testifies to there is lies; I just want to tell you that." Refusing to acknowledge Whitley directly, Alexander turned to a bystander and huffed, "I don't want any such man to approach me."[10] In a clumsy effort at revenge, Whitley lodged formal perjury charges against Michael Hayes, only to have the trial judge accuse Whitley himself of "interference with this court," and hold him in contempt.[11]

After thirty-six days, the trial ended—in a hung jury. The twelve men split 9–3 in favor of "not guilty."[12] Democratic newspapers ridiculed the result, attributing it to the fact that the jurors had been drawn from a largely Republican jury pool. It was an understandable complaint, given that the defense scenario—Whitley was not a conspirator, but the victim of a conspiracy engineered by Michael Hayes—was so far-fetched.

Nevertheless, a reasonable juror could have had doubts. Even if the charges against Whitley were true, as they probably were, did they really amount to a crime, as opposed to a political dirty trick? Newspapers called it the Washington Safe Burglary Case, but it was an odd sort of burglary in which the alleged perpetrators had permission to enter. The plot may have been designed to plant incriminating documents on Columbus Alexander, but that had never actually occurred. If anything, Alexander emerged with his reputation enhanced.

Whitley probably also benefited from a widespread suspicion that whatever he had done must have been on orders from above. "If Whitley were involved, and the whole secret service [*sic*] with him," a *Baltimore Sun* editorial wondered, "what influence enlisted their agency in a vulgar conspiracy to rob a safe and 'put up the job' on a Washington taxpayer?"[13] Speculation centered on Orville E. Babcock, President Grant's right-hand man, as the real mastermind.

This wasn't true, as Whitley knew. Yet many people believed it, which gave the former Secret Service chief leverage over Babcock. Consequently, the president's aide lived "in fear of Whitley for the past," as solicitor of the Treasury Bluford Wilson noted in a March letter to his brother.[14]

For about half a year after his trial, Whitley maneuvered at the edges of official Washington, attempting to exploit his inside knowledge, actual and perceived. He sought a new federal job, and permanent immunity from criminal liability in the safe burglary case, which was technically still open because his trial had ended in a hung jury, not acquittal.

Whitley's first ploy was to persuade Kate Williams, wife of the attorney general, to write anonymous blackmail notes to the wives of various cabinet officers and to First Lady Julia Grant. The notes threatened to expose alleged corruption in the administration. Then, Whitley approached Babcock, told him who the author of the notes was, and offered to blackmail Kate Williams into ceasing her threats. Babcock, beholden to Whitley for reasons of his own, agreed to pursue the idea.

Benjamin Bristow and Bluford Wilson got wind of these doings and reacted with alarm. Their alarm grew when their investigation showed that the anonymous letters to cabinet wives had been delivered on or near the dates of Whitley's periodic visits to Washington.[15] "I am willing enough...to see the scandal suppressed," Wilson wrote to his brother. "I am not willing however to invoke the aid of an infernal damned scoundrel like Whitley...nor am I willing to see the President placed unwittingly in the power of such a man." Threatening to go over his head to President Grant, Bristow and Wilson prevailed upon Babcock to abandon Whitley's plan.[16]

Undaunted, Whitley continued to pressure Babcock, either personally or through a trusted intermediary, his erstwhile Secret Service operative, Abner B. Newcomb. In August 1875 Whitley told Babcock he was willing to leave Washington for the frontier boomtown of Pueblo, in the remote Colorado Territory. The region was familiar to Whitley from pre–Civil War days, when it was his refuge from Kansas abolitionists. All he asked for in return was appointment to a federal job there.[17]

By this time, however, Babcock was facing his own scandal. In May 1875 Secretary of the Treasury Bristow had revealed a massive embezzlement conspiracy in his department known as the Whiskey Ring, and was pursuing indications Babcock might be involved. Unable to do much else, Babcock apparently told Whitley he would take care of him eventually, if he would just lie low in Pueblo until the Whiskey Ring uproar blew over.

Whitley was in Pueblo when the House of Representatives reconvened in Washington on December 4, 1875. That body was no longer under Republican control. The Democrats had won the November 1874 midterm elections, overwhelmingly, benefiting politically from the safe burglary and other scandals, as well as from the brutal economic recession that began in late 1873. What had been a 110-seat Republican majority in the House was now a 77-seat Democratic majority, though the Republicans held on to the Senate.

Democratic control of the House for the first time since before the Civil War meant that that chamber would favor the South's white supremacists. The Democratic members, many of them former Confederate military officers, could not pass legislation over Senate opposition and President Grant's veto, but they could use investigation and oversight to harass and discredit the Republican administration. One of the first cases the Democratic House reopened was the safe burglary.

Whitley's erstwhile lieutenant, Ichabod C. Nettleship, saw this as an opportunity. Though indicted with Whitley in 1874, Nettleship had not stood trial: he had absconded to his hometown, Newark, New Jersey, where his cronies in the local police helped him evade the United States Marshals. By 1876, Nettleship was growing tired of life on the lam. He offered to tell the House Judiciary Committee what he knew about the safe burglary, if the committee would ask the attorney general to grant him immunity from prosecution.[18]

When word that Nettleship was turning state's evidence reached Whitley in Pueblo, he hurried back to Washington, arriving on March 21, 1876, to explore a similar deal for himself.[19] Having failed to secure immunity from prosecution and a new job from Babcock, despite months of mutual manipulation between the two men, Whitley apparently felt he had a right to turn against the president's aide.

The result was a series of sensational hearings before the House Judiciary Committee, in April 1876. First Nettleship, then Whitley, admitted they had staged the safe burglary to frame Columbus Alexander, and that the whole business got started due to Babcock's wish to discredit the congressional investigation of the public works program in Washington. Babcock had "great influence over the Secret Service," Whitley said in a press interview. "Anything that he required of us had to be done."[20] On April 15, 1876, the Washington grand jury brought new indictments for conspiracy, this time with Babcock's name atop the list of defendants. The Department of Justice quickly agreed to give Whitley and Nettleship immunity from prosecution in return for their testimony against Babcock.

Babcock's trial convened in September 1876. Incredibly enough, the two lawyers who contested Joshua D. Miner's 1871 counterfeiting case in New York faced each other again in this one. Edwards

Pierrepont, Miner's erstwhile prosecutor, had replaced George H. Williams as attorney general of the United States; in that capacity, he oversaw the prosecution of Babcock. Babcock, meanwhile, had hired William S. Fullerton as his defense attorney, the same expert in cross-examination who had picked Whitley apart during the Miner trial, and would have to break him down in this case, too, if Babcock was to win.

Whitley and Nettleship hardly made the most credible prosecution witnesses. Their confessions before the House Judiciary Committee obviously meant that both men had heretofore flagrantly lied—to Congress, to Bluford Wilson, and to the public—about their involvement in the plot against Columbus Alexander. Fullerton wasted no time in confronting Whitley with that fact. Whitley hemmed and hawed, as he had done at the Miner trial. He admitted "evasions" and "mental reservations" in his past testimony about the safe burglary, but attempted to justify them by claiming that he had been in "personal danger." In any case, Whitley testified, "I had not believed that any man could commit burglary on his own safe. I knew of no safe burglary, in that sense."[21]

Babcock's defense was that he had merely ordered the former Secret Service chief to spy on hostile newspaper reporters, and only learned that Whitley had interpreted this as authority to hatch the frame-up of Columbus Alexander after the whole plot came undone. Babcock's version was not admirable, but it did have the advantage of being truthful. Under cross-examination by Fullerton, Whitley conceded that Babcock never expressly told him to frame Alexander. For his part, Ichabod C. Nettleship testified that the whole conspiracy had been Whitley's idea.[22]

The jury took less than an hour to return a "not guilty" verdict on September 30, 1876. A crowd of Babcock's friends cheered at his second acquittal in less than a year.[23] He had also been indicted in the Whiskey Ring scandal, but a jury found him not guilty in that case, too, in part because President Grant testified in his defense.

Babcock's political enemies complained that the Grant administration, through Edwards Pierrepont, the attorney general, had somehow fixed the safe burglary trial so that none of the alleged principals—not Babcock, not Whitley, not Nettleship—would ever go to the penitentiary. There was, a prominent journalist later wrote, "a general belief that the whole affair was a shrewdly managed game, in which the first move had been to procure immunity for Whitley and Nettleship, and then, by pre-arranged admissions and contradictions on their part, to insure the escape of Babcock."[24]

If the fix had been in, Babcock certainly went to a lot of unnecessary expense to hire an expert on cross-examining Whitley as his lawyer. Nor was there anything feigned about the fury Babcock and his partisan allies directed at the turncoat detective. The pro-Babcock *National Republican* filled its pages with stories of Whitley's purported past misdeeds, from shooting an innocent man in New Orleans and claiming it was Pedro Capdeville during the Civil War, to robbing a safe the government assigned him to protect after the conflict ended.[25] Supposedly he had even set up a traveling hypnotism show during which he "mesmerized a lady" in Selma, Alabama, and "endeavored to violate her person."

After Babcock's acquittal, the *National Republican* opined:

> The chief plotter and perjurer Hiram C. Whitley has secured his freedom while attempting to blast the reputation of honorable men, and today walks the earth an outcast from respectable society, with the mark of Cain indelibly stamped upon his brow, while those he tried to injure have passed through the refiner's fire, and come forth to occupy high stations among men and enjoy their confidence and esteem.[26]

Actually, Orville E. Babcock did not emerge with his public "esteem" intact. Concluding that his longtime friend and ally had become a political liability, President Grant fired Babcock, though, in March 1877, during his last few days in office, the president made him a supervisor of federal lighthouses on the Atlantic Coast. The aide who had previously wielded vast behind-the-scenes power in

Washington lost his life in 1884 when his boat capsized as he was surveying a lighthouse site near Mosquito Inlet, Florida.

Secretary of the Treasury Benjamin Bristow did not win his campaign for the presidency in 1876. Supporters offered him as a candidate at the Republican National Convention, touting his purge of the Secret Service and other efforts to clean up Washington, but party regulars, bitter that Bristow had embarrassed Grant by pursuing Babcock and Whitley, blocked his candidacy. Finished in politics, Bristow practiced law in New York City until he died in 1896. Bluford Wilson went home to Springfield, Illinois, where he, too, practiced law until his death in 1924.

The eventual 1876 Republican nominee, Governor Rutherford B. Hayes of Ohio, captured the White House after a prolonged dispute over the results that threatened to plunge the country into renewed civil war. That struggle did not end until March 1877, when Republicans acquiesced in a return of Democratic rule in the last three Southern states that had not yet been "redeemed" for white supremacy, and Democrats, in turn, acquiesced in a Hayes presidency. Congress remained divided between a Democratic House and a Republican Senate.

For Whitley, the situation offered no hope of a comeback. Democrats could never forgive him for waging clandestine war against the Ku Klux Klan. Both wings of the divided Republican Party, meanwhile, had something against him. Bristow-like reformers wanted nothing to do with the author of the safe burglary and other skulduggery; pro-Grant party stalwarts might still appreciate his anti-Klan effort, but could not forgive his betrayal of Orville E. Babcock.

Whitley could not even count on all of his old friends from the Secret Service anymore. His relationship with Ichabod C. Nettleship was damaged beyond repair: Nettleship paid dearly for Whitley's refusal to heed his doubts about the safe burglary plan, and could not quite forgive his ex-boss for it. The best Nettleship could manage after escaping prosecution in that case was to go back home to Newark and take a position as justice of the peace. He died in 1887, at the age of fifty-four.[27]

In all the world, Whitley enjoyed the support of just four people: Abner B. Newcomb, his trusty subordinate at the Secret Service; his mother, Hannah; his wife, Catherine; and their adopted daughter, Kittie, who turned seven on December 2, 1876. He collected his mother, wife, and child at their house in Cambridge, Massachusetts, and, sometime after Hayes's inauguration on March 5, 1877, set out for a new home in the West. It was the second time in his life that Whitley made the move from Massachusetts to Kansas. The first sojourn ended in 1859, when Whitley fled to New Orleans after making himself a pariah to both pro- and antislavery forces. Now, a pariah once again, for different reasons, he was going back.

He had recently gone through Emporia, Kansas, on his way to and from Pueblo, Colorado, on the new Atchison, Topeka, and Santa Fe Railway. Whitley noted Emporia's thriving commercial center and strategic position at a major railroad intersection. There could be business opportunities in such a location.

Above all, its people seemed not to know or care much about his past, which meant that Emporia was one of the few places in America where Hiram C. Whitley could have a future.

The Democrats' political resurgence, both in the Southern states and in Washington, showed that the Grant administration victory over the Ku Klux Klan in 1871 and 1872 had been far more transitory than many Republicans believed at the time.

Taking his reelection as proof that he had almost vanquished white supremacist terrorism, and that it was both safe and politic finally to do so, President Grant during his second term ordered the release from Albany Penitentiary of forty-three Klansmen. By the end of 1874, all but two of the seventy-nine Klan terrorists from North Carolina, South Carolina, and Alabama imprisoned for federal crimes against African Americans and white Republicans had gotten out from behind bars, either by completing brief sentences or through executive clemency. (One died in prison; Grant pardoned another in March 1875.) Even the high-level offenders for whom Hiram C. Whitley had opposed clemency, Samuel G. Brown and Randolph A. Shotwell, received pardons in 1873.[28]

Grant and his advisers hoped Southern Democrats would reciprocate by ceasing opposition to Reconstruction and accepting the new political and racial order. Similar thinking may have influenced the Grant administration's choice of a successor for Whitley, amid the 1874 midterm election campaign. Solicitor of the Treasury Bluford Wilson tapped the uncontroversial police chief of Chicago, Illinois.

In doing so, he rebuffed the many Republicans who wanted Joseph G. Hester to take the job: they considered the aggressive detective a hero for his anti-Klan covert operations for the Secret Service in North Carolina, and hoped that he might continue to lead the division in such work as chief. As a North Carolina Republican member of the House of Representatives wrote to Grant: "The Country and our State owe him a debt of gratitude for his brilliant achievements and valuable services during the Ku Klux reign of terror at the South."[29]

Passed over as Whitley's replacement, Hester continued as a federal detective, infiltrating white supremacist terror groups in the South through the end of the 1876 election. Thereafter, he conducted a census of the Eastern Cherokee for the Interior Department in 1883, then settled in Washington, D.C., where he ran a real estate business until his death in 1901.[30]

After the pardons, Southern white supremacists made a show of responding favorably to the Grant administration's more conciliatory posture. "The ear of the president is open to the appeal of the Southern men who now obey the laws as faithfully as, during the war, they served the South," a Charleston, South Carolina, newspaper exulted. "The action of the president does him honor and time will show that his conduct in the Kuklux [sic] matter was as wise as it is generous and just."[31] Actually, they interpreted the Grant administration's gestures, not inaccurately, as signs of Republican weakness, division, and exhaustion with Reconstruction. With federal pressure abating, they reorganized and resumed political violence, much as Whitley had predicted they would in his secret reports to Washington during the anti-Klan effort. Terror groups took different names—the White League in Louisiana, the Red Shirts in South Carolina—but they had the same goals as the Klan. Their attacks suppressed African American voting, paving the way for Southern Democratic gains at the polls in both 1874 and 1876.

During Rutherford B. Hayes's single-term presidency, from March 1877 to March 1881, Democrats used their new power in Congress to attack the federal law enforcement authority upon which Southern Republicans, white and black, had relied for protection. The Democrats tried to cut the United States Army's budget, and passed the Posse Comitatus Act, which prohibited the United States Marshals from summoning troops to enforce court orders or to suppress white supremacist insurrection.

Congress slashed the Justice Department's budget for investigating "other crimes against the United States"—understood to encompass white supremacist violence in the South. Lawmakers also cut appropriations for the Secret Service, the erstwhile infiltrators of the Klan, specifying that the detective force's funds could be used to fight counterfeiting "and for no other purpose whatever."[32]

After Democrats took control of the Senate in the 1878 election, with the aid of fraud and violence in the South, they intensified their attack on institutions the Republicans had built during Reconstruction, including the Secret Service. In a long speech on the House floor decrying the Republicans' post–Civil War deviation from Jeffersonian small-government principles, New York Democratic Representative Benjamin Willis went out of his way to condemn the "employment of unprincipled detectives who for partisan purposes have not hesitated to attempt the ruin of innocent civilians."[33] Federal "spies and detectives" had not gone South to investigate terrorism, Democratic Representative James Ronald Chalmers of Mississippi, a former Confederate cavalry officer, declared, but to "brand the whole community with the faults of a few."[34] Democrat Ebenezer Finley of Ohio complained that there was "no law authorizing the employment of these secret detectives," and that Congress had never received a report on how, exactly, the Secret Service spent its money.[35]

Led by James B. Beck of Kentucky, now a senator, Democrats tried repeatedly during 1879 and 1880 to repeal Reconstruction-era civil rights laws, through riders attached to must-pass government funding bills. President Hayes, repenting his attempts to conciliate the South, vetoed these measures, even at the risk of shutting down the government.[36] Hayes's gambit worked: most voters blamed Democrats for the impasse. In May 1880, with elections just six months away, Democrats bowed to political reality and agreed to negotiate.

In the resulting compromises, the Democratic Congress abandoned any effort to abolish the Secret Service, while the Republicans accepted continued cuts in the detective force's funding, as well as the statutory language restricting its mission to fighting counterfeiting and "no other purpose whatever."

The trade-off was finalized on the Senate floor in June 1880, when Senator Beck of Kentucky and a fellow Democrat, Senator Wilkinson Call of Florida (a former Confederate officer), rose to speak in favor of it. Any national police force, Senator Call said, "is a dangerous power and one subject to great abuse," which could be acceptable only in the limited context of counterfeiting. "I think it has not been the history of this Government that secret service money or money for the detection of crime should be used by the Government, except in that class of cases," he concluded.[37]

These events disproved Hiram C. Whitley's claim, in *Memoirs of the United States Secret Service*, that the existence of the force re-flected a decision by the American people, through their elected leaders, to create "an elaborate plan of detection, similar to that supported advantageously in European countries."[38] He was cor-rect to assume that no such institution could endure except on a strong political basis, of the kind that monarchy supplied in places like Russia or Spain. In the United States, however, the Secret Service was not the product of a king's decree or a true national consensus, but of a rare and fleeting political circumstance: con-trol of the federal government by one party, the Republicans, whose principles and interests it favored. White Democrats in the South, however, came to think of the Secret Service, like the rest of the federal government, as their enemy. Restored to a share of power in Washington, they legislated accordingly.

Consequently, of the Republicans' two great post–Civil War nation-building projects—a national currency and equal national citizenship for whites and blacks—only the national currency would continue to enjoy protection from a federal undercover force. Only the national currency enjoyed sufficient bipartisan support.

With that understanding, a Republican Congress authorized the Secret Service Division of the Treasury Department explic-itly, by statute, for the first time, in 1882, removing any question as to its legality.[39] For the rest of the nineteenth century, the Se-cret Service had to make do with a budget no more than about half of what it had in Hiram C. Whitley's day. Between 1878 and 1893, its roster averaged two dozen full-time detectives.[40]

They performed well, especially after James J. Brooks, a for-mer internal revenue agent with actual undercover experience, took over in late 1876. Secret Service detectives pursued coun-terfeiters using the same methods Whitley had so staunchly advocated: entrapping low-level criminals, turning them into informants, following up leads until they reached the top of a gang's chain of command.

Subsequent editions of the Secret Service's instruction book in the nineteenth century included only minor changes from the one Whitley produced in 1873. Also maintained was the three-tier hierarchy Whitley established within the division, along with the distribution of regional field offices he devised. When the Secret Service moved its headquarters from New York to Washington, per Secretary Bristow's orders, Whitley's files on counterfeiters and other suspected criminals, complete with detailed biographies and photographs, traveled to the Treasury Department building, too. They represented an irreplaceable legacy of his tenure.

Solicitor of the Treasury Bluford Wilson's notion that the United States Marshals could effectively lead the fight against counterfeiting died a quiet bureaucratic death. Instead, Whitley's successors rehired Whitley-era detectives who were untainted by the safe burglary or other scandal. Michael G. Bauer, the German-born sleuth who infiltrated Klan dens in South Carolina and Kentucky; William Kennoch, the erstwhile tobacco smuggler who wrestled Joshua D. Miner to the muddy ground in Manhattan; and Henry Finnegass, Whitley's crony from Civil War days in New Orleans—all returned.[41] Bauer served almost continuously until he died in 1898.[42] Among the holdovers from Whitley's team only Charles Anchisi went bad. His superiors caught him engaging in fraud and counterfeiting, for which he was tried and convicted in 1881.[43]

Over time, the Secret Service reduced the formerly rampant scourge of counterfeiting to a relatively infrequent crime. There were four thousand different counterfeit issues in circulation in 1865; by 1911, the Treasury Department estimated that only one out of every one hundred thousand bills in circulation was a phony.[44] Past kingpins of the illicit business were neutralized. Harry Cole, who traded his testimony against Miner for immunity from prosecution, tried to go back to counterfeiting, but Secret Service men ran him down. Given a twelve-year sentence in 1879, he died in prison in 1885.[45]

Yet there would be precious little federal intervention on behalf of black Americans, the great majority of whom remained poor agricultural workers in the rural South. At the mercy of white supremacist–dominated state governments, they faced violence, segregation, and, over time, disenfranchisement. White authors of terrorist violence during Reconstruction, by contrast, escaped punishment and often went on to fame and fortune. William D. Chipley of Columbus, Georgia, constructed railroads in the Florida panhandle, won a seat in the Florida state senate, and, eventually, became mayor of Pensacola.[46] The town of Chipley, Florida, bears his name.

Chipley and his fellow defendants in the Ashburn case celebrated their good fortune by purchasing a magnificent silver-handled mahogany walking stick for Senator James B. Beck of Kentucky. "A grateful remembrance from the Columbus Prisoners, as a gift for their defender," the inscription reads.[47] Beck died in 1890.

As the events of Reconstruction faded into historical oblivion, or succumbed to the outright historical distortion of Thomas Dixon Jr. and other Southern apologists, myths about the origins of the Secret Service also took hold. The most stubborn was the tale that President Abraham Lincoln gave the order to establish it, on the final day of his life. Purportedly this occurred at a cabinet meeting on the morning before Lincoln's fateful April 14, 1865, outing to Ford's Theatre: Secretary of the Treasury Hugh McCulloch reported to Lincoln that the government's efforts against counterfeiting were inadequate, and proposed a "permanent force" to improve them. "Work it out your own way, Hugh," the president supposedly said. That night, John Wilkes Booth assassinated him, leaving McCulloch to carry out his wishes.[48]

Not a shred of contemporaneous documentation supports this story. None of those present at Lincoln's last cabinet meeting subsequently recalled the exchange about counterfeiting. Hugh

McCulloch's own 1889 memoir included a detailed account of his final conversation with Lincoln on the day of the assassination; it lacks any reference to counterfeiting.[49]

The myth probably persists because it is considerably more dramatic than the truth, which is that the United States government's first civilian secret agency began its existence as a bureaucratic improvisation. It reflected the policy and partisan interests of the Republican politicians who found themselves in charge of the federal government in the tumultuous aftermath of the Civil War. Until 1882, its only legal basis was a flexible interpretation of appropriations for the Treasury and Justice departments.

Hiram C. Whitley had grand ambitions for the force, and he realized some of them before his career came crashing down. There would have to be further political development before the United States could truly acquire the centralized, covert, investigative bureaucracy whose necessity Whitley so fervently affirmed.

As the twentieth century approached, the sectional and partisan divisions of the previous Civil War generations abated; and America's international involvement grew. The Spanish-American War, beginning in 1898, created a common enemy, Spain, against whom the federal government could deploy undercover agents legitimately, in the eyes of both political parties and all sections of the country. Secret Service detectives, many of them Spanish-speakers newly hired for the war, conducted espionage and counterespionage against Spanish agents throughout the Western Hemisphere.

After an anarchist assassinated President William McKinley in 1901, the Secret Service received a mandate from Congress to act as a presidential bodyguard. This formalized in law a mission detectives had previously performed informally for President Grover Cleveland during summer vacations, and, indeed, for President McKinley, on occasion.

During World War I, the Secret Service again engaged in war-related intelligence-gathering, until eventually ceding that kind of work to the Department of Justice, and its new Federal Bureau of Investigation—whose first eight detectives were reassigned to it from the Secret Service in 1908. For the remainder of the twentieth century, the Secret Service would have two missions: protection of the president and other dignitaries, and, as always, fighting counterfeiters.[50]

Not until the "Mississippi Burning" case of the 1960s, when the FBI investigated the Ku Klux Klan murder of three civil rights workers, would federal agents again operate against that form of domestic terrorism in the South, as the Secret Service had done in the 1870s. By then, of course, the United States had completed the rise to global power that began with the war against Spain. Two world wars, a Great Depression, and the Cold War, had convinced Democrats and Republicans to accept a vast new national government, complete with a huge military establishment and multiple clandestine law enforcement and intelligence agencies.

By then, too, many of the inherent dangers to civil liberties of such an apparatus had also been made manifest, whether through the Palmer Raids against anarchists just after World War I, the internal security investigations of leftists and Communists in the 1950s, or the wiretapping of Dr. Martin Luther King Jr. and other African American civil rights leaders.

The dilemmas of a permanent federal covert apparatus are with us still, as the debate over alleged Central Intelligence Agency, National Security Agency, and FBI excesses in the "war on terror" since September 11, 2001, demonstrate. Americans across the ideological spectrum alternate between lauding the skill and patriotism of their intelligence services, and expressing fear, or anger, at their alleged co-optation for partisan use or, worse, their evolution into a self-perpetuating "surveillance state" beyond democratic control.

All of this seems new and modern. Yet it all has precedent in the rise of the Reconstruction-era Secret Service, and in the long-ago conflicts over its power and purposes. In the twenty-first century, Americans debate using military commissions, selective suspensions of habeas corpus, isolated interrogation centers, and torture against terrorists—including, potentially, American citizens considered terrorists. Each one of these issues had its historical counterpart in the Reconstruction-era debates over the Grant administration's response to Ku Klux Klan terror. None of the legal, moral, and constitutional arguments for and against these methods today is fundamentally different from the ones that were advanced almost one hundred fifty years ago by men like Hiram C. Whitley, or Amos T. Akerman, or Bluford Wilson, or, for that matter, James B. Beck, on behalf of their respective causes.

We, like they, are torn between Alexander Hamilton's appreciation, expressed in *The Federalist Papers*, of the executive branch's capacity for "decision, activity, secrecy, and despatch," and James Madison's equally valid belief that "all men having power ought to be distrusted to a certain degree."[51] Like Hiram C. Whitley and his contemporaries, we decide whether the ends justify the means based on a mix of rational thought, moral principle, ideological belief, and partisan self-interest.

Living in de facto internal exile on the Kansas prairie, Hiram C. Whitley finally achieved the respectable business success that eluded him in younger days. With the wealth he accumulated, licitly or otherwise, as Secret Service chief, Whitley acquired Emporia's Coolidge House Hotel, at the corner of Fifth Avenue and Merchant Street, soon after he arrived in town. He renamed it the Whitley Hotel and turned it into a profitable establishment, catering to business travelers on the transcontinental railroads. Purchase of another hotel soon followed, as did Whitley's promotion of Emporia's modern water, gas and electric lighting, and streetcar systems. He and four partners built the Whitley Opera House, which bore his name because he provided most of the funds. Opened in January 1882, it was the largest facility of its kind in the state; Emporia began to call itself "the Athens of Kansas."[52]

The Whitley Hotel in downtown Emporia was one of several enterprises through which Whitley finally achieved the respectable business success that had eluded him earlier in life. (*The Emporia Times*)

Whitley built his family a Victorian mansion on the outskirts of Emporia. The place had ten rooms, identical in size to the rooms in the Whitleys' previous home in Cambridge, Massachusetts: the carpets from that abode could be shipped West and installed without trimming.[53] In time, he and Catherine adopted yet another daughter, whom they named Sabra, after Whitley's maternal aunt. Like Kittie's adoption, Sabra's adoption occurred under remarkable circumstances. A woman in her twenties from Massachusetts, who called herself Lizzie W. Newcomb, migrated to Emporia at roughly the same time the Whitleys did and, on November 11, 1878, awarded them custody over her fifteen-month-old child. Then she moved into their big Victorian house, too, and remained there for the rest of her life, described in various local newspaper articles and official documents as a visitor, a widow, or even as the niece of Whitley's confidant, Abner B. Newcomb, who also hailed from Massachusetts.

As Sabra matured, people would remark on how much she resembled her adoptive father, and whisper that, possibly, there was more of a connection between the founder of the Whitley Opera House, Lizzie, and Sabra, than any of them acknowledged. Certainly, it was unusual that Whitley would draw up a will in 1895 granting Lizzie a sixth of his estate, and making both her and his wife, Catherine, coexecutors, contingent on Lizzie's promise to renounce "any possible claim she might have" against him. For the old Secret Service man, concealing paternity and an extramarital affair, while enlisting his very own wife in the plot, would have been the ultimate covert operation.[54]

The Whitleys' home was a Victorian mansion on the outskirts of Emporia; the former Secret Service chief is visible seated in the middle foreground. (*Danforth W. Austin Family Collection*)

For the most part, Whitley seemed content to reign over this unconventional family and supervise his business empire, basking in his prestige as a civic leader and avoiding any thought of a return to federal service or even state-level police work. "Because their earlier years were filled with excitement," the *Emporia Gazette* noted, "Mr. and Mrs. Whitley have preferred and enjoyed quiet in the later years."[55] Still, Whitley enjoyed regaling Emporians with his version of events during his tenure at the Secret Service. He would occasionally lend his interrogation talents to local police, when they needed help questioning particularly uncooperative suspects.[56]

Whitley's public involvement in his previous line of work otherwise took the limited and retrospective form of an autobiography, which appeared in 1894. As his title, he chose *In It*, a bit of detective slang referring to a state of constant watchfulness.[57] Hiram C. Whitley certainly thought of himself as having been "in it" his whole life. By the last decade of the nineteenth century, the detective memoir, and—thanks to Arthur Conan Doyle and Sherlock Holmes—detective fiction had become popular genres. Publishing his book, Whitley was taking advantage of an opportunity for profit, and following the literary trail previously blazed by other famous undercover operators who had written up their exploits, such as his American contemporary, Allan Pinkerton, and, many years earlier, Vidocq of France.

Hiram C. Whitley lived out his life in de facto internal exile in Emporia, Kansas, with his wife, Catherine, and adopted daughters, Kittie (left) and Sabra (right). (*Danforth W. Austin Family Collection*)

In the text Whitley not only relived his glory days but also relitigated them, bemoaning once again the wrong done to him and his men by Judge Benedict's jury instructions, which resulted in Joshua D. Miner's acquittal. "Justice had probably retired to the mountains for a time," he wrote.[58]

Once again, he defended detectives against their moralizing opponents. Covert operations were not only a necessary evil, he now contended, but quite literally the Lord's work: "Suspicions come from Heaven, and the use of detective intelligence was coextensive with the origins of mankind." Whitley's proof came from the original police report—the Book of Genesis. "The first sin committed by men was detected by the Almighty," he wrote.

He walked into his garden one evening to take an airing. As He strolled about admiring the beautiful flowers and delicious fruits He had created for the good of man, He, as if by chance, spied Adam and Eve skulking about in the sombre shadows of the trees, among the shrubbery. He called them. As they came forth and drew near to him, He saw they had donned fig-leaf aprons and suspected and questioned them. The young couple cast their eyes on the ground as He accused them of partaking of the fruit which had been forbidden them. The fig-leaf aprons somehow bespoke craft and it is assumed that they were taken as an indication of guilt. It seems that Adam at first tried to defend himself by charging blame upon the woman; and the woman in her turn declared that she had been beguiled by the snake. It seems, however, that the Lord did not accept their excuses, as He inflicted punishment on all who had assisted in committing the offense.[59]

In It focused on Whitley's battles against counterfeiting, and told the tale of the dirty trick he played on James Ivins (albeit with the names of Ivins and the Williamses omitted), but mostly avoided two other great dramas of his career: the covert campaign against the Ku Klux Klan and the safe burglary affair. Whitley's slighting of the latter episode, his disgrace and his downfall, was understandable. The less said about such things, the better for Whitley. Otherwise, a key theme of his memoir— that the most dangerous "rogues" were not common criminals, but "high-toned" ones like Joshua D. Miner, who cloaked their wrongdoing in the raiment of respectability, or escaped punishment "through technicalities"—could too easily apply to him.[60]

As for his campaign against the Klan, that was a genuine accomplishment, but no longer a politically popular one. By 1894, Blue and Gray were busily reconciling on the basis, partly, of their shared contempt for black people's capacity to participate in self-government. As a hotelier, Whitley had to do business with men from all sections of the country as they passed through his town. The less *In It* said about his part in the covert federal crackdown on Klan terrorism, the better that would be for him, too. His book briefly decried the Klan—"infamous," he called it—and then moved on, while expressing the view, widely held among whites, that blacks were destined by racial inferiority to second-class status.[61]

A dozen years after *In It*, though, as Whitley sat watching *The Clansman*, something made him abandon this artificially evenhanded posture. Whitley concluded that he should speak out about the Ku Klux Klan. As was so often the case with this calculating man, his true motivation was not easy to discern. Perhaps the sheer brazenness with which Thomas Dixon Jr., who was not even born until after Reconstruction, distorted events irritated Whitley. Possibly Whitley thought that, having let his theater host the play, in defiance of respectable religious and journalistic opinion in Emporia, and having profited from doing so, he owed it to the town to counteract any ideological harm Dixon's play might do. Or maybe the reminders of the Klan's violence had reactivated the same corner of Whitley's conscience that an overseer's racist savagery had stirred many years earlier in Louisiana.

And, of course, Hiram C. Whitley always had to have the last word.

Whatever his reason, Whitley denounced Dixon's play in the *Emporia Gazette* on the first Monday after the Friday night performance.[62] *The Clansman* was "misleading," Whitley told the paper, "a sort of palliation if not a justification for the existence of the most formidable and dangerous secret order that ever infested this or any other country." The Ku Klux Klan, he explained, was not defensive; it arose when Southern whites both refused to accept Republican "carpetbagger" governments in their states, and "determined that others should not do it and live in peace." The Klan had "perpetrated crimes with impunity," he reminded readers, "shielded by terror." The Secret Service's files contained documentary proof that "23,000 persons, black and white, were scourged or murdered by the Ku Klux Klan within 10 years following the close of the rebellion," Whitley claimed. "It would seem impossible that such deeds of slaughter could have been perpetrated in a civilized country," he wrote. But they had been.

Whitley's political analysis of the Klan's origins greatly oversimplified matters. Morally, however, his statement brought a much-needed note of candor to public discussion of Reconstruction. Whitley avoided a common fallacy: attributing Klan crime to the purported lower-class origins of rank-and-file members. Rather, he identified "wealthy and educated men" as its true support base. Tinged with racial condescension as they were, Whitley's comments, unlike those of all but a few of his contemporaries, acknowledged black officeholders in Reconstruction governments had tried to serve "with honest intentions to do their duty."

Throughout his life, Hiram C. Whitley practiced situational honesty. Now, a few months shy of his seventy-fourth birthday, he faced the uncomfortable subject of white racist terrorism and spoke about it with more than usual clarity, relative both to his own practice since leaving the government, and to the standards of other men of his race and social standing in the early twentieth century. This was Whitley at his best, defending historical facts that many preferred to ignore, at a time when monuments were going up to the likes of William Dudley Chipley, the erstwhile Columbus, Georgia, Klan leader and initiator of a wave of murders whose political and social repercussions distorted the next hundred and fifty years of American history.

The plaque on the twenty-foot obelisk in a downtown Pensacola, Florida, public park honoring Chipley, who died in 1897, declares him a "statesman" and "public benefactor."[63]

Whatever else he might have done, for good or for evil, in his long life, Hiram C. Whitley had at least endeavored to bring Chipley and his coconspirators, and others like them, to justice, when the United States government asked him to do so.

He died on April 19, 1919, to be followed in death three days later by his wife, Catherine. Whitley's family buried him in Emporia, at the Maplewood Memorial Lawn Cemetery. The only marker on the detective's grave is a rectangular granite headstone, engraved with his name, the year of his birth, the year of his passing—and nothing else.

★ ★ ★ ★ ★

ACKNOWLEDGMENTS

It would not have been possible to finish this book without assistance and support. Before I do finish it, I would like to express my appreciation to the many good and generous people who helped.

My editor at the *Washington Post* editorial page, Fred Hiatt, gave me a leave from my duties at the paper for the last four months of 2017, during which I finished a first draft of the manuscript. That expedited schedule would never have been feasible without a helping hand from Professor Kenneth Anderson of the American University Washington College of Law in Washington, D.C., who arranged for me to work as a visiting scholar in a comfortable, quiet office at the school's Pence Law Library. Dean Billie Jo Kaufman and administrative assistant Charmaine Baxter at the library welcomed me, provided logistical support, and made sure that I had all the books and articles I needed.

As always, Scott Waxman, my literary agent, would not take no for an answer—either from me, when my belief in this project occasionally flagged, or from potential publishers. At Hanover Square Press, Peter Joseph was a supportive and astute editor; he has done much to improve this project. Copy editor Anne-Marie

Rutella and proofreader Leah Mol ably scrubbed the text. My research assistant, Drew Goins, rummaged energetically through archival arcana and found what I needed when I needed it.

Special thanks are due to Danforth W. Austin of Scottsdale, Arizona, Hiram C. Whitley's great-grandson, who answered my questions about the family's history, shared records and photographs, and permitted me to include much of this material in the book. I hope I have done his ancestor justice.

Archivists, librarians, and historians across the country unhesitatingly aided my research. I would like to thank the staffs of the Library of Congress and National Archives, as well as Daniel S. Holt, Assistant Historian of the United States Senate Historical Office; James Amermason and Gregory Guderian of the New Jersey Historical Society in Newark, New Jersey; Ronald E. Romig, Site Director for the Kirtland Temple Visitor's Center, Kirtland, Ohio; Laura E. West, Managing Editor of *Mississippi Quarterly* in Oxford, Mississippi; Patricia E. Powers, Managing Editor of the *Journal of Policy History* in Tempe, Arizona; Rebecca Bush, Curator of History/Exhibitions Manager at The Columbus Museum in Columbus, Georgia; Theresa Altieri Taplin, Archivist and Collections Manager at The Abraham Lincoln Foundation of The Union League of Philadelphia; Jennifer M. Cole, Associate Curator of Special Collections at The Filson Historical Society in Louisville, Kentucky; Lora Kirmer, Research Librarian at the Lyon County History Center in Emporia, Kansas; Fran Leadon, Associate Professor, City College of New York; Jocelyn Wilk, Research Archivist at Columbia University in New York; Mark Osler, Professor and Robert and Marion Short Distinguished Chair in Law at St. Thomas University in Minneapolis, Minnesota; Margaret Shannon of Washington Historical Research in Arlington, Virginia; Stephan Loewentheil and Thomas Edsall of The 19th Century Rare Book & Photography Shop in New York and Baltimore; and Howard Roloff of Victoria, British Columbia.

The United States Secret Service's public affairs staff in Washington, D.C., generously provided a trove of documents from the organization's early history. Following Secret Service policy, they requested anonymity, but I know who they are, and I very much appreciate their assistance.

We all need someone we can talk to, writers especially. As I worked, the following gave advice, information, and encouragement: Tom Sietsema, Morris Panner, Lara Ballard, Jonathan G. Cedarbaum, Michael A. Ross, Lawrence Powell, Ross Davies, S. L. Price, and Stephen F. Hayes. Dan and Andrea Elish, dear friends of mine for many years, went above and beyond by hosting me at their place in New York City while I was doing research in that part of the country.

I am indebted to Professor Gary Gerstle, Paul Mellon Professor of American History at the University of Cambridge, in Cambridge, England, who agreed to read and comment upon an early draft of the book, as well as to advise me on various points of interpretation and analysis throughout the writing of the manuscript. Gary's perspective was indispensable, as it has been for more than thirty-five years—since he was my undergraduate thesis adviser. It has been a privilege to learn from him about America's past.

It's challenging to write a book. It can be even more challenging to live in the same house with someone who's writing a book. For tolerating me, humoring me, and loving me, I am eternally grateful to David, Nina, and Johanna Lane, my children, and to Catarina Bannier, my wife and, truly, my coauthor.

Charles Lane
Washington, D.C.
December 2018

SELECTED BIBLIOGRAPHY

Manuscript Collections

Danforth W. Austin Family Collection (Private)
    Hiram C. Whitley Papers

Filson Historical Society, Louisville KY
    M. G. Bauer Papers
    James B. Beck Papers

Library of Congress, Manuscripts Division, Washington DC
    Benjamin H. Bristow Papers
    Hamilton Fish Papers
    James H. Wilson Papers

Lyon County History Center, Emporia KS
    Hiram C. Whitley Scrapbooks

National Archives, College Park MD
    Records of the Department of State, Record Group 59
    Records of the Department of Justice, Record Group 60
    Records of the U.S. Secret Service, Record Group 87
    Records of the Solicitor of the Treasury, Record Group 206

National Archives, Southeast Region, Atlanta GA
    Records of the U.S. Circuit Court for North Carolina, Record
    Group 21

National Archives, Washington DC
    Records of the Department of Veterans Affairs, Record Group 15
    Records of the Office of the Judge Advocate General (U.S.
    Army), Record Group 153
    Records of the U.S. Army, Department of the South, Record
    Group 393

New Jersey Historical Society, Newark NJ
    I. C. Nettleship Papers

The Heritage Center of The Union League of Philadelphia, Philadelphia PA
    Abraham Lincoln Foundation Collection

U.S. Secret Service Archives, Washington DC

Government Documents

U.S. Army Department of the South. Major General Meade's Report
on the Ashburn Murder (1868).

U.S. Congress. Sen. Ex. Doc., 41st Cong., 3d sess., no. 16, "Outrages Committed by Disloyal Persons in North Carolina and other
Southern States."

————. Senate Reports, 42d Cong., 1st sess., no. 1, "Condition
of Affairs in the Southern States: North Carolina."

————. Senate Reports, 42d Cong., 2d sess., no. 41, "Report
of the Joint Select Committee to Inquire into the Condition of Affairs in the Late Insurrectionary States" (Vols. 1–13).

————. Senate Reports, 42d Cong., 2d sess., no. 227, "Testimony in Relation to the Alleged Frauds in the New York Custom
House Taken by the Committee on Investigation and Retrenchment" (Vol. 2).

——————. House Reports, 43d Cong., 1st sess., no. 559, "The Sanborn Contracts."

——————. House Reports, 43d Cong., 1st sess., no. 785, "Testimony in Relation to the Alleged Safe-Burglary at the Office of the United States Attorney."

——————. House Reports, 43d Cong., 2d sess., no. 262, "Affairs in Alabama" (Vol. 3).

U.S. Naval War Records Office. Official Records of the Union and Confederate Navies in the War of the Rebellion. Washington: Government Printing Office (1894–1922).

U.S. Census

Kansas State Census

Massachusetts State Census

New York State Census

Books

Alexander, Shawn Leigh, ed. *Reconstruction Violence and the Ku Klux Klan Hearings*. Boston: Bedford/St. Martin's, 2015.

Anderson, Eric and Alfred A. Moss Jr., eds. *The Facts of Reconstruction: Essays in Honor of John Hope Franklin*. Baton Rouge LA: Louisiana State University Press, 1991.

Anonymous. *The Nation's Peril: The Ku Klux Klan*. New York: n.p., 1872.

——————. *Radical Rule: Military Outrage in Georgia*. Louisville KY: John Morton & Co., 1868.

Blackmar, Frank W., ed. *Kansas: A Cyclopedia of State History, Embracing Events, Institutions, Industries, Counties, Cities, Vol. III*. Chicago: Standard Publishing Company, 1912.

Bowen, Walter S. and Harry Edward Neal. *The United States Secret Service*. New York: Popular Library, 1960.

Bradley, Mark L. *Bluecoats and Tar Heels: Soldiers and Civilians in Reconstruction North Carolina*. Lexington KY: University of Kentucky Press, 2009.

Burnham, George P. *Memoirs of the United States Secret Service*. Boston: Lee & Shephard, 1872.

Caldwell, Wilber W. *The Courthouse and the Depot: The Architecture of Hope in an Age of Despair: A Narrative Guide to Railroad Expansion and Its Impact on Public Architecture in Georgia, 1833–1910*. Macon GA: Mercer University Press, 2001.

Chernow, Ron. *Grant*. New York: Penguin Press, 2017.

Connelley, William E. *A Standard History of Kansas and Kansans, Vol. V.* Chicago: Lewis Publishing Company, 1918.

Conway, Alan. *The Reconstruction of Georgia*. Minneapolis: University of Minnesota Press, 1966.

Creswell, Stephen F. *Mormons and Cowboys, Moonshiners and Klansmen: Federal Law Enforcement in the South and West, 1870–1893*. Tuscaloosa AL: University of Alabama Press, 1991.

Cummings, Homer and Carl McFarland. *Federal Justice: Chapters in the History of Justice and the Federal Executive*. New York: MacMillan, 1937.

Cutler, William G. *History of the State of Kansas*. Chicago: A. T. Andreas, 1883.

Doy, John. *The Narrative of John Doy of Lawrence, Kansas*. New York: Thomas Holman, 1860.

Dray, Philip. *Capitol Men*. New York: Houghton Mifflin, 2008.

Drummond, A. L. *True Detective Stories*. Chicago: M. A. Donahue, 1908.

DuBois, W.E.B. *Black Reconstruction in America.* New York: Harcourt, Brace, 1935.

Emsley, Clive and Haia Shpayer-Makov, eds. *Police Detectives in History, 1750–1950.* Aldershot: Ashgate, 2006.

Farmer, John Stephen and William Ernest Henley. *A Dictionary of Slang and Colloquial English.* London: Routledge, 1905.

Foner, Eric. *Reconstruction: America's Unfinished Revolution, 1863–1877.* New York: Harper & Row, 1988.

Friedman, Lawrence. *Crime and Punishment in American History.* New York: Basic Books, 1993.

Frothingham, Octavius Brooks. *Gerrit Smith: A Biography.* New York: G. P. Putnam's Sons, 1877.

Gillette, William. *Retreat from Reconstruction: 1869–1879.* Baton Rouge LA: Louisiana State University Press, 1979.

Grant, Ulysses S. *The Papers of Ulysses S. Grant.* Edited by John Y. Simon. 32 vols. Carbondale IL: Southern Illinois University Press, 1967–2012.

Guelzo, Allen. *Reconstruction: A Concise History.* New York: Oxford University Press, 2018.

Hackett, Frank Warren. *A Sketch of the Life and Public Services of William Adams Richardson.* Washington: n.p., 1898.

Hamilton, Joseph Grégoire de Roulhac, ed. *The Papers of Randolph Abbott Shotwell,* Vols. 1–3. Raleigh NC: North Carolina Historical Commission, 1929.

Helwig, E., et al. *Annals of Cleveland, 1818–1935.* Cleveland: Cleveland WPA Project, 1938.

Hurt, R. Douglas. *The Ohio Frontier: Crucible of the Old Northwest, 1720–1830.* Bloomington IN: Indiana University Press, 1996.

Jeffreys-Jones, Rhodri. *The FBI: A History.* New Haven CT: Yale University Press, 2007.

—————. *In Spies We Trust: The Story of Western Intelligence.* New York: Oxford University Press, 2013.

Johnson, David R. *Illegal Tender: Counterfeiting and the Secret Service in Nineteenth-Century America.* Washington: Smithsonian Institution Press, 1995.

Kaczorowski, Robert J. *The Politics of Judicial Interpretation: The Federal Courts, Department of Justice, and Civil Rights, 1866–1876.* New York: Fordham University Press, 2005.

Kousser, J. Morgan and James M. McPherson, eds. *Region, Race, and Reconstruction: Essays in Honor of C. Vann Woodward.* New York: Oxford University Press, 1982.

Lemann, Nicholas. *Redemption.* New York: Farrar, Strauss and Giroux, 2006.

Lessoff, Alan. *The Nation and Its City: Politics, "Corruption," and Progress in Washington D.C., 1861–1902.* Baltimore: The Johns Hopkins University Press, 1994.

Link, William A. *Atlanta, Cradle of the New South: Race and Remembering in the Civil War's Aftermath.* Chapel Hill NC: University of North Carolina Press, 2013.

Martinez, J. Michael. *Carpetbaggers, Cavalry, and the Ku Klux Klan: Exposing the Invisible Empire during Reconstruction.* Lanham MD: Rowman & Littlefield, 2007.

Masur, Kate. *An Example for All the Land: Emancipation and the Struggle over Equality in Washington, D.C.* Chapel Hill NC: University of North Carolina Press, 2010.

McCulloch, Hugh. *Men and Measures of Half a Century.* New York: C. Scribner's Sons, 1889.

McPherson, James. *Battle Cry of Freedom: The Civil War Era*. New York: Oxford University Press, 1988.

Melanson, Philip H. and Peter F. Stevens. *The Secret Service: The Hidden History of an Enigmatic Agency*. New York: MJF Books, 2002.

Mihm, Stephen. *A Nation of Counterfeiters*. Cambridge MA: Harvard University Press, 2007.

Nash, Steven E. *Reconstruction's Ragged Edge: The Politics of Postwar Life in the Southern Mountains*. Chapel Hill NC: University of North Carolina Press, 2016.

Newcomb, John Bearse. *Genealogical Memoir of the Newcomb Family*. Chicago: Knight & Leonard, 1874.

Owings, David M. *Images of America: Columbus*. Charleston SC: Arcadia Publishing, 2015.

Parrillo, Nicholas. *Against the Profit Motive: The Salary Revolution in American Government, 1780–1940*. New Haven CT: Yale University Press, 2013.

Parsons, Elaine Frantz. *Ku-Klux: The Birth of the Klan during Reconstruction*. Chapel Hill NC: University of North Carolina Press, 2015.

Pinkerton, Allan. *Thirty Years a Detective*. New York: G. W. Dillingham, 1884.

Prince, K. Stephen, ed. *Radical Reconstruction: A Brief History with Documents*. Boston: Bedford/St. Martin's, 2016.

Rable, George C. *But There Was No Peace: The Role of Violence in the Politics of Reconstruction*. Athens GA: University of Georgia Press, 1984.

Rossiter, Clinton L., ed. *The Federalist Papers: Alexander Hamilton, James Madison, John Jay*. New York: Mentor, 1999.

Slide, Anthony. *American Racist: The Life and Films of Thomas Dixon*. Lexington KY: University Press of Kentucky, 2004.

Smith, Jean Edward. *Grant*. New York: Simon and Schuster, 2001.

Stampp, Kenneth M. *The Era of Reconstruction, 1865–1877*. New York: Vintage, 1965.

Swinney, Everette. *Suppressing the Ku Klux Klan: The Enforcement of the Reconstruction Amendments, 1870–1877*. New York: Garland, 1987.

Tarnoff, Ben. *A Counterfeiter's Paradise: The Wicked Lives and Surprising Adventures of Three Early American Moneymakers*. New York: Penguin Books, 2011.

Telfair, Nancy. *A History of Columbus, Georgia, 1828–1928*. Columbus GA: Historical Publishing Company, 1929.

Trefousse, Hans L. *Andrew Johnson: A Biography*. New York: W. W. Norton, 1989.

Trelease, Allen W. *White Terror: The Ku Klux Klan Conspiracy and Southern Reconstruction*. Baton Rouge LA: Louisiana State University Press, 1971.

Tsouras, Peter G., ed. *Scouting for Grant and Meade: The Reminiscences of Judson Knight, Chief of Scouts, Army of the Potomac*. New York: Skyhorse Publishing, 2014.

Vidocq, Eugène François. *Memoirs*. Baltimore: Carey, Hart & Co., 1834.

Way, Frederick. *Way's Packet Directory, 1848–1939*. Athens OH: Ohio University Press, 1983.

Webb, Ross A. *Benjamin Helm Bristow: Border State Politician*. Lexington KY: University Press of Kentucky, 1969.

Wellman, Manly Wade. *The County of Moore, 1847–1947: A North Carolina Region's Second Hundred Years*. Southern Pines NC: Moore County Historical Association, 1962.

West, Jerry. *The Reconstruction Ku Klux Klan in York County, South Carolina, 1865–1877*. Jefferson NC: McFarland & Co., 2002.

White, Richard. *The Republic for Which It Stands: The United States during Reconstruction and the Gilded Age, 1865–1896*. New York: Oxford University Press, 2017.

Whitley, Hiram C. *In It*. Cambridge MA: Riverside Press, 1894.

Whyte, James H. *The Uncivil War: Washington during the Reconstruction, 1865–1878*. New York: Twayne Publishers, 1958.

Williams, Lou Falkner. *The Great South Carolina Ku Klux Klan Trials, 1871–1872*. Athens GA: University of Georgia Press, 1996.

Woolen, William Wesley. *William McKee Dunn, Brigadier-General, U. S. A.; A Memoir*. New York: Putnam, 1892.

Worsley, Etta Blanchard. *Columbus on the Chattahoochee*. Columbus GA: Columbus Office Supply Company, 1951.

Zuczek, Richard. *State of Rebellion: Reconstruction in South Carolina*. Columbia SC: University of South Carolina Press, 1996.

Articles

Ansley, Norman. "The United States Secret Service: An Administrative History." *Journal of Criminal Law, Criminology, and Police Science* 47, no. 1 (May–June 1956): 93–109.

Bagger, Louis. "The 'Secret Service' of the United States." *Appletons' Journal* 10, no. 235 (Sept. 20, 1873): 360–65.

Blain, William T. "Challenge to the Lawless: The Mississippi Secret Service, 1870–1871." *Mississippi Quarterly* 40, no. 2 (May 1978): 119–31.

Bond, Almand. "The Ashburn Murder Case and Military Trial." *Georgia Bar Journal* 10 (Aug. 1947): 43–48.

Boynton, H. V. "The Washington 'Safe Burglary' Conspiracy." *American Law Review* XI, no. 3 (Apr. 1877): 401–46.

Buttaro, Andrew. "The Posse Comitatus Act of 1878 and the End of Reconstruction." *St. Mary's Law Journal* 47 (2015): 135–86.

Cohen, Andrew Wender. "Smuggling, Globalization, and America's Outward State, 1870–1909." *Journal of American History* 97, no. 2 (2010): 371–98.

Cresswell, Stephen. "Enforcing the Enforcement Acts: The Department of Justice in Northern Mississippi, 1870–1890." *Journal of Southern History* 53, no. 3 (1987): 421–40.

Dailey, Douglass C. "The Elections of 1872 in North Carolina." *North Carolina Historical Review* 40, no. 3 (July 1963): 338–60.

Davis, Curtis Carroll. "The Craftiest of Men: William P. Wood and the Establishment of the United States Secret Service." *Maryland Historical Magazine* 83, no. 2 (Summer 1988): 111–26.

Davis, Henry E. "The Safe Burglary Case: An Episode and a Factor in the District's Development." *Records of the Columbia Historical Society* 25 (1923): 140–81.

Jackson, Joy J. "Keeping Law and Order in New Orleans under General Butler, 1862." *Louisiana History* 34, no. 1 (Winter 1993): 51–67.

Jaeger, Jens. "Photography: A Means of Surveillance? Judicial Photography, 1850–1900." *Crime, History & Societies* 5, no. 1 (2001): 27–51.

Kaczorowski, Robert J. "Federal Enforcement of Civil Rights during the First Reconstruction." *Fordham Urban Law Journal* 23, no. 1 (1995): 155–86.

Lane, Roger. "Urban Police and Crime in Nineteenth-Century America." *Crime and Justice* 15 (1992): 1–50.

Massengill, Stephen E. "The Detectives of William W. Holden, 1869–1870." *North Carolina Historical Review* 62, no. 4 (Oct. 1985): 448–87.

Obert, Jonathan. "A Fragmented Force: The Evolution of Federal Law Enforcement in the United States, 1870–1900." *Journal of Policy History* 29, no. 4 (Oct. 2017): 640–75.

Pearl, Matthew. "K Troop: The Story of the Eradication of the Original Ku Klux Klan." *Slate*, Mar. 4, 2016.

Swinney, Everette. "Enforcing the Fifteenth Amendment, 1870–1877." *Journal of Southern History* 28, no. 2 (May 1962): 202–18.

Vazzano, Frank P. "President Hayes, Congress, and the Appropriations Riders Vetoes." *Congress and the Presidency* 20, no. 1 (Spring 1993): 25–37.

Williamson, Edward C. "William D. Chipley, West Florida's Mr. Railroad." *Florida Historical Quarterly* 25, no. 4 (Apr. 1947): 333–55.

Zuczek, Richard. "The Federal Government's Attack on the Ku Klux Klan: A Reassessment." *South Carolina Historical Magazine* 97, no. 1 (Jan. 1996): 47–64.

Newspapers and Periodicals

Atlanta Constitution
Baltimore Sun
Bank Note Reporter
Boston Herald
Brooklyn Eagle
Carolina Era (Raleigh NC)
Carolina Watchman (Salisbury NC)
Centinel of Freedom (Newark NJ)
Charleston (SC) *Daily News*
Charlotte Democrat
Chicago Tribune
Cincinnati Commercial Tribune
Cincinnati Daily Enquirer
Cincinnati Daily Gazette
Cincinnati Daily Times
Cleveland Leader
Cleveland Plain Dealer
Congressional Globe
Congressional Record
Daily Argus (Albany NC)
Daily Carolinian (Raleigh NC)

Daily Phoenix (Columbia SC)
Daily Sun (Columbus GA)
Emporia Gazette
Evening Star (Washington DC)
Fayetteville (NC) *Eagle*
Forney's Sunday Chronicle (Washington DC)
Freeman's Champion (Prairie City KS)
Greensboro Patriot
Harper's Weekly
Herald of Freedom (Lawrence KS)
Indiana State Sentinel (Indianapolis IN)
Liberator (Boston MA)
Louisville Courier-Journal
Macon Weekly Telegraph
Milwaukee Sentinel
Morning Star (Wilmington NC)
National Police Gazette
National Republican (Washington DC)
New Orleans Daily Picayune
New York Evening Post
New York Herald
New York Sun
New York Times
New York Tribune
New York World
North Carolinian (Elizabeth City NC)
Philadelphia Inquirer
Pittsburgh Weekly Gazette
Pomeroy's Democrat (Chicago IL)
Raleigh Daily Standard
Raleigh News
Raleigh Sentinel
Rocky Mountain Gazette (Helena MT)
Rutherford Star (Rutherfordton NC)
Southern Home (Charlotte NC)
Southerner (Tarboro NC)
Topeka Daily Capital
Tri-Weekly Era (Raleigh NC)
Washington Daily Critic
Weekly Kansas Chief (Troy KS)

Weekly Pioneer (Asheville NC)
Wheeling Register
Wilmington (NC) *Journal*
Wilmington (NC) *Post*

Theses and Dissertations

Brisson, Jim D. "The Kirk-Holden War of 1870 and the Failure of Reconstruction in North Carolina." M.A. thesis, University of North Carolina, Wilmington, 2010.

Hamilton, Lois Neal. "Amos T. Akerman and His Role in American Politics." M.A. thesis, Columbia University, 1939.

Kemmerling, James Delbert. "A History of the Whitley Opera House in Kansas, 1881–1913." M.S. thesis, Kansas State Teachers College, 1967.

Moore, T. Ross. "The Congressional Career of James B. Beck, 1867–1875." M.A. thesis, University of Kentucky, 1950.

Proctor, Bradley David. "Whip, Pistol, and Hood: Ku Klux Klan Violence in the Carolinas during Reconstruction." Ph.D. diss., University of North Carolina, Chapel Hill, 2013.

NOTES

Prologue

1. This description of Hiram C. Whitley's mission in Virginia moonshiner country and subsequent events, including his meeting with President Grant, derives from Hiram C. Whitley, *In It* (Cambridge MA: Riverside Press, 1894), 92–101.

2. George P. Burnham, *Memoirs of the United States Secret Service* (Boston: Lee & Shepard, 1872), 33.

3. George S. Boutwell to Hiram C. Whitley, May 6, 1869, U.S. Secret Service Archives, Washington DC; Untitled news item, *Alexandria* (VA) *Gazette*, May 6, 1869; "Affairs in the Government Departments," *National Intelligencer*, May 13, 1869.

Chapter 1

1. U.S. Congress, Sen. Repts., 42d Cong., 2d sess., no. 41, "Report of the Joint Select Committee to Inquire into the Condition of Affairs in the Late Insurrectionary States" (Hereafter cited as "KKK Hearings"), Vol. 6, 451–53 (Testimony of J. H. Caldwell).

2. "A Dark and Bloody Tragedy," *Cincinnati Daily Gazette*, Apr. 21, 1868.

3. "G.W. Ashburn, of Georgia," *Raleigh Daily Standard*, Apr. 10, 1868.

4. "Letter from Washington," *Massachusetts Spy*, Apr. 10, 1868.

5. Allen C. Guelzo, *Reconstruction: A Concise History* (New York: Oxford University Press, 2018), 25.

6. Allen Trelease, *White Terror: The Ku Klux Klan Conspiracy and Southern Reconstruction* (Baton Rouge LA: Louisiana State University Press, 1971), 3–27.

7. Ibid., 50.

8. "Rebel Vengeance in Georgia," *Cincinnati Daily Gazette*, Apr. 9, 1868.

9. This account of the murder of George W. Ashburn derives from the following sources: U.S. Army Department of the South, Major General Meade's Report on the Ashburn Murder (1868) (Hereafter cited as "*Gen. Meade's Book*"), passim; Anonymous, *The Nation's Peril: The Ku Klux Klan* (New York: n.p., 1872), 65–69; Anonymous, *Radical Rule: Military Outrage in Georgia* (Louisville KY: John Morton & Co., 1868) (Hereafter cited as "*Radical Rule*"), passim; Records of the Office of the Judge Advocate General (U.S. Army), Record Group 153, Court Martial Case Files, George W. Ashburn court martial transcript, National Archives, Washington DC, passim; Trelease, *White Terror*, passim; William A. Link, *Atlanta, Cradle of the New South: Race and Remembering in the Civil War's Aftermath* (Chapel Hill NC: University of North Carolina Press, 2013), 93–95; Nancy Telfair, *A History of Columbus, Georgia: 1828–1928* (Columbus GA: Historical Publishing Company, 1929), 155–72; Etta Blanchard Worsley, *Columbus on the Chattahoochee* (Columbus GA: Columbus Office Supply Company, 1951), 311–15; KKK Hearings, Vol. 6, 451–53 (Testimony of J. H. Caldwell); "The Leader of Radicalism in Georgia," *Daily Sun* (Columbus GA), Aug. 22, 1866; "Georgia Negro-Radical Convention," *Macon Weekly Telegraph*, Jan. 17, 1868; "The Murder of George W. Ashburn of Georgia," *New York Times*, Apr. 6, 1868; "Rebel Vengeance in Georgia," *Cincinnati Daily Gazette*, Apr. 9, 1868; "The Killing of George W. Ashburn," *Daily Sun* (Columbus GA), Apr. 1, 1868; "A Dark and Bloody Tragedy," *Cincinnati Daily Gazette*, Apr. 21, 1868; "The

Ku-Klux Klan: Trial of the Prisoners Charged with the Murder of George W. Ashburn," *New York Tribune*, July 3, 1868; KKK Hearings, Vol. 6, 532–35 (Testimony of Hannah Flournoy); KKK Hearings, Vol. 7, 1031–42 (Testimony of Henry McNeal Turner).

10. "A Dark and Bloody Tragedy," *Cincinnati Daily Gazette*, Apr. 21, 1868.

11. "The Ku-Klux-Klan," *Detroit Advertiser & Tribune*, Apr. 17, 1868.

12. "Political Murders in the South," *New York Times*, Apr. 7, 1868.

13. Capt. William Mills to Gen. George G. Meade, Mar. 31, 1868, *Gen. Meade's Book*, 6.

14. "The Killing of George W. Ashburn," *Daily Sun* (Columbus GA), Apr. 1, 1868.

15. Ibid.

16. Capt. William Mills to Gen. George G. Meade, Apr. 10, 1868, *Gen. Meade's Book*, 12.

17. Telfair, *History of Columbus*, 160.

18. "Recent Scenes in Georgia," *Massachusetts Spy*, May 15, 1868.

19. Ibid.

20. Guelzo, *Reconstruction*, 62.

21. Gen. George G. Meade to Gen. U. S. Grant, Apr. 4, 1868, *Gen. Meade's Book*, 8–9.

22. Gen. George G. Meade to Gen. U. S. Grant, Apr. 13, 1868, ibid., 16–17.

23. William H. Reed to Gen. George G. Meade, Apr. 22, 1868, ibid., 20–21.

24. Gen. U. S. Grant to Gen. George G. Meade, Apr. 23, 1868, ibid., 22.

Chapter 2

1. For an excellent overview of federal policing in the nineteenth century, see Jonathan Obert, "A Fragmented Force: The Evolution of Federal Law Enforcement in the United States, 1870–1900," *Journal of Policy History* 29, no. 4 (Oct. 2017), 640–75.

2. Lawrence Friedman, *Crime and Punishment in American History* (New York: Basic Books, 1993), 204–208.

3. On the career of Eugène François Vidocq, see Michael Dirda, "The First Detective: A Devil Extraordinaire," review of *The First Detective*, by James Morton, *Washington Post*, June 2, 2011; Clive Emsley, "From Ex-Con to Expert: The Police Detective in Nineteenth-Century France," in Clive Emsley and Haia Shpayer-Makov, eds., *Police Detectives in History, 1750–1950* (Aldershot: Ashgate, 2006), 61–78; Eugène François Vidocq, *Memoirs* (Baltimore: Carey, Hart & Co., 1834).

4. A vast literature covers the lives and careers of Allan Pinkerton and Lafayette Baker. For concise biographies, see Norman Polmar and Thomas B. Allen, *Spy Book: The Encyclopedia of Espionage* (New York: Random House, 1997), 45, 439–40.

5. "Solicitor Jordan's Detective Force," *New York World*, July 8, 1867.

6. The account of the Doy party's ambush is derived from: John Doy, *The Narrative of John Doy of Lawrence, Kansas* (New York: Thomas Holman, 1860); "From Kansas," *Milwaukee Sentinel*, Feb. 11, 1859; "Old Brown," *New York Herald-Tribune*, Feb. 12, 1859; "Kansas Intelliience [*sic*]," *Cleveland Leader*, Feb. 15, 1859; "The Kidnapping of Dr. Doy and Son," *Liberator* (Boston MA), Feb. 18, 1859; "From the Kansas Prisoners," *New York Herald-Tribune*, Feb. 19, 1859; "Letter from Dr. Doy and Son: A Painful Statement," *Liberator* (Boston MA), Mar. 18, 1859; "Trial of Dr. Doy—Read This!" *Liberator* (Boston MA), July 22, 1859; "Betrayer of Dr. Doy," *Chicago Tribune*, Sept. 1, 1859; "From Kansas," *New York Times*, Sept. 2, 1859; Untitled news item, *Portland* (ME) *Advertiser*, Sept. 13, 1859; "The Letter Writers on Lawrence," *Herald of Freedom* (Lawrence KS), Oct. 1, 1859; "H.C. Whit-

ley, or What's His Name," *National Republican*, Apr. 11, 1876; "Whitley," *Weekly Kansas Chief* (Troy KS), May 4, 1876; "The Famous Doy Rescue," *Kansas City* (KS) *Journal*, June 3, 1895.

7. *Freeman's Champion* (Prairie City KS), Feb. 4, 1858 (advertisement for "The Boston Dining Saloon").

8. Hiram C. Whitley's biographical information derives from: Pension File for Hiram C. Whitley, Records of the Veterans Administration, Records Relating to Pensions and Bounty Claims, Record Group 15, National Archives, Washington DC (Hereafter cited as "Whitley Pension File"); U.S. Congress, Sen. Repts., 42d Cong., 2d sess., no. 227, "Testimony in Relation to the Alleged Frauds in the New York Custom House Taken by the Committee on Investigation and Retrenchment," Vol. 2 (Hereafter cited as "Custom House Hearing"), 719–23 (Testimony of H. C. Whitley); Burnham, *Memoirs*, 13–41; Whitley, *In It*, passim; "Counterfeiting," *New York Herald*, Dec. 19, 1871; "The Whitleys' Anniversary: Sixtieth Wedding Anniversary Observed by Quiet Day with Children and Grandchildren," *Emporia Gazette*, Mar. 25, 1916; "Whitley," *Weekly Kansas Chief* (Troy KS), May 4, 1876; "Was Chief of Secret Service," *Topeka Daily Capital*, Aug. 11, 1907; 1870 U.S. Census for Cambridge, Middlesex County, MA; Burke Aaron Hinsdale, "The History of Popular Education in the Western Reserve," An Address Delivered in the Series of Educational Conferences Held in Association Hall, Cleveland, Sept. 7 and 8, 1896, 50; "Hiram C. Whitley," in William E. Connelley, *A Standard History of Kansas and Kansans, Vol. V* (Chicago: Lewis Publishing Company, 1918), 2217–19; "Hiram C. Whitley," in Frank W. Blackmar, ed., *Kansas: A Cyclopedia of State History, Embracing Events, Institutions, Industries, Counties, Cities, Vol. III* (Chicago: Standard Publishing Company, 1912), 1388–89; "Obituary (Hannah Dixon Whitley)," *Camden* (ME) *Herald*, May 10, 1889; "Was a Hero to Emporia," *Kansas City Star*, Oct. 29, 1919; "Col. H.C. Whitley Dead," *Emporia Gazette*, Oct. 16, 1919; Whitley Family Genealogy, Vertical Files, Lyon County History Center, Emporia KS.

9. Case Western Reserve University, *The Encyclopedia of Cleveland History: Teacher Education*, https://case.edu/ech/articles/t/teacher-education; author correspondence with Ronald E. Romig, Site Director, Kirtland Temple, Kirtland OH, 2016.

10. R. Douglas Hurt, *The Ohio Frontier: Crucible of the Old Northwest, 1720–1830* (Bloomington IN: Indiana University Press, 1996), 223.

11. Benjamin Shurtleff, *Descendants of William Shurtleff of Plymouth and Marshfield, Massachusetts* (Revere MA: 1912), 754.

12. R. M. Campbell, "To My Patrons and the Public," *Boston Herald*, Aug. 15, 1856.

13. Burnham, *Memoirs*, 33.

14. R. M. Campbell, "To My Patrons and the Public," *Boston Herald*, Aug. 15, 1856; Hiram C. Whitley, "To My Patrons and the Public," *Boston Herald*, Aug. 15, 1856; R. M. Campbell, "Hiram C. Whitley, Again!" *Boston Herald*, Aug. 21, 1856; Hiram C. Whitley, "R.M. Campbell Again," *Boston Herald*, Aug. 22, 1856.

15. "Whitley," *Weekly Kansas Chief* (Troy KS), May 4, 1876.

16. Untitled news item, *Lawrence* (KS) *Republican*, Feb. 3, 1859; "More of the Kidnapping Case," *Lawrence* (KS) *Republican*, Feb. 10, 1859; "From Kansas," *Milwaukee Sentinel*, Feb. 11, 1859.

17. "Old Brown," *New York Herald-Tribune*, Feb. 12, 1859.

18. "From Kansas," *New York Times*, Sept. 2, 1859.

19. Ibid.

20. Ibid.; Untitled news item, *Portland* (ME) *Advertiser*, Sept. 13, 1859; "The Letter Writers on Lawrence," *Herald of Freedom* (Lawrence KS), Oct. 1, 1859.

21. Charles Gardner, *New Orleans Directory for 1861* (New Orleans: C. Gardner, 1861), 454. The Whitleys lived in a house at 175 St. Peter Street.

22. "Recorder Emerson's Court," *New Orleans Daily Delta*, Dec. 27, 1861.

23. "The Whitleys' Anniversary: Sixtieth Wedding Anniversary Observed by Quiet Day with Children and Grandchildren," *Emporia Gazette*, Mar. 25, 1916.

24. Burnham, *Memoirs*, 21–22; Whitley, *In It*, 25–27.

25. Ibid., 27–32.

26. "Counterfeiting Tickets," *New Orleans Daily Delta*, Oct. 23, 1862.

27. This account of Whitley's clash with the man known as Pedro Capdeville is derived from Whitley, *In It*, 48–49; Burnham, *Memoirs*, 24–26; "The City," *New Orleans Times-Picayune*, Jan. 9, 1863; "The City," *New Orleans Times-Picayune*, Jan. 16, 1863; "City Intelligence," *New Orleans Daily Delta*, Jan. 16, 1863; "Hiram C. Whitley," *National Republican*, Apr. 20, 1876.

28. Whitley Pension File; Whitley, *In It*, 74.

29. Ibid. See also Connelley, *Kansas and Kansans*, 2218.

30. "Counterfeiting: Trial of Miner, the Alleged Counterfeiter," *New York Herald*, Dec. 19, 1871; Custom House Hearings, 719–23 (Testimony of Hiram C. Whitley).

31. U.S. Congress, House Ex. Doc., 40th Cong., 2d sess., no. 267, "Appointments in the Treasury: Special Agents under Internal Revenue Appointed since February 20, 1868," 4; Whitley, *In It*, 85–86, 91.

32. "Provost Court," *New Orleans Times-Picayune*, Aug. 6, 1863.

Chapter 3

1. *Daily Sun* (Columbus GA), Mar. 24, 1868, quoted in KKK Hearings, Vol. 6, 452 (Testimony of J. H. Caldwell).

2. Wilber W. Caldwell, *The Courthouse and the Depot: The Architecture of Hope in an Age of Despair: A Narrative Guide to Railroad Expansion and Its Impact on Public Architecture in Georgia, 1833–1910* (Macon GA: Mercer University Press, 2001), 191.

3. Capt. William Mills to Lt. John E. Hosmer, Apr. 6, 1868, *Gen. Meade's Book*, 9–10; "Historic Claflin School Restoration Project Gets Momentum at Last," *Columbus Ledger-Enquirer*, Dec. 7, 2017.

4. "The Killing of G.W. Ashburn," *Daily Sun* (Columbus GA), Apr. 1, 1868 (as reprinted in *Macon Weekly Telegraph*, Apr. 10, 1868).

5. Ibid.

6. Capt. William Mills to Gen. George G. Meade, Apr. 10, 1868, *Gen. Meade's Book*, 14.

7. William H. Reed to Gen. George G. Meade, Apr. 22, 1868, *Gen. Meade's Book*, 20–21.

8. Hiram C. Whitley to Gen. George G. Meade, May 4, 1868, *Gen. Meade's Book*, 23.

9. When General Meade later published his correspondence on the Ashburn case, he attempted to portray Whitley's use of "severity" as a typographical error. Whitley had actually said "celerity"—speed—the general claimed. See "Errata," *Gen. Meade's Book*.

10. *U.S. Statutes at Large*, 14: 428–30. See also Andrew Johnson's veto message for the first Reconstruction Act, *Congressional Globe*, Mar. 2, 1867, 1969.

11. Capt. William Mills to Gen. R. C. Drum, May 14, 1868, *Gen. Meade's Book*, 24–25.

12. Brochure, Fort Pulaski National Monument, U.S. National Park Service, https://www.nps.gov/fopu/index.htm.

13. Burnham, *Memoirs*, 35–36.

14. Hiram C. Whitley to Gen. George G. Meade, May 18, 1868, *Gen. Meade's Book*, 25.

15. Ibid.

16. The account of the Columbus Klan's efforts to intimidate witness Alexander Bennett is derived from *Gen. Meade's Book*, 92–107 (Military Commission Testimony of Alexander Bennett), 108–15 (Military Commission Testimony of Amanda Patterson).

17. *Gen. Meade's Book*, 108–15 (Military Commission Testimony of Amanda Patterson).

18. Biographical information for William Dudley Chipley is derived from *Proceedings of the Eighth Annual Meeting of the Florida State Horticultural Society, May 1895* (DeLand FL: E. O. Painter, n.d.), 135–36; Edward C. Williamson, "William D. Chipley, West Florida's Mr. Railroad," *Florida Historical Quarterly* 25, no. 4 (Apr. 1947), 333–55.

19. During the military commission trial, Chipley himself was allowed out of the barracks, on the condition that he not leave Atlanta. Gen. George G. Meade to Gen. W. M. Dunn, July 11, 1868, *Gen. Meade's Book*, 48.

20. *Congressional Globe*, May 13, 1868, 2450.

21. *Congressional Globe*, May 18, 1868, 2751–52.

22. Details of Hiram C. Whitley's interrogation of George Betts are derived from *Gen. Meade's Book*, 75–91 (Military Commission Testimony of George Betts).

23. Link, *Atlanta*, 103.

24. Ibid.

25. Information on Whitley's interrogation of Charles Marshall is derived from *Gen. Meade's Book*, 52–75 (Military Commission Testimony of Charles Marshall).

26. Ibid., 106 (Military Commission Testimony of Alexander Bennett).

27. *Gen. Meade's Book*, 51.

28. The pro-Klan version of events spread well beyond Georgia. See, for example, "The Ashburn Tragedy," *New York World*, June 18, 1868. This article, based on a letter from an unknown correspondent in Columbus, refers to "drumhead justice," the "indiscriminate arrest of innocent persons," and the "tyranny of General Meade."

29. "The Inquisition Revived," *Atlanta Constitution*, June 22, 1868.

30. "Atlanta, Ga.: The Murderers of Hon. G.W. Ashburn," *Chicago Tribune*, June 22, 1868.

31. "The Ashburn Murderers," *New York Tribune*, June 18, 1868; "The Ku Klux Klan," *New York Tribune*, July 18, 1868.

32. Hiram C. Whitley to Gen. George G. Meade, June 27, 1868, *Gen. Meade's Book*, 33–36.

33. *Gen. Meade's Book*, 128–29 (Military Commission Testimony of Burrill Davis).

34. Ibid., Hiram C. Whitley to Gen. George G. Meade, May 18, 1868, *Gen. Meade's Book*, 25–26.

35. James W. Barber, Civil War Soldiers Service Cards, Alabama Department of Archives and History, Montgomery AL, http://www.archives.alabama.gov/civilwar/soldier.cfm?id=8337.

36. Hiram C. Whitley to Gen. George G. Meade, May 18, 1868, *Gen. Meade's Book*, 25–26.

37. Ibid., 120 (Military Commission Testimony of Wade Stevens); *Radical Rule*, 156 (Military Commission Testimony of John Peabody). Pro-Klan Democrats published *Radical Rule* as a rebuttal to General Meade's report in the fall of 1868. Despite its inaccuracies and falsehoods, and obvious political purposes, which included influencing that year's presidential election, *Radical Rule* reproduced a complete and reliable transcript of testimony at the military commission trial, including that of the defense witnesses, which was omitted from *Gen. Meade's Book*.

38. The account of Hiram C. Whitley's abuse of prisoners at Fort Pulaski derives from the following sources: "Mysteries of the Sweat Box Revealed," *Atlanta Constitution*, July 16, 1868 (John Stapler affidavit); "Putting Negroes to Torture," *National Intelligencer*, June 17, 1868 (John Wells affidavit); "The Ashburn Murder Trial: Confession of One of the Suborners," *National Intelligencer*, Aug. 14, 1868 (William H. Reed affidavit); Hiram C. Whitley to Gen. George G. Meade, June 27, 1868, *Gen. Meade's Book*, 35.

39. "Putting Negroes to Torture," *National Intelligencer*, June 17, 1868.

40. "The Radical Steam Torture Box at Fort Pulaski," *Macon Weekly Telegraph*, July 17, 1868.

41. Hiram C. Whitley to Gen. George G. Meade, June 27, 1868, *Gen. Meade's Book*, 33–36.

42. Gen. George G. Meade to Gen. U. S. Grant, July 21, 1868, *Gen. Meade's Book*, 5.

43. Gen. George G. Meade to Hon. Secretary of War and Gen. U. S. Grant, June 30, 1868, *Gen. Meade's Book*, 37.

44. "The Ku-Klux Klan: Trial of the Columbus (GA.) Prisoners for the Murder of G. W. Ashburn, a Member of the Georgia Constitutional Convention," *New York Tribune*, July 6, 1868.

45. For biographical information on Rufus Saxton, see Thomas Wentworth Higginson, *Carlyle's Laugh, and Other Surprises* (Boston: Houghton Mifflin, 1909), 175–82; Link, *Atlanta*, 114.

46. William Wesley Woolen, *William McKee Dunn, Brigadier-General, U. S. A.; A Memoir* (New York: Putnam, 1892), 64.

47. Richard Brookhiser, "Confederate Cornerstone," www.nationalreview.com, Mar. 21, 2011.

48. "The Ashburn Tragedy," *Cincinnati Daily Gazette*, July 8, 1868.

49. "The South: Trial of the Ashburn Murderers at Columbus, Georgia," *Chicago Tribune*, July 3, 1868.

50. *Gen. Meade's Book*, 70 (Military Commission Testimony of Charles Marshall).

51. "The Ashburn Tragedy," *Cincinnati Daily Gazette*, July 8, 1868.

52. "The Ashburn Murder: Tenth Day of the Trial—Southern Society," *New York Tribune*, July 21, 1868.

53. *Radical Rule*, 111, 115.

54. "Affairs in Atlanta," *Macon Weekly Telegraph*, July 10, 1868.

55. "The South," *Chicago Tribune*, July 11, 1868.

56. Gen. George G. Meade to Hon. Secretary of War and Gen. U. S. Grant, June 20, 1868, *Gen. Meade's Book*, 37.

57. Gen. John A. Rawlins to Gen. George G. Meade, July 2, 1868, Ulysses S. Grant, *The Papers of Ulysses S. Grant*. Edited by John Y. Simon (Carbondale IL: Southern Illinois University Press, 1967–2012) (Hereafter cited as "Grant Papers"), Vol. 18, 230.

58. Telfair, *History of Columbus*, 166–67; "Stand Firm!" *Atlanta Constitution*, July 21, 1868; "In the Union," *Atlanta Constitution*, July 22, 1868; "Suspension of the Military Commission," *Atlanta Constitution*, July 23, 1868.

59. "Georgia Legislature," *Atlanta Constitution*, July 22, 1868. See also Alan Conway, *The Reconstruction of Georgia* (Minneapolis: University of Minnesota Press, 1966), 161–63.

60. "Return of the Prisoners," *Columbus Daily Enquirer*, July 26, 1868; Telfair, *History of Columbus*, 167.

61. *Nation's Peril*, 68–69.

62. "The Georgia Legislature—Progress of the Ashburn Murder Trial," *New York Times*, July 17, 1868.

63. "The Ashburn Tragedy," *Cincinnati Daily Gazette*, July 8, 1868.

64. Gen. George G. Meade to Gen. U. S. Grant, July 21, 1868, *General Meade's Book*, 5.

Chapter 4

1. Ben Tarnoff, *A Counterfeiter's Paradise: The Wicked Lives and Surprising Adventures of Three Early American Moneymakers* (New York: Penguin Books, 2011), 86.

2. Clinton L. Rossiter, ed., *The Federalist Papers: Alexander Hamilton, James Madison, John Jay* (New York: Mentor, 1999), 84.

3. Stephen Mihm, *A Nation of Counterfeiters* (Cambridge MA: Harvard University Press, 2007), 63–102.

4. James McPherson, *Battle Cry of Freedom: The Civil War Era* (New York: Oxford University Press, 1988), 593–94.

5. Eric Foner, *Reconstruction: America's Unfinished Revolution, 1863–1877* (New York: Harper & Row, 1988), 24.

6. David R. Johnson, *Illegal Tender: Counterfeiting and the Secret Service in Nineteenth-Century America* (Washington: Smithsonian Institution Press, 1995), 72–73. See also reports submitted on legal origins of the Secret Service Division by Chief James J. Brooks: James J. Brooks to R. C. McCormick, et al., Sept. 17, 1877, and James J. Brooks to William Windom, Mar. 19, 1881, both in U.S. Secret Service Archives, Washington DC.

7. Johnson, *Illegal Tender*, 69–77; Curtis Carroll Davis, "The Craftiest of Men: William P. Wood and the Establishment of the United States Secret Service," *Maryland Historical Magazine* 83, no. 2 (Summer 1988), 111–26.

8. Johnson, *Illegal Tender*, 76–77; "The Secret Service," newspaper clipping, dated June 20, 1869, contained in the Hiram C. Whitley Scrapbooks, Lyon County History Center, Emporia KS.

9. In response to a demand from Congress, President Johnson submitted a complete report on these pardons, including capsule biographies of each convicted counterfeiter, details of the alleged offense, and the reason for granting clemency: U.S. Congress, House Ex. Doc., 40th Cong., 2d sess., no. 179, "Pardons for Making or Passing Counterfeit Money, Forgery, and Perjury."

10. "The Counterfeiting Cases," *New York Times*, July 2, 1867.

11. "Counterfeiters in the Employ of the Government," *New York Times*, June 28, 1867.

12. Frank Warren Hackett, *A Sketch of the Life and Public Services of William Adams Richardson* (Washington DC: n.p., 1898), 135.

13. "The Secret Service," newspaper clipping, dated June 20, 1869, contained in the Hiram C. Whitley Scrapbooks, Lyon County History Center, Emporia KS.

14. U.S. Congress, House Reports, 43d Cong., 1st sess., no. 559, "The Sanborn Contracts," 189 (Testimony of Everett C. Banfield).

15. 1870 U.S. Census for Cambridge, Middlesex County, MA.

16. "More Revenue Frauds—Important Arrests by United States Detectives," *New York Times*, Aug. 5, 1869.

17. Hiram C. Whitley to Everett C. Banfield, June 14, 1870, Letters Sent from Headquarters of the Chief in New York, Records of the U.S. Secret Service, Record Group 87, National Archives, College Park MD (Hereafter cited as "Whitley Official Correspondence").

18. Hiram C. Whitley to Everett C. Banfield, June 16, 1870, Whitley Official Correspondence.

19. Custom House Hearings, 633.

20. Hiram C. Whitley to Everett C. Banfield, June 16, 1870, Whitley Official Correspondence.

21. *U.S. Statutes at Large*, 16: 291.

22. "Crime Against the Government," *New York Herald*, Mar. 9, 1871.

23. Burnham, *Memoirs*, 122–24.

24. Ibid., 301–303, 310.

25. "M.G. Bauer Removed," *Louisville Courier-Journal*, Feb. 15, 1894; "Captain Bauer's Sudden Death," *Louisville Courier-Journal*, May 17, 1898; House Reports, 43d Cong., 1st sess., no. 785, "Testimony in Relation to the Alleged Safe-Burglary at the Office of the United States Attorney" (Hereafter cited as "Safe Burglary Hearings"), 267–68 (Testimony of Michael G. Bauer); James J. Brooks to R. C. McCormick, Sept. 26, 1877, U.S. Secret Service Archives, Washington DC.

26. Burnham, *Memoirs*, 160–64; I. C. Nettleship Daybook, June 25, 1869, I. C. Nettleship Papers, New Jersey Historical Society, Newark NJ; "Obituary Notes (I. C. Nettleship)," *New York Times*, Nov. 10, 1887.

27. Burnham, *Memoirs*, 278–85; Safe Burglary Hearings, 256–57 (Testimony of Abner B. Newcomb).

28. Burnham, *Memoirs*, 63–77.

29. Ibid., 103–11.

30. Ibid., 78–89; "Bill Gurney, the Counterfeiter, at Work in Jail," *Evening Star* (Washington DC), Oct. 7, 1870; "An Important Arrest," *New York Herald*, Aug. 26, 1870.

31. Biographical information for Joshua D. Miner is derived from the following sources: Untitled news item, *New York Tribune*, Nov. 2, 1867 (reporting Miner's candidacy for local office as a Republican); "Counterfeiters Seized," *New York Sun*, Oct. 27, 1871; "Counterfeiting Annihilated," *New York Dispatch*, Oct. 29, 1871; "Joshua D. Miner: A Wealthy Tammany Contractor," *New York Sunday Dispatch*, Dec. 31, 1871; Burnham, *Memoirs*, 420–34; "Death of Miner, the Counterfeiter," *New York Tribune*, Mar. 13, 1886; "Death of a Noted Counterfeiter: Joshua D. Miner, Autocrat of the Coney Men, Dies in New York," *Cleveland Plain Dealer*, Mar. 13, 1886; A. L. Drummond, *True Detective Stories* (Chicago: M. A. Donahue, 1908), 47–65.

32. Details of Whitley's first encounter with Joshua D. Miner, and their subsequent meetings leading up to Miner's surrender of the counterfeit National Shoe and Leather Bank note plates, are derived from "Counterfeiting: The Trial of Miner, the Alleged Counterfeiter," *New York Herald*, Dec. 16, 1871; Custom House Hearings, 697 (Testimony of Hiram C. Whitley).

33. Burnham, *Memoirs*, 46–56.

34. "Miner the Counterfeiter," *New York Register*, Dec. 15, 1871. Bill Gurney would eventually be sentenced to ten years—five years fewer than Fred Biebusch got for his similar offenses. Whitley, *In It*, 89.

35. "Counterfeit Plates, Dies, &c. to be Destroyed," *Evening Star* (Washington DC), Nov. 3, 1870.

36. Whitley, *In It*, 5.

37. Burnham, *Memoirs*, 35.

38. "The Alleged Head Centre of the Counterfeiters," *New York Herald*, Dec. 12, 1871.

39. Details of the undercover investigation and arrest of Joshua D. Miner are derived from the following sources: Burnham, *Memoirs*, 427–34; Whitley, *In It*, 223–35; Drummond, *True Detective Stories*, 47–57; "Counterfeiters Seized," *New York Sun*, Oct. 27, 1871; "A Seizure of Men and Money," *New York World*, Oct. 27, 1871; "Arrest of Counterfeiters," *New York Times*, Oct. 27, 1871; "Counterfeiting Annihilated," *New York Dispatch*, Oct. 29, 1871; "Counterfeiting," *New York Herald*, Dec. 13, 1871; "Joshua D. Miner: Wealthy Tammany Contractor," *New York Sunday Dispatch*, Dec. 31, 1871; Custom House Hearing, 697 (Testimony of Hiram C. Whitley).

40. "Counterfeiting," *New York Herald*, Dec. 13, 1871.

41. "Miner the Counterfeiter," *New York Sun*, Dec. 16, 1871.

42. "Counterfeiting Annihilated," *New York Dispatch*, Oct. 29, 1871.

43. "Counterfeiters Seized," *New York Sun*, Oct. 27, 1871.

44. "Counterfeiting Annihilated," *New York Dispatch*, Oct. 29, 1871.

45. Whitley, *In It*, 233.

46. "The Alleged Head Centre of the Counterfeiters," *New York Herald*, Dec. 12, 1871.

47. Custom House Hearings, 733 (Testimony of Hiram C. Whitley).

48. "The Alleged Head Centre of the Counterfeiters," *New York Herald*, Dec. 12, 1871.

49. "Counterfeiting: Continuation of the Trial of Miner, the Alleged Counterfeiter," *New York Herald*, Dec. 14, 1871.

50. "Counterfeiting: The Trial of Miner, the Alleged Counterfeiter," *New York Herald*, Dec. 16, 1871.

51. Details of Abraham Beatty's career, as well as his involvement with Joshua D. Miner's legal team and his falling-out with Hiram C. Whitley, are derived from the following sources: Custom House Hearings, 609–33 (Testimony of Abraham Beatty), 687–736 (Testimony of Hiram C. Whitley); "The Custom House

Frauds," *Brooklyn Daily Eagle*, Feb. 9, 1872; "Whitley's Subordinates," *New York Sun*, Feb. 10, 1872.

52. For the history of moieties and their eventual abolition, see Nicholas Parrillo, *Against the Profit Motive: The Salary Revolution in American Government, 1780–1940* (New Haven CT: Yale University Press, 2013), 221–54.

53. "The Diamond Smuggling Case," *New York Herald*, May 27, 1871.

54. Custom House Hearings, 726 (Testimony of Hiram C. Whitley).

55. Ibid., 692–93.

56. Ibid., 625–26 (Testimony of Abraham Beatty).

57. "The Twenty Dollar Counterfeit," *New York Herald*, Oct. 18, 1870.

58. For details of William Kennoch's illicit activities prior to joining the Secret Service, see "Counterfeiting: Continuation of the Trial of Miner, the Alleged Counterfeiter," *New York Herald*, Dec. 14, 1871; James J. Brooks to R. C. McCormick, Sept. 26, 1877, U.S. Secret Service Archives, Washington DC.

59. "Counterfeiting: Continuation of the Trial of Miner, the Alleged Counterfeiter," *New York Herald*, Dec. 14, 1871.

60. "Counterfeiting: Trial of Miner, the Alleged Counterfeiter; Cross-Examination of Colonel Whitley, Chief of the Secret Service Division," *New York Herald*, Dec. 19, 1871.

61. "Counterfeiting: The Trial of Miner, the Alleged Counterfeiter," *New York Herald*, Dec. 20, 1871.

62. "The Miner Case: Judge Pierrepont's Argument for the Prosecution," *New York Evening Post*, Dec. 27, 1871.

63. "Judge C.L. Benedict to Resign," *New York Times*, Jan. 22, 1895.

64. "Counterfeiting: Trial of J.D. Miner, the Alleged Counterfeiter," *New York Herald*, Dec. 28, 1871.

65. Custom House Hearing, 733.

66. Details of the scene on the last day of the Miner trial are from "Joshua D. Miner: Wealthy Tammany Contractor," *New York Sunday Dispatch*, Dec. 31, 1871; "Counterfeiting: Trial of J.D. Miner, the Alleged Counterfeiter," *New York Herald*, Dec. 28, 1871.

67. "Chief Detective Whitley," *Daily Sun* (Columbus GA), Feb. 13, 1872. Whitley's penciled-in comments are visible on a clipping of this article contained in the Hiram C. Whitley Scrapbooks, Lyon County History Center, Emporia KS.

68. Hiram C. Whitley to Everett C. Banfield, Oct. 19, 1871, Whitley Official Correspondence.

69. Hiram C. Whitley to James J. Fitzpatrick, Aug. 8, 1871, Whitley Official Correspondence.

70. Custom House Hearing, 733 (Testimony of Hiram C. Whitley).

71. "Counterfeiting: Letter to the People by the Chief of the U.S. Secret Service," Pamphlet, Hiram C. Whitley (New York: n.p., 1872). For an example of how the press reprinted the pamphlet, see "Counterfeiting: Letter to the People," *Cleveland Leader*, Jan. 17, 1872.

72. "Counterfeiting and Its Antidote," *Boston Times*, Jan. 14, 1872; "A Defense of Detectives," *Pittsburgh Chronicle*, Jan. 16, 1872.

73. Hiram C. Whitley to Everett C. Banfield, Feb. 9, 1872, Whitley Official Correspondence.

74. Custom House Hearings, 696 (Testimony of Hiram C. Whitley).

75. "The Custom House Gang," *New York World*, Feb. 8, 1872.

76. "Whitley's Subordinates," *New York Sun*, Feb. 10, 1872.

77. "Joshua D. Miner: Wealthy Tammany Contractor," *New York Sunday Dispatch*, Dec. 31, 1871.

78. Roderick Henry Burnham, *The Burnham Family: Or, Genealogical Records of the Descendants of the Four Emigrants of the Name* (Hartford: Lockwood & Brainard, 1869), 238; Emelyn Rude, "The Forgotten History of the Hen Fever," *National Geographic*, Aug. 5,

2015, https://www.nationalgeographic.com/people-and-culture/
food/the-plate/2015/08/05/the-forgotten-history-of-hen-fever/.

79. Burnham, *Memoirs*, 13–41.

80. Ibid., 434.

81. By the end of his tenure, Whitley had accumulated roughly two hundred fifty photographs of counterfeiters and other criminals, some in their prison garb, others in the formal suit and tie men customarily donned for portrait sittings in that era. "National Rogues Gallery," *New York Sunday News*, Feb. 1, 1874.

82. Jens Jaeger, "Photography: A Means of Surveillance? Judicial Photography, 1850–1900," *Crime, History & Societies* 5, no. 1 (2001), 32–35.

83. "Coincident Indictments: Miner Not to Be Tried Twice for the Same Offense," *New York Tribune*, Mar. 12, 1874.

84. "The Secret Service: The Charge of Judge Nixon, of New Jersey," *National Republican*, Apr. 22, 1873; Johnson, *Illegal Tender*, 157–59.

85. Burnham, *Memoirs*, 44.

Chapter 5

1. Trelease, *White Terror*, 117; Link, *Atlanta*, 108; Conway, *Georgia*, 168–70.

2. For these and other cases of white supremacist terrorism in the South between 1868 and 1871, see Trelease, *White Terror*, passim.

3. Nathan Bedford Forrest claimed in an August 1868 interview that there were forty thousand Klansmen in Tennessee and five hundred fifty thousand in the South as a whole. See "An Oracle of the South: Interesting Interview with General N. B. Forrest," *New York Herald*, Sept. 3, 1868.

4. "The Ku-Klux," *Harper's Weekly*, Apr. 1, 1871.

5. Robert J. Kaczorowski, *The Politics of Judicial Interpretation: The Federal Courts, Department of Justice, and Civil Rights, 1866–1876* (New York: Fordham University Press, 2005), 64.

6. This measure was known as the Enforcement Act of 1870, *U.S. Statutes at Large*, 16: 140–46.

7. For details of the attempted crackdown on the Klan under Governor William Woods Holden in North Carolina, see Trelease, *White Terror*, 208–25; Mark L. Bradley, *Bluecoats and Tar Heels: Soldiers and Civilians in Reconstruction North Carolina* (Lexington KY: University of Kentucky Press, 2009), 217–34; Jim D. Brisson, "The Kirk-Holden War of 1870 and the Failure of Reconstruction in North Carolina" (M.A. thesis, University of North Carolina, Wilmington, 2010), passim.

8. Stephen E. Massengill, "The Detectives of William W. Holden, 1869–1870," *North Carolina Historical Review* 62, no. 4 (Oct. 1985), 448–87.

9. U.S. Congress, Sen. Ex. Doc., 41st Cong., 3d sess., no. 16, "Outrages Committed by Disloyal Persons in North Carolina and other Southern States."

10. Grant Papers, Vol. 21, 246.

11. *Congressional Globe*, Apr. 4, 1871, 441–51.

12. The provision was Section 6 of the Enforcement Act of 1870, which made it a crime for two or more persons to "band or conspire together, or go in disguise upon the public highway, or upon the premises of another, with intent to violate any provision of this act, or to injure, oppress, threaten, or intimidate any citizen with intent to prevent or hinder his free exercise and enjoyment of any right or privilege granted or secured to him by the Constitution or laws of the United States, or because of his having exercised the same." *U.S. Statutes at Large*, 16: 140. By comparison, the North Carolina law, enacted Apr. 12, 1869, criminalized "wearing any mask or any other device for the concealment of the face or person with intent to terrify or frighten any citizen or the community." *Public laws of the State of North Carolina, Passed by the General Assembly, 1868–1869*, Ch. 267, 613.

13. Amos T. Akerman to Cornelius Cole, Jan. 23, 1871, Letters Sent by the Department of Justice, General and Miscellaneous, 1818–1904, Microfilm Publication M699, Vol. I, Roll 14, Records of the Department of Justice, Record Group 60, National Archives,

College Park MD. See also Homer Cummings and Carl McFarland, *Federal Justice: Chapters in the History of Justice and the Federal Executive* (New York: MacMillan, 1937), 231.

14. Biographical information for Amos T. Akerman comes from the following sources: William S. McFeely, "Amos T. Akerman: The Lawyer and Racial Justice," in J. Morgan Kousser and James M. McPherson, eds., *Region, Race, and Reconstruction: Essays in Honor of C. Vann Woodward* (New York: Oxford University Press, 1982), 395–415; Lois Neal Hamilton, "Amos T. Akerman and His Role in American Politics" (M.A thesis, Columbia University, 1939); "Death of Amos T. Akerman," *Cincinnati Daily Gazette*, Dec. 23, 1880; "The Capital: Hon. Amos T. Akerman the Choice," *Philadelphia Inquirer*, June 17, 1870; "From New Hampshire," *Boston Journal*, June 25, 1870; "Amos. T. Akerman," *Newport* (RI) *Mercury*, June 25, 1870; "The Georgia Press on Mr. Akerman: What a Southern Political Enemy Says," *New York Tribune*, June 22, 1870; "A Grant Elector Ostracized in Georgia," *Boston Journal*, Oct. 31, 1868.

15. McFeely, "The Lawyer," 411.

16. Amos T. Akerman to Cornelius Cole, Jan. 23, 1871, Letters Sent by the Department of Justice, General and Miscellaneous, 1818–1904, Microfilm Publication M699, Vol. I, Roll 14, Records of the Department of Justice, Record Group 60, National Archives, College Park MD.

17. *U.S. Statutes at Large*, 16: 495, 497 (Mar. 3, 1871).

18. John Pool to Amos T. Akerman, Mar. 31, 1871 (forwarding Tod R. Caldwell to John Pool, Mar. 29, 1871), Letters Received from the Senate, 1871–1884, Records of the Department of Justice, Record Group 60, National Archives, College Park MD.

19. "The Irrepressible Conflict Still in Progress in North Carolina," *New York Times*, July 20, 1871; "A Shabby Trick," *Weekly Era* (Raleigh NC), Aug. 3, 1871.

20. *U.S. Statutes at Large*, 17: 6 (Apr. 19, 1871).

21. KKK Hearings, Vol. 2 (North Carolina), 13–19 (Testimony of Joseph G. Hester).

22. Biographical information for Joseph G. Hester derives from the following sources: KKK Hearings, Vol. 2 (North Carolina), 19 (Testimony of Joseph G. Hester); U.S. Congress, House Reports, 43d Cong., 2d sess., no. 262, "Affairs in Alabama," Vol. 3 (Hereafter cited as "Affairs in Alabama"), 1007–29 (Testimony of Joseph G. Hester); U.S. Naval War Records Office, Official Records of the Union and Confederate Navies in the War of the Rebellion, Series I, Vol. 1, 508–509, 688–90; Series I, Vol. 15, 563–64; Series II, Vol. 3, 582–83, 616–17, 857–58, 860; "The Ku-Klux in Alabama," *National Republican*, Oct. 16, 1874; "Captain J.G. Hester," *National Republican*, July 21, 1875; "Hester's History," *Indiana State Sentinel* (Indianapolis IN), Feb. 16, 1876; Grant Papers, Vol. 27, 328–29.

23. Details of President Grant's encounter with Joseph G. Hester and related correspondence are derived from "Affairs in Alabama," 1021 (Testimony of Joseph G. Hester); Grant Papers, Vol. 22, 11–13.

24. William T. Blain, "Challenge to the Lawless: The Mississippi Secret Service, 1870–1871," *Mississippi Quarterly*, 40, no. 2 (May 1978), 119–31. Mississippi budgeted $40,000 for state detectives in 1870, according to Sen. Adelbert Ames. *Congressional Globe*, Mar. 21, 1871, 196.

25. "Crime Against the Government," *New York Herald*, Mar. 9, 1871.

26. Amos T. Akerman to Hiram C. Whitley, June 28, 1871, Letters Sent from the Department of Justice, General and Miscellaneous, 1818–1904, Microfilm Publication M699, Vol. I, Roll 14, Records of the Department of Justice, Record Group 60, National Archives, College Park MD.

27. *Congressional Globe*, Mar. 9, 1866, 1294.

28. Hiram C. Whitley to Amos T. Akerman, June 30, 1871, Letters Received from the Department of Treasury, 1871–1884, Records of the Department of Justice, Record Group 60, National Archives, College Park MD.

29. *Nation's Peril*, 117.

30. Safe Burglary Hearings, 275 (Testimony of Michael G. Bauer).

31. Joseph G. Hester, "Weekly Report to the Department of Justice for Month Ending June 30," July 20, 1871, Letters Received by the Department of Justice from North Carolina, 1871–1884, Microfilm Publication M1345, Roll 1, Records of the Department of Justice, Record Group 60, National Archives, College Park MD.

32. Ibid.

33. For the exchange between Hiram C. Whitley and Joseph G. Hester, as well as details of their meeting, see Joseph G. Hester, "Weekly Report to the Department of Justice for First Six Days of July," July 25, 1871, Letters Received by the Department of Justice from North Carolina, 1871–1884, Microfilm Publication M1345, Roll 1, Records of the Department of Justice, Record Group 60, National Archives, College Park MD.

34. Amos T. Akerman to Benjamin F. Butler, Aug. 9, 1871, in Lois Neal Hamilton, "Amos T. Akerman and His Role in American Politics" (M.A thesis, Columbia University, 1939), 71–72.

35. Biographical information for John A. Campbell, and the account of Joseph G. Hester's operation in Moore County derive from the following sources: Hiram C. Whitley to Amos T. Akerman, Sept. 29, 1871, Letters Received from the Department of Treasury, 1871–1884, Records of the Department of Justice, Record Group 60, National Archives, College Park MD (Hereafter cited as "Whitley KKK Report I"); "Arrival of Ku Klux in Our Midst," *Tri-Weekly Era* (Raleigh NC), Aug. 12, 1871; N. R. Bryan, Letter to the Editor, *Raleigh Sentinel*, Aug. 12, 1871; *National Republican*, Sept. 9, 1871; "How Radical Thunder Is Manufactured," *Wilmington* (NC) *Journal*, Oct. 6, 1871; "To the Public: A Card and an Affidavit," *Tri-Weekly Era* (Raleigh NC), Dec. 28, 1871; "The Ku Klux in Alabama," *National Republican*, Oct. 16, 1874; Manly Wade Wellman, *The County of Moore, 1847–1947: A North Carolina Region's Second Hundred Years* (Southern Pines NC: Moore County Historical Association, 1962), 77–80; KKK Hearings, Vol. 2 (North Carolina), 75 (Testimony of Elias Bryan).

36. "No Revolution! Convention Defeated!" *Carolina Era* (Raleigh NC), Aug. 10, 1871.

37. The following account of the atrocity against Sally Gilmore and her family derives from: Whitley KKK Report I; *Nation's Peril*, 79–83.

38. "Arrival of Ku Klux in Our Midst," *Tri-Weekly Era* (Raleigh NC), Aug. 12, 1871.

39. KKK Hearings, Vol. 2 (North Carolina), 316 (Testimony of Plato Durham).

40. "Arrival of Ku Klux in Our Midst," *Tri-Weekly Era* (Raleigh NC), Aug. 12, 1871.

41. "How Radical Thunder Is Manufactured," *Wilmington* (NC) *Journal*, Oct. 6, 1871.

42. "The Ku Klux Klan," *National Republican*, Sept. 9, 1871. The widely circulated broadside was titled "Plan of the Contemplated Murder of John Campbell," and included both the woodcut and a brief account of Joseph G. Hester's action. Possibly the only surviving print of the actual photograph is on file in the archives of the Union League of Philadelphia. A handwritten notation on the reverse indicated it was deposited by a descendant of Capt. Fred G. Smith, commander of the 4th Artillery Regiment Company that helped Hester capture the Klansmen. See VI.4.7.001, Photograph, "A Ku Klux Party, 1871," The Union League of Philadelphia Archives, Courtesy of The Abraham Lincoln Foundation of The Union League of Philadelphia.

43. "Sally Gilmore," *Raleigh Sentinel*, Aug. 12, 1871; "The Ku Klux," *Wilmington* (NC) *Journal*, Oct. 6, 1871.

44. "Horried Sight," *Raleigh Sentinel*, Aug. 12, 1871.

45. "Arrests and Infamous Despotism," *Fayetteville* (NC) *Eagle*, Aug. 24, 1871.

46. "Planning Murder: Wrong Man Caught," *Raleigh Semi-Weekly Sentinel*, Nov. 1, 1871.

47. Wicker's affidavit is transcribed in Whitley KKK Report I.

48. Bryan's affidavit is transcribed in Whitley KKK Report I.

49. Ibid.

50. Details of the Ferguson family's ordeal are derived from Whitley KKK Report I; *Nation's Peril*, 51–65; "Punishing Witnesses—Another Outrage," *Tri-Weekly Era* (Raleigh NC), Sept. 28, 1871; "Another Ku-Klux Outrage," *Tri-Weekly Era* (Raleigh NC), Oct. 19, 1871.

51. "Kitty Furgerson [*sic*]," *Raleigh Sentinel*, Sept. 25, 1871; *Nation's Peril*, 63.

52. "The Kuklux," *New York Times*, Oct. 7, 1871.

53. Amos T. Akerman to Ulysses S. Grant, Oct. 16, 1871, Grant Papers, Vol. 22, 179.

54. U.S. Congress, Sen. Ex. Doc., 42d Cong., 3d sess., no. 55, "Letter of the Attorney General," 10; Hiram C. Whitley to the Attorney General, Jan. 15, 1872, Letters Received from the Department of Treasury, 1871–1884, Records of the Department of Justice, Record Group 60, National Archives, College Park MD (Hereafter cited as "Whitley KKK Report II").

55. Whitley KKK Report II; "Hester and Keith Bagged 'Em," *Tri-Weekly Era* (Raleigh NC), Dec. 7, 1871. For details of the crime for which Hester arrested these Klansmen, the murder of Menas Herring in Sampson County, see Edward Cantwell, Letter to the Editor, *Tri-Weekly Era* (Raleigh NC), Sept. 30, 1871.

56. Joseph G. Hester, "To the Public: A Card and an Affidavit," *Tri-Weekly Era* (Raleigh NC), Dec. 28, 1871.

57. "The Troubles in Alabama," *Chicago Tribune*, July 23, 1870; Trelease, *White Terror*, 269–70.

58. The account of George W. Carter's infiltration of the Calhoun County Ku Klux Klan and participation in the atrocity against William F. Fletcher derives from: Whitley KKK Report II; *Nation's Peril*, 85–88; Safe Burglary Hearings, 136–51 (Testimony of George W. Carter).

59. Whitley KKK Report I.

60. Carter biographical data are derived from: 1870 U.S. Census for Brooklyn Ward 22, Kings County, NY; Safe Burglary Hearings, 149 (Testimony of George W. Carter).

61. John A. Minnis to Hiram C. Whitley, Jan. 2, 1872, Whitley KKK Report II.

62. Ibid.

63. Whitley KKK Report I.

64. Ibid.

65. U.S. Congress, Sen. Ex. Doc., 42d Cong., 3d sess., no. 32, "Annual Report of the Attorney General for the Fiscal Year July 1, 1871 through June 30, 1872." See also Trelease, *White Terror*, 406–407.

66. Nettleship Daybook, Sept. 19, 21, 22, 28, Oct. 2, 1871, I. C. Nettleship Papers, New Jersey Historical Society, Newark NJ.

67. See Peter G. Tsouras, ed., *Scouting for Grant and Meade: The Reminiscences of Judson Knight, Chief of Scouts, Army of the Potomac* (New York: Skyhorse Publishing, 2014).

68. The details of Henry Lowther's ordeal are derived from the following sources: Whitley KKK Report II; *Nation's Peril*, 49–50; KKK Hearings, Vol. 6, 356–63 (Testimony of Henry Lowther). Whitley KKK Report II refers to the fact that Whitley made his first report to Akerman of the atrocity against Henry Lowther in a previous report dated Oct. 16, 1871, of which only the cover sheet survives in the National Archives.

69. KKK Hearings, Vol. 6, 368–75 (Testimony of John D. Pope).

70. Ibid.

71. Hiram C. Whitley to Amos T. Akerman, Oct. 12, 1871, Letters Received by the Department of Justice from the Southern District of New York, Records of the Department of Justice, Record Group 60, National Archives, College Park MD.

72. Ron Chernow, *Grant* (New York: Penguin Press, 2017), 705.

73. Grant Papers, Vol. 22, 201.

74. McFeely, "The Lawyer," 410.

75. Ulysses S. Grant, "Third Annual Message," Dec. 4, 1871, online by Gerhard Peters and John T. Woolley, The American Presidency Project, http://www.presidency.ucsb.edu/ws/?pid=29512. See also KKK Hearings, Vol. 1, 99.

76. Richard Zuczek, "The Federal Government's Attack on the Ku Klux Klan: A Reassessment," *South Carolina Historical Magazine* 97, no. 1 (Jan. 1996), 58–59.

77. Whitley KKK Report II.

78. "Secret Service Division," *Washington Chronicle*, Jan. 19, 1872.

79. "The Administration Still After the Ku Klux: Letter from Attorney General Williams," *New York Herald*, Jan. 4, 1872.

80. Kaczorowski, *Judicial Interpretation*, 80; "United States Attorneys Resigning," *New York Daily Herald*, Feb. 29, 1872.

81. McFeely, "The Lawyer," 410.

82. Trelease, *White Terror*, 417. See also Charles Lane, *The Day Freedom Died* (New York: Henry Holt, 2008), 139–42.

83. Hiram C. Whitley to George H. Williams, Feb. 21, 1872, Whitley Official Correspondence; Hiram C. Whitley to Joseph G. Hester, Mar. 7, 1872, ibid.; George H. Williams to Hiram C. Whitley, Feb. 26, 1872, Letters Sent by the Department of Justice, General and Miscellaneous, 1818–1904, Microfilm Publication M699, Vol. 1, Roll 14, Records of the Department of Justice, Record Group 60, National Archives, College Park MD.

84. A. J. Falls to Hiram C. Whitley, Mar. 21, 1872, Letters Sent by the Department of Justice, General and Miscellaneous, 1818–1904, Microfilm Publication M699, Vol. I, Roll 14, Records of the Department of Justice, Record Group 60, National Archives, College Park MD.

85. Hiram C. Whitley to E. A. Ireland, May 15, 1872, Whitley Official Correspondence.

86. Hiram C. Whitley to Michael G. Bauer, July 8, 1872, Whitley Official Correspondence.

87. Everette Swinney, *Suppressing the Ku Klux Klan: The Enforcement of the Reconstruction Amendments, 1870–1877* (New York: Garland, 1987), 184–85.

88. Hiram C. Whitley to George H. Williams, July 10, 1872, Letters Received from the Department of Treasury, 1871–1884, Records of the Department of Justice, Record Group 60, National Archives, College Park MD; Hiram C. Whitley to George H. Williams, Aug. 15, 1872, Letters Received from the Department of Treasury, 1871–1884, Records of the Department of Justice, Record Group 60, National Archives, College Park MD (Hereafter cited as "Whitley KKK Report III"). This document summarizes field reports from spring and early summer of 1872; it includes references to Whitley's report dated May 6, 1872, which has been lost.

89. Hiram C. Whitley to George H. Williams, July 10, 1872, Letters Received from the Department of Treasury, 1871–1884, Records of the Department of Justice, Record Group 60, National Archives, College Park MD.

90. Whitley KKK Report III.

91. Hiram C. Whitley to George H. Williams, July 2, 1872, Letters Received from the Department of the Treasury, 1871–1884, Records of the Department of Justice, Record Group 60, National Archives, College Park MD.

92. Hiram C. Whitley to Michael G. Bauer, July 8, 1872, Whitley Official Correspondence; Hiram C. Whitley to Judson Knight, July 9, 1872, ibid.; Hiram C. Whitley to E. A. Ireland, July 9, 1872, ibid.; George H. Williams to Hiram C. Whitley, July 10, 1872, Letters Sent by the Department of Justice, General and Miscellaneous, 1818–1904, Microfilm Publication M699, Vol. 1, Roll 14, Records of the Department of Justice, Record Group 60, National Archives, College Park MD.

93. Custom House Hearings, 701 (Testimony of Hiram C. Whitley).

94. Many years later, a published biography of Whitley noted that he "has written extensively, including a book about the Ku Klux

Klan, which was largely circulated by the republican [*sic*] leaders in pamphlet form." See William E. Connelley, *A Standard History of Kansas and Kansans, Vol. V* (Chicago: Lewis Publishing Company, 1918), 2219.

95. *Nation's Peril*, 143.

96. "The Ku Klux Convicts," *New York World*, Aug. 10, 1872.

97. "Grant's Prisoner's [*sic*] in Town," *New York Sun*, June 12, 1872.

98. "Republican Party Platform of 1872," June 5, 1872. Online by Gerhard Peters and John T. Woolley, The American Presidency Project, http://www.presidency.ucsb.edu/ws/?pid=29623.

99. Untitled news item, *Washington Daily Critic*, Aug. 12, 1872.

100. Jacob R. Davis to U. S. Grant, May 29, 1872, and H. K. Thurber to U. S. Grant, Oct. 9, 1872, Grant Papers, Vol. 23, 212–13.

101. Rossiter, ed., *The Federalist*, 449.

102. Grant Papers, Vol. 23, 214.

103. Octavius Brooks Frothingham, *Gerrit Smith: A Biography* (New York: G. P. Putnam's Sons, 1877), 301–10; Joseph Grégoire de Roulhac Hamilton, ed., *The Papers of Randolph Abbott Shotwell, Vol. 3* (Raleigh NC: North Carolina Historical Commission, 1929) (Hereafter cited as "Shotwell Papers"), 234–35. See also "The Albany Bastille," *Daily Phoenix* (Columbia SC), Aug. 17, 1872; "Greeley and the Prisoners at Albany," *Southerner* (Tarborough NC), Sept. 12, 1872.

104. "Grant's Prisoner's [*sic*] in Town," *New York Sun*, June 12, 1872.

105. U. S. Grant to Gerrit Smith, July 22, 1872, Grant Papers, Vol. 23, 210.

106. George H. Williams to Hiram C. Whitley, Aug. 2, 1872, Letters Sent by the Department of Justice, General and Miscellaneous, 1818–1904, Microfilm Publication M699, Vol. 1, Roll 14, Records of the Department of Justice, Record Group 60, National Archives, College Park MD.

107. This account of Hiram C. Whitley's visit to the Albany Penitentiary, and descriptions of the facility, derive from "The Ku Klux: What Colonel Whitley Says about the Albany Prisoners," *New York Herald*, Aug. 14, 1872; Shotwell Papers, Vol. 3, 245–47, 253; Carl Johnson, "The Albany Penitentiary," Nov. 3, 2010, www.alloveralbany.com; David Dyer, *History of the Albany Penitentiary* (Albany NY: J. Munsell, 1867); "Annual report of the Attorney General of the United States for the Fiscal Year Ending June 30, 1873," 16–17, 38–39.

108. "The Ku-Klux at Albany," *National Republican*, Aug. 10, 1871.

109. "Washington: The Ku Klux Prisoners at Albany," *New York Herald*, Aug. 13, 1871.

110. "The Ku Klux: What Colonel Whitley Says about the Albany Prisoners," *New York Herald*, Aug. 14, 1872.

111. "Trial of the Ku Klux Case," *Carolina Era* (Raleigh NC), Sept. 21, 1871; Shotwell Papers, Vol. 3, 54.

112. "The Ku Klux: What Colonel Whitley Says about the Albany Prisoners," *New York Herald*, Aug. 14, 1872. (There had been sixty-five prisoners at the time of Gerrit Smith's visit, but one died before Whitley's arrival.)

113. "Ku Klux Prisoners in the Albany Penitentiary," *New York Herald*, Aug. 14, 1872.

114. Grant Papers, Vol. 23, 228–29.

115. "Why the Albany Ku Klux Have Not Been Pardoned," *Chicago Post*, Aug. 30, 1872. South Carolina Republican officials also weighed in against the pardons. Trelease, *White Terror*, 416.

116. Hiram C. Whitley to A. J. Falls, Aug. 20, 1872, Letters Received from the Treasury Department, 1871–1884, Records of the Department of Justice, Record Group 60, National Archives, College Park MD.

117. "Alexander H. Stephens's Plea for the Ku Klux," *Intelligencer* (Anderson SC), Oct. 3, 1872.

118. Ulysses S. Grant, "Fourth Annual Message," Dec. 2, 1872, online by Gerhard Peters and John T. Woolley, The American Presidency Project, http://www.presidency.ucsb.edu/ws/?pid=29513.

119. Hiram C. Whitley to Amos T. Akerman, July 14, 1871, Whitley Official Correspondence.

120. Hiram C. Whitley to George H. Williams, Jan. 2, 1873, Letters Received from the Department of Treasury, 1871–1884, Records of the Department of Justice, Record Group 60, National Archives, College Park MD (Hereafter cited as "Whitley Final KKK Report").

121. Ibid.

122. Ibid.

123. Hiram C. Whitley to A. J. Falls, Nov. 28, 1872, Whitley Official Correspondence.

124. Whitley Final KKK Report.

Chapter 6

1. Mrs. J. B. Luckey to Hiram C. Whitley, Dec. 9, 1872, Hiram C. Whitley Papers, Danforth W. Austin Family Collection.

2. Indenture contract, Supreme Court of New York County, New York, Dec. 13, 1872, Hiram C. Whitley Papers, Danforth W. Austin Family Collection.

3. Hiram C. Whitley to M. G. Bauer, et al., Aug. 27, 1873, Letters Sent from Headquarters of the Chief in New York, Vol. II, Records of the U.S. Secret Service, Record Group 87, National Archives, College Park MD.

4. Hiram C. Whitley to M. G. Bauer, et al., Aug. 28, 1873, Letters Sent from Headquarters of the Chief in New York, Vol. II, Records of the U.S. Secret Service, Record Group 87, National Archives, College Park MD.

5. Hiram C. Whitley to George H. Williams, Report on Outrages in Kentucky, Sept. 24, 1873, Letters Received by the Department

of Justice from Kentucky, 1871–1884, Microfilm Publication M1362, Roll 1, Records of the Department of Justice, Record Group 60, National Archives, College Park MD.

6. Hiram C. Whitley to Everett C. Banfield, May 14, 1874, U.S. Secret Service Archives, Washington DC.

7. Hiram C. Whitley to Everett C. Banfield, Apr. 1870, Whitley Official Correspondence.

8. Louis Bagger, "The 'Secret Service' of the United States," *Appletons' Journal* 10, no. 235 (Sept. 20, 1873), 360–65.

9. "The Custom House Gang," *New York World*, Feb. 8, 1872.

10. *Appendix to the Congressional Globe*, May 20, 1872, 374.

11. KKK Hearings, Vol. 1, 507.

12. "Congressman Beck's Exposures," *New Orleans Times-Picayune*, July 18, 1872.

13. *Congressional Globe*, Feb. 22, 1873, 1636.

14. Ibid.

15. Walter S. Bowen and Harry Edward Neal, *The United States Secret Service* (New York: Popular Library, 1960), 173. None of the original Secret Service badges survive, but the design Whitley adopted, a five-pointed star, is still incorporated in the agency's insignia today.

16. Burnham, *Memoirs*, 354–56.

17. *Circular of Instructions to Operatives*, Secret Service Division, Treasury Department, Letters Received, Secret Service Division, 1863–1895, Records of the Solicitor of the Treasury, Record Group 206, National Archives, College Park MD.

18. Hiram C. Whitley to Albert C. Falls, May 19, 1873, Letters Received by the Attorney General from the Department of the Treasury, 1871–1884, Records of the Department of Justice, Record Group 60, National Archives, College Park MD.

19. H. V. Boynton, "The Washington 'Safe Burglary' Conspiracy," *American Law Review* XI, no. 3 (Apr. 1877), 403; *The Campaign Text Book: Why the People Want a Change* (Democratic Party pamphlet) (New York: 1876), 424–26; "Washington: Astounding Developments by the Ex-Chief of the Detectives," *New York Herald*, Apr. 15, 1876.

20. Whitley, *In It*, 292–98; "A Daring Swindler," *National Republican*, Apr. 17, 1873; Hiram C. Whitley to Orville E. Babcock, Apr. 14, 1873, Letters Sent from Headquarters of the Chief in New York, Secret Service Division, Vol. II, Records of the U.S. Secret Service, Record Group 87, National Archives, College Park MD; Drummond, *True Detective Stories*, 69–82.

21. George H. Williams to Hiram C. Whitley, Feb. 19, 1873, Letters Sent by the Department of Justice, General and Miscellaneous, 1818–1904, Microfilm Publication M699, Vol. I, Roll 14, Records of the Department of Justice, Record Group 60, National Archives, College Park MD; Hiram C. Whitley to George H. Williams, Mar. 4, 1873, Letters Received from the Department of Treasury, Records of the Department of Justice, Record Group 60, National Archives, College Park MD.

22. The account of Hiram C. Whitley's use of Secret Service personnel to kidnap Kate Williams's son James Ivins and remove him from the country is derived from the following sources: Whitley, *In It*, 257–66; "Gathered Together," *Pomeroy's Democrat*, Apr. 22, 1876; "The Skeleton in the Closet," *St. Louis Globe-Democrat*, May 22, 1909.

23. Biographical data for Kate and George Williams, and for her son, James Ivins, are derived from the following sources: Whitley, *In It*, 257–58; J. M. Reid, *Sketches and Anecdotes of the Old Settlers and Newcomers, the Mormon Bandits, and Danite Band* (Keokuk IA: Ogden, 1877), 72–73, 176–77; Vertical File Biography for Mrs. George H. Williams, Oregon Historical Society, Portland OR; "Planned Social Conquest: The Bitter Experience of Mrs. Williams in Washington," *Boston Herald*, Dec. 18, 1893; 1860 U.S. Census for Kirtland OH; 1920 U.S. Census for Los Angeles CA.

24. The account of Joseph G. Hester's forcible attempted extradition of Klansman James Rufus Bratton from Canada to South

Carolina is derived from the following sources: Trelease, *White Terror*, 404; Jerry West, *The Reconstruction Ku Klux Klan in York County, South Carolina, 1865–1877* (Jefferson NC: McFarland & Co., 2002), 126–29; J. Michael Martinez, *Carpetbaggers, Cavalry, and the Ku Klux Klan: Exposing the Invisible Empire during Reconstruction* (Lanham MD: Rowman & Littlefield, 2007), 193–94; Richard Zuczek, *State of Rebellion: Reconstruction in South Carolina* (Columbia SC: University of South Carolina Press, 1996), 119–21; "The Canada Outrage," *New York Sun*, June 12, 1872; "Abduction of an American Refugee," *New York Herald*, June 14, 1872; "The Mysterious Prisoner," *Charleston* (SC) *Daily News*, June 15, 1872; "Kidnapping in Canada," *New York World*, June 20, 1872; "A High-Handed Outrage," *Daily Rocky Mountain Gazette* (Helena MT), June 26, 1872; Untitled news item, *Intelligencer* (Anderson SC), June 27, 1872; "Where is Hester?" *Raleigh News*, July 1, 1872; "The Abduction Case of Dr. Bratton of SC," *Charlotte Democrat*, July 30, 1872; Matthew Pearl, "K Troop: The Story of the Eradication of the Original Ku Klux Klan," *Slate*, Mar. 4, 2016.

25. George H. Williams to Hamilton Fish, Nov. 2, 1872, Letters Sent by the Department of Justice, Microfilm Publication M702, Roll 2, Records of the Department of Justice, Record Group 60, National Archives, College Park MD; Daniel T. Corbin to George H. Williams, Nov. 5, 1872, Letters Received by the Department of Justice from South Carolina, Microfilm Publication M947, Roll 2, Records of the Department of Justice, Record Group 60, National Archives, College Park MD; "British Protection for an American Citizen," *Augusta* (GA) *Chronicle*, Nov. 9, 1872.

26. Untitled news item (Hester letter of resignation as Deputy U.S. Marshal), *Greensboro* (NC) *North State*, Aug. 8, 1872; D. H. Starbuck to John Pool, Nov. 26, 1872 (endorsed and forwarded to George H. Williams by Pool), Letters Received by the Department of Justice from North Carolina, 1871–1884, Microfilm Publication M1345, Roll 1, Records of the Department of Justice, Record Group 60, National Archives, College Park MD.

27. 1920 U.S. Census for Los Angeles CA; U.S. Passport Application for James C. H. Ivins, June 29, 1920, Records of the Department of State, Microfilm Publication M1490, Roll 1488, Record Group 59, National Archives, College Park MD; "James C. H.

Ivins," in James Miller Guinn, *A History of California and an Extended History of Los Angeles and Environs* (Los Angeles: Historic Record Co., 1915), Vol. 3, 582–83.

28. "Safe Burglary Trial," *National Republican*, Sept. 22, 1876.

29. "Counterfeit Money: The Secret Service Division," *Pittsburgh Evening Telegraph*, July 8, 1874.

30. "The Safe Burglary: Startling Testimony of Colonel Whitley," *New York World*, Apr. 8, 1876.

31. The Washington Safe Burglary Case may qualify as the first scandal involving alleged abuses by a federal covert agency in American history. Certainly it was a pivotal moment in the development of the United States' national law enforcement and intelligence capabilities, which it may have set back decades. Whatever its long-term impact, the safe burglary counts as a bizarre episode even by the rough-and-tumble political standards of Reconstruction. Even now, almost a century and a half after the events, it is difficult to piece together precisely what happened, much less narrate it succinctly. The most important source of information is the extensive witness testimony gathered by the joint committee of Congress responsible for investigating the affair, compiled in U.S. Congress, House Reports, 43d Cong., 1st sess., no. 785, "Testimony in Relation to the Alleged Safe-Burglary at the Office of the United States Attorney." The best journalistic narrative is Boynton, "Safe Burglary," 401–46. The account presented here derives from those two documents, as well as Alan Lessoff, *The Nation and Its City: Politics, "Corruption," and Progress in Washington D.C., 1861–1902* (Baltimore: The Johns Hopkins University Press, 1994), passim; James H. Whyte, *The Uncivil War: Washington during the Reconstruction, 1865–1878* (New York: Twayne Publishers, 1958), 262–68; Henry E. Davis, "The Safe Burglary Case: An Episode and a Factor in the District's Development," *Records of the Columbia Historical Society* 25 (1923), 140–81; and numerous press clippings about the case found in the Hiram C. Whitley Scrapbooks, Lyon County History Center, Emporia KS. Many newspapers covered the 1874 and 1876 safe burglary conspiracy trials; for the sake of ideological balance and factual completeness I relied on the de-

tailed coverage of the proceedings by the *National Republican* of Washington DC, and the Democratic *Baltimore Sun.*

32. "Letter from Washington," *Baltimore Sun*, Sept. 22, 1876. See also "Safe Burglary Trial," *National Republican*, Sept. 22, 1876.

33. Lessoff, *The Nation and Its City*, 125.

34. "Letter from Washington," *Baltimore Sun*, Sept. 22, 1876.

35. Biographical information for Michael Hayes derived from the following sources: U.S. Congress, House Reports, 43d Cong. 1st sess., no. 785, "Testimony in Relation to the Alleged Safe-Burglary at the Office of the United States Attorney," passim; Whitley KKK Report I; Hiram C. Whitley to George H. Williams, Aug. 15, 1872, Letters Received from the Department of Treasury, Records of the Department of Justice, Record Group 60, National Archives, College Park MD; Michael Hayes to M. G. Bauer, Sept. 6, 1872, and Michael Hayes to M. G. Bauer, Sept. 9, 1872, M. G. Bauer Papers, Filson Historical Society, Louisville, Kentucky.

36. "The Safe Burglary: A Nolle Pros. Entered in Whitley's Case," *New York Times*, Sept. 21, 1876.

37. U.S. Congress, House Reports, 43d Cong., 1st sess., no. 785, "Testimony in Relation to the Alleged Safe-Burglary at the Office of the United States Attorney," 120.

38. "Detective Nettleship," *New York News*, June 30, 1874.

39. "Special Report on the Harrington Safe Burglary," *Baltimore Sun*, June 24, 1874.

40. Hiram C. Whitley to William B. Allison, June 23, 1874, Benjamin H. Bristow Papers, Library of Congress, Manuscripts Division, Washington DC.

41. David Davis to Benjamin H. Bristow, June 15, 1874, Bristow Papers, Library of Congress, Manuscripts Division, Washington DC.

42. Hiram C. Whitley to Benjamin H. Bristow, June 2, 1874, Bristow Papers, Library of Congress, Manuscripts Division, Washington DC.

43. Bluford Wilson to Benjamin H. Bristow, July 27, 1874 (copy), Letters Received from the Secret Service Division, 1865–1895, Records of the Solicitor of the Treasury, Record Group 206, National Archives, College Park MD.

44. Bluford Wilson to Benjamin H. Bristow, June 8, 1874, Bristow Papers, Library of Congress, Manuscripts Division, Washington DC.

45. "Developments in the Secret Service," *New Hampshire Patriot and State Gazette* (Concord NH), Sept. 30, 1874.

46. Bluford Wilson to George Bliss and others, July 3, 1874 (copy), Letters Received from the Secret Service Division, 1865–1895, Records of the Solicitor of the Treasury, Record Group 206, National Archives, College Park MD.

47. "The District of Columbia Safe Burglary," *New York Times*, July 9, 1874. See also "The District of Columbia Safe Robbery," *New York Times*, July 15, 1874.

48. Benjamin H. Bristow to James H. Wilson, July 18, 1874, Bristow Papers, Library of Congress, Manuscripts Division, Washington DC.

49. *Letter of Wm. P. Wood, to the Hon. Geo. S. Boutwell, Secretary of the Treasury, Relating to one of his favorite officials, with facts and quotations submitted for reference and study*, Broadside pamphlet [Washington DC], 1872, 2. Wood claimed, apparently falsely, that Whitley had a venereal disease. Ibid.

50. "The Safe Burglary Investigation," *Baltimore Sun*, July 20, 1874.

51. Hiram C. Whitley to Benjamin H. Bristow, telegram, July 20, 1874, Bristow Papers, Library of Congress, Manuscripts Division, Washington DC.

52. Bluford Wilson to Benjamin H. Bristow, telegram, July 18, 1874, Bristow Papers, Library of Congress, Manuscripts Division, Washington DC.

53. Bluford Wilson to Benjamin H. Bristow, July 27, 1874 (copy), Letters Received from the Secret Service Division, 1865–1895,

Records of the Solicitor of the Treasury, Record Group 206, National Archives, College Park MD.

54. Hiram C. Whitley to Bluford Wilson, July 24, 1874, Letters Received from the Secret Service Division, 1865–1895, Records of the Solicitor of the Treasury, Record Group 206, National Archives, College Park MD.

55. Bluford Wilson to Benjamin H. Bristow, July 27, 1874 (copy), Letters Received from the Secret Service Division, 1865–1895, Records of the Solicitor of the Treasury, Record Group 206, National Archives, College Park MD.

56. "The Safe Burglary: Col. Whitley Makes a Statement," *Evening Star* (Washington DC), Sept. 10, 1874.

57. "Counterfeit Money: The Secret Service Division," *Pittsburgh Evening Telegraph*, July 8, 1874.

58. Boynton, "Safe Burglary," 426–27.

59. "The Secret Service System," *Philadelphia Inquirer*, Sept. 14, 1874.

60. "The Safe Burglary Investigation," *Baltimore Sun*, July 20, 1874.

61. "The Secret Service: A Project for Its Reorganization Approved by Secretary Bristow," *New York Evening Post*, Dec. 16, 1874.

Chapter 7

1. "The Clansman in Emporia," *Emporia Gazette*, Mar. 24, 1906.

2. Anthony Slide, *American Racist: The Life and Films of Thomas Dixon* (Lexington KY: University Press of Kentucky, 2004), 59–60. *The Clansman*'s success as a stage play led to the production of D. W. Griffith's 1915 film based on the same novel, *Birth of a Nation*.

3. "Emporia: Downtown Historic Survey," Christy Davis, Davis Preservation, Inc., 2011, https://www.kshs.org.

4. "Ku Klux on the Stage," *Emporia Gazette*, Mar. 19, 1906.

5. "Knocking the Clansman," *Emporia Gazette*, Mar. 17, 1906.

6. Untitled news item, *Emporia Gazette*, Mar. 20, 1906.

7. "The Clansman in Emporia," *Emporia Gazette*, Mar. 24, 1906.

8. James Delbert Kemmerling, "A History of the Whitley Opera House in Emporia, Kansas, 1881–1913" (M.S. thesis, Kansas State Teachers College, 1967), 28–48.

9. Indictment quoted in "Letter from Washington," *Baltimore Sun*, Sept. 17, 1874.

10. "Whitley and Alexander," *Washington Critic-Record*, Oct. 28, 1874.

11. "Letters from Washington," *Baltimore Sun*, Nov. 18, 1874.

12. "The Safe Burglars' Jury," *Forney's Sunday Chronicle* (Washington DC), Nov. 29, 1874.

13. "The End of the Safe Burglary Trial," *Baltimore Sun*, Nov. 28, 1874.

14. Bluford Wilson to James H. Wilson, Mar. 28, 1875, Grant Papers, Vol. 26, 106.

15. "A Curious Narrative," *New York Herald*, Aug. 19, 1876.

16. Bluford Wilson to James H. Wilson, Mar. 28, 1875, Grant Papers, Vol. 26, 107.

17. "Safe Burglary Trial," *National Republican*, Sept. 22, 1876.

18. "Telegraphic News from Washington: The Safe Burglary," *Baltimore Sun*, Apr. 10, 1876.

19. Boynton, "Safe Burglary," 442.

20. "Washington: Astounding Developments by the Ex-Chief of the Detectives," *New York Herald*, Apr. 15, 1876.

21. "Letter from Washington," *Baltimore Sun*, Sept. 22, 1876. See also "From Our Regular Correspondent," *New York Herald*, Apr. 13, 1876.

22. "Letter from Washington," *Baltimore Sun*, Sept. 22, 1876; "Fourth Day of the Trial," *National Republican*, Sept. 23, 1876.

23. "The Safe Burglary," *National Republican*, Oct. 2, 1876.

24. Boynton, "Safe Burglary," 444.

25. "H.C. Whitley, or Hale," *National Republican*, Apr. 12, 1876.

26. "The Safe Burglary," *National Republican*, Oct. 2, 1876.

27. "Obituary Notes (I. C. Nettleship)," *New York Times*, Nov. 10, 1887.

28. Shotwell Papers, Vol. 3, 458–59; Trelease, *White Terror*, 417.

29. William A. Smith to Ulysses S. Grant, Jan. 21, 1874, Grant Papers, Vol. 27, 328; "The Secret Service Division," *Washington Daily Critic*, Sept. 10, 1874; "The Move on the Secret Service Bureau," *Baltimore Sun*, Sept. 11, 1874.

30. "Washington Notes," *New York Tribune*, Sept. 30, 1882; "Funeral of Capt. Hester," *Evening Star* (Washington DC), June 17, 1901. Between September and November of 1874, Hester worked as an undercover agent of the Post Office Department, investigating a suspected white terrorist murder of an African American political leader and U.S. mail agent in Sumter County, Alabama. As he had done during the 1871 campaign against the Klan in North Carolina, Hester penetrated the Alabama white vigilante network disguised as a tobacco peddler, and helped federal marshals and troops round up the guilty parties. Hester returned to North Carolina as a Department of Justice detective in 1876. When he was temporarily laid off in August of that year due to budget cuts, he wrote President Grant warning of impending "Ku Klux" plots in the state and pleading for his job. The president, praising Hester's "exertions and fearlessness," ordered his reinstatement. Grant Papers, Vol. 27, 328–29; "Affairs in Alabama," 1007–46; "The Ku Klux in Alabama," *National Republican*, Oct. 16, 1874.

31. "The Release of Kuklux Prisoners," *New York Times*, Aug. 5, 1873.

32. *U.S. Statutes at Large*, 20: 377, 384.

33. *Appendix to the Congressional Record*, Vol. 8 (1879), Feb. 24, 1879, 205.

34. *Appendix to the Congressional Record*, Vol. 8 (1879), Feb. 27, 1879, 227.

35. *Congressional Record*, May 25, 1880, 3771–72.

36. Frank P. Vazzano, "President Hayes, Congress, and the Appropriations Riders," *Congress and the Presidency* 20, no. 1, (Spring 1993), 25–37.

37. *Congressional Record*, June 10, 1880, 4377–78.

38. Burnham, *Memoirs*, 14.

39. *U.S. Statutes at Large*, 22: 219.

40. Johnson, *Illegal Tender*, 96.

41. James J. Brooks to R. C. McCormick, Sept. 26, 1877, U.S. Secret Service Archives, Washington DC.

42. "Capt. Bauer's Sudden Death," *Louisville Courier-Journal*, May 17, 1898.

43. Johnson, *Illegal Tender*, 101.

44. Ibid., 144; Mihm, *Nation of Counterfeiters*, 373.

45. Johnson, *Illegal Tender*, 139.

46. Williamson, "William D. Chipley," 333–55.

47. This remarkable artifact, known as the "Columbus Prisoners' Cane," is housed in the Columbus Museum, Columbus GA. A photograph is available at http://www.columbusmuseum.com.

48. Bowen and Neal, *Secret Service*, 26.

49. Hugh McCulloch, *Men and Measures of Half a Century* (New York: C. Scribner's Sons, 1889), 222. See also Mihm, *Nation of Counterfeiters*, 345.

50. Norman Ansley, "The United States Secret Service: An Administrative History," *Journal of Criminal Law, Criminology, and Police Science* 47, no. 1 (May–June 1956), 94–96.

51. Rossiter, ed., *The Federalist*, 424; Max Farrand, ed., *Records of the Federal Convention of 1787, Vol. 1* (New Haven CT: Yale University Press, 1911), 584.

52. Jan Huston, "Hiram C. Whitley, a Builder of Emporia," *Emporia Living*, Feb. 2, 2014, 82–88.

53. "Story of a House," *Emporia Weekly Gazette*, Nov. 20, 1947.

54. Order, Lyon County KS, Probate Court, July 17, 1894, certifying adoption of Sabra and Kittie Whitley; Delayed Certificate of Birth for Sabra Whitley, Kansas State Department of Health, Topeka KS, Mar. 15, 1946; Last Will and Testament of Hiram C. Whitley, Jan. 3, 1895, all in Hiram C. Whitley Papers, Danforth W. Austin Family Collection. Sabra Whitley's birth certificate, a post hoc document reconstructing the facts of her birth from various witnesses' memories, lists her birthplace as Emporia, her name at birth as "Sadie Gardner," and her parents as Lizzie W. Gibbs and John E. Gardner. According to U.S. Census and Massachusetts Census records, Lizzie W. Gibbs was born in 1853 in Sagamore, Massachusetts, near Sandwich, which was the family home of Abner B. Newcomb. Later she took the last name "Newcomb," while she lived with the Whitleys, despite never having married anyone by that name. No census or other records documenting the existence of "John E. Gardner" could be found, though the 1902 Emporia city directory lists her as his "widow." Kittie Whitley's parentage is mysterious, as well. No trace of any family with her last name at birth, Gladde, can be found in the U.S. and New York state census records of the relevant period. It is unclear who the girl's biological father was and how he came to be separated from her mother, Lottie N. Luckey, who later married J. B. Luckey. The speed with which Whitley placed a newspaper ad seeking to adopt a girl of a particular age, found a woman willing to provide one, and closed the adoption—all within a single week—is impressive. In photographs, Kittie Whitley, too, bears a faint physical resemblance to her adoptive father.

55. "The Whitleys' Anniversary," *Emporia Gazette*, Mar. 25, 1916.

56. "'Colonel' Whitley Was One of Emporia's Most Picturesque Personalities in the 1880s and 90s," *Emporia Daily Gazette*, June 26, 1957.

57. John Stephen Farmer and William Ernest Henley, *A Dictionary of Slang and Colloquial English* (London: Routledge, 1905), 237.

58. Whitley, *In It*, 243.

59. Ibid., 2–3.

60. Ibid., 9.

61. Ibid.,104.

62. "Colonel Whitley's View," *Emporia Gazette*, Mar. 26, 1906.

63. "Who Was William Chipley?" *Pensacola News-Journal*, Apr. 18, 2015. A photograph of the inscription is available at www.hmdb.org.

INDEX

A

abductions, Secret Service
  botched, 219–21
  James Ivins, 218–19, 221–24
African Americans, federal intervention for, 264
African Americans, voting rights of, 23–24, 77, 91
Akerman, Amos Tappan, 149–53, *150*, 155–56, 158–63, 172, 175, 180, 182–83, 186–92, 205–206, 238, 267
Albany Penitentiary, 119, 196, 198–200, 258
Alexander, Columbus, 227–37, 241–42, 250–52, 254–55
Allison, William B., 236, 239
Anchisi, Charles E., 107, *107*, 110–11, 141, 263
anti-counterfeiting force, formation of, 99–100
Appletons' Journal, 211–13
Army of the Cumberland, 21

Army of the Potomac, 39, 185
Ashburn, George W., 21–22, 28–36
Ashburn murder
  artist's rendition of, *30*
  confessions obtained, 77–87
  investigation and arrests, 63–77
  as threat to Reconstruction, 101
  trial, 87–94
  See also Democrats; Ku Klux Klan; Republicans; Whitley, Hiram Coombs
Atlanta Constitution, 80, 92
Avery, James William, 220–21

B

Babcock, Orville E., 217, 225–37, 252–53
  trial and acquittal, 254–57
Baker, Lafayette, 39–40, 99

Ballard, Thomas, 114, 121, 124, 138, 211, *212*

Baltimore Sun, 252

Banfield, Everett C., 102–106, 110, 117, 126, 134, 136, 141, 157, 216, 224–25, 237, 239

Banks, Gen. Nathaniel, 57

Barber, James W., 75–77, 79, 81–82, 84–85

Bates, Catherine Webster. *See* Whitley, Catherine Webster Bates

Battle of New Orleans, 57

Bauer, Michael G., 107, *125*, 181–83, 192, 210, 263

Bay State Republican Party, 102

Beatty, Abraham, 124–29, *125*, 133–37, 158, 237

Beck, James Burnie, 75–76, 213–15, *214*, 235, 245, 261, 264, 267

Beckwith, James R., 244

Bedell, Christopher Columbus "Lum," 74–76, 78–79

Benedict, Judge Charles Linneaus, 131–35, 139, 141–42, 190, 213, 270–71

Bennett, Alexander, 64–66, 70–74, 78–79, 88

Benning, Gen. Henry L., 88

Betts, George, 75–78, 88–89

Biebusch, Fred, 110

Biggerstaff, Aaron, 153

Bill of Rights, 38–39

"black codes," 23

Bleecker Street, Secret Service Headquarters, 102, 109, 116, 118–21, 124–25, 133, 137, 139, 141, 161–62, 211, 215, 223, 229, 236, 240

"bleeding Kansas"/Lawrence, Kansas, 40

Blue, Dan, 145

Bonaparte, Napoleon, 38

Booth, John Wilkes, 264

Boston Herald, 46

Boston Times, 136

Boutwell, George S., 17, 101–102, 116–17, 141, 214–15, 237

Bow Street Runners, 38, 213

Boyd, Jim, 110–11

Boynton, Henry V., 246

branch office, chief operatives, 110

Bratton, James Rufus, 221

Bristow, Benjamin H., 238–42, 245–47, 252–53, 257, 263

Brooks, James J., 262

Brown, John, 40–41, 48, 198

Brown, Joseph E., 87–90

Brown, Samuel G., 200–202, 259

Bryan, Jesse, 171–72

Buck, Jake, 111–12, 125

Burnham, George P., 139

Butler, Gen. Benjamin, 53–57, 59–60, 101, 106, 148, 150, 196, 246

Butts, William H., 223

C

Caldwell, Tod R., 151–52, 168

Call, Wilkinson, 261

Campbell, John A., 164–69, 171

Campbell, R. M., 45–46, 48, 51, 59, 128–29, 134

Capdeville, Pedro, 56–57, 212, 256

carpetbagger governments, 273

Carter, George W., 176–80, 192, 232–37

Casserly, Sen. Eugene, 137–38

Central Intelligence Agency, 266

Chalmers, James Ronald, 261

Chicago Post, 203

Chicago Tribune, 81, 91

Children's Aid Society, 209

Chipley, William D., 71–72, 74–76, 79–81, 92, 213–14, 235, 264, 274

Cincinnati Daily Gazette, 30, 89–90, 94

"Circular of Instructions," 215–17, 232, 262–63

Civil Rights Act, 1866, 24, 159

Civil War, 39, 61, 68–69, 83, 114, 122, 159

Civil War debt, 60

The Clansman, 248–51, *251*, 272–73

Cleveland, President Grover, 265

Clough, W. F., 47–48

Cockspur Island, Georgia, 68–69

Cold War, 266

Cole, Cornelius, 149–51

Cole, Harry, 118–20, 123–24, 128, 130–31, 138, 263

Collins, David, 202–203

Columbus, Georgia, 20–36

Columbus Prisoners, 80–81, 88, 91–92

Company G, 16th Infantry Regiment, 31–34

coniackers/coney men/counterfeiters, 97

counterfeiter arrests, 110–11, 141–42

counterfeiting, 96–100, 103–105

counterfeiting gangs, 55–56, 104

counterfeiting investigation, 117–22

D

Daily Sun
accusations of torture of prisoners, 81, 85
editors as white supremacist, 22
on KKK, 63
on Miner trial, 133
on terror in the night, 20–21
threats against African Americans, 32–33
threats against Ashburn, 27–28

Daniel, Robert, 72–73, 75–76

Davis, David, 238

Davis, Jacob R., 197

Davis, President (Confederate) Jefferson, 198

Declaration of Independence, 25

Del'Omo, Louis, 110–11, 176–77, 180

Democratic Party, Georgia, 21–23

Democratic press, 80, 85, 91, 94
See also Atlanta Constitution; *Daily Sun*

Democrats, 237
affiliates with anti-Grant Republicans, 194, 213
and African American rights, 25
and Ashburn murder, 32–34, 65, 71, 77–78, 85, 93
attacks on federal law enforcement, including Secret Service, 260–61
control of House, 1874, 246–47, 253–54
Forrest recruits in Columbus, 27
government as enemy, 262
on Grant's "corruption," 245
impeachment of Holden, 147
Miner trial, 136
political resurgence, 1877, 258
seek to overturn Reconstruction political order, 144–47, 152

testimony during Ashburn trial, 90

tie to white supremacists, 205

See also Ashburn murder; Ku Klux Klan; Southern Democrats; Whitley, Hiram Coombs

Department of Justice created, 146, 158

Dixon, Thomas, Jr., 248–50, 264, 272–73

Doy, Charles, 40, 47

Doy, John, 40–43, 47, 49–50, *52*, 86, 129–30, 140, 159

Doyle, Arthur Conan, 270

Duke, William A., 79

Dunn, Gen. William M., 87–88

Durell, Judge Edward Henry, 134

Durham, Plato, 168

E

Eagle Mills textile plant/Eagle & Phenix Mills, 27

Emporia Gazette, 249, 269, 273

F

"Farmer's Clubs," 193

Fayetteville Eagle, 170

Federal Bureau of Investigation, 266

federal forces, 37–38

The Federalist Papers, 197, 267

Feeley, Andrew, 55–56

Ferguson, Catherine, 172–74

Ferguson, Dennis, 172

Ferguson, Sarah Jane, 172–74

Fifteenth Amendment, 146, 159

Fillmore, President Millard, 41

Finley, Ebenezer, 261

Finnegass, Henry F., 106, 215, 263

Fish, Hamilton, 183, 187–89

Fletcher, William F., 176–79

Flournoy, Hannah, 22, 28–29, 64–66, 70, 73–74

Ford's Theatre, 264

Forrest, Nathan Bedford, 26–28, 178

Fort Pulaski, 68–69, 72–73, 80–85

Fouché, Joseph, 38, 140, 213

Fourteenth Amendment, 24, 91–93, 144, 159

"Free State men," 40

Freedmen's Bureau, 23–25, 64, 68, 87

Fugitive Slave Act, 1850, 41, 61, 140, 159

Fullerton, William S., 128–30, 133, 158, 254–55

G

Garfield, President James A., 187, 214–15

gens de couleur libre/free people of color, 57, 86

"ghouls" (KKK), 27

Gilmore, Frances, 166

Gilmore, Sally, 166–67, 169–72, 174

"Grand Wizard," 26–27

Grant, First Lady Julia, 252

Grant, President Ulysses S.

adopts a cautious posture toward KKK, 187–89

anti-Grant sentiment. *See* Democrats; Liberal Republicans faction

dissolution of military commission, Ashburn trial, 94–95

elected President, 96

fires Babcock, 256–57

hesitance to intervene in South, 146–47

inauguration, 13

and Klan violence, 146–49

and Ku Klux Klan Act, 151–56

orders investigation of Ashburn's death, 32–36

pardons four Klansmen, Williams retracts the pardons, 202–204

pardons more Klansmen, 1873, 258–59

questions Whitley about Virginia moonshiner case, 17–19

threatens to suspend habeas corpus in South Carolina, 182–84, 186

wins 1872 election, 204–205, 207

Great Depression, 266

Greeley, Horace, 194, 196, 198, 205

Gregorio, Nicolas, 55

Gurney, Bill, 111–15, 124–25, 138, 212

H

habeas corpus, 30, 147–48, 182–83, 186–88, 190, 192, 205, 267

Hamilton, Alexander, 197, 267

Harpers Ferry, 41, 198

Harper's Weekly, 145–46

Harrington, Richard, 226–33, 237, 241

Harris, Essic, 153

Hayes, Michael, 228–37, 240–41, 250–51

Hayes, President Rutherford B., 257–58, 260–61

Hester, Joseph Goodman, 153–56, 161–76, 180, 191, 206, 214, 220–21, 259

History of the Hen Fever, 139

Holden, William Woods, 147, 149, 152, 164

Honoré de Balzac, 38

Hudson, Robert, 76–77, 79

I

illegal whiskey epidemic, 60

Internal Revenue, 13, 17, 36–37, 60, 94

"Invisible Empire," 26

Ireland, E. A., 195

Ivins, James, 221–24, 271

J

"Jake Buck," 111–12, 125

"James Simpson," 220–21

Johnson, President Andrew, 23–26, 32, 35, 60, 65, 79, 81, 96, 99–101, 105

Johnson, Thomas, 64–66

Johnson's Island, Ohio, 74

Jordan, Edward, 99, 102

Justice, James M., 201

"Justin Knight," 195

K

The Kansas Narrative: "A Plain, Unvarnished Tale" (Doy), *52*

Kansas–Nebraska Act, 1854, 42
Keene, David, 118
Kennoch, William, 123–24, 127–28, 263
King, Dr. Martin Luther, Jr., 266
Kirkbride, David, 118
Kirkscey, Elisha, 71, 74–79, 81, 90, 92
"Klan" parade
  second organized by Hester, 175
  Southern response to, 169–71
  staged by Hester, 167–68
Knight, Judson, 184–88
"Ku Klux Committee" (Joint Select Committee to Inquire into the Condition of Affairs in the Late Insurrectionary States), 153–54, 168, 188, 213
Ku Klux Klan
  actions suppressed, 1872, 192
  activities in GA, 184–89
  arrests, Ashburn assassination, 75
  Ashburn assassination, 29–30
  Ashburn trial, 89–92
  costume of, *26, 169*
  as Democratic party terrorist wing, 144–56
  investigated in "Mississippi Burning" by FBI, 266
  investigation and arrests, Ashburn assassination, 63–77
  in KY, 1873, 210
  Mills crackdown, 34
  oath of silence, 82, 171, 175
  origins of, 25–28
  pardons for four Klansmen, retracted by Williams, 203–204
  photograph of, *169*
  plans to silence Patterson, 70–73
  as political insurrection and criminal conspiracy, 197
  as saviors of the white race, 249
  Secret Service proof of crimes, 273
  South Carolina, ordered to disperse and retire by Grant, 147–48
  as threat to Reconstruction, 101
  threats in the night, 20–22, 27–28
Ku Klux Klan Act, 1871, 148–52, 180, 182–83, 187–88, 205

L

La Sûreté Nationale, 38
Lawrence, Amos, 46
Leonard, Major John, 64
Liberal Republicans faction, 187–88, 193–94, 196–97, 245
Lincoln, President Abraham, 21, 23, 39, 53, 61, 93, 98–99, 131, 264–65
Lonergan, Thomas, 106, 141
Lowther, Henry, 185–89
Luckey, J. B., 209
Luckey, Lottie N., 209

M

Macon Weekly Telegraph, 91
Madison, President James, 97, 267
Marshall, Sgt. Charles, 77–78, 88–89
McCartney, Pete, 115
McClellan, Gen. George, 39
McCoombs, Hannah Dixon. *See* Whitley, Hannah Dixon McCoombs

McCulloch, Hugh, 264–65
McKinley, President William, 265
McLean, Murchison, 166–67, 171
McPherson Barracks, 75, 80–81, 87–88
Meade, Gen. George
  Ashburn assassination investigation, 66–88
  and Ashburn murder, 94–95, 183, 190
  dissolution of military commission, Ashburn trial, 92–93
  military authority under Reconstruction Acts, 32–36
Memoirs of the United States Secret Service (Burnham), 139–43, 195, 261–62
Merrill, Major Lewis, 181, 183, 205
Mills, Capt. William, 32–35, 63–64, 66–68, 70–73, 77–78, 81, 83, 86
Miner, Joshua D. "Jot," *113, 122,* 211, 241, 263
  as "autocrat of American coney men," 141–42
  found "not guilty" at trial, 132–34
  investigated and arrested for counterfeiting, 112–22
  ruined as criminal, 138–39, 142
  trial, 122–34
Miner counterfeit investigation, 112
"Mississippi Burning," 266
mock executions, Ashburn investigation, 84–86
moiety, 125–26, 136
Moore County KKK confessions, 171–72

Moore County Klansmen, 153, 163–75
"museum of crime and cupidity," Secret Service HQ as, 211

N

National Banking Act, 1863, 98
National Police Gazette, 38
National Republican, 168, 200, 256
National Security Agency, 266
National Shoe and Leather Bank, 112, 115–16, 118, 127–29
The Nation's Peril, 195–96, 206
"Negro rule," 22, 201
Nettleship, Ichabod C., *108,* 108–109, 128, 141, 184, 209, 217, 240, 246, 257–58
  resigns, 245
  turns state's evidence, 254–56
  and "Washington Safe Burglary Case," 227–37
New Falls City, 54, 60
New Orleans, 50–53
New York Dispatch, 122
New York Herald, 122, 127, 157–58, 208
  on clemency, 202–203
  on pardon requests, 200
New York Sun, 196–97
New York Sunday Dispatch, 138
New York Times, 30, 100, 174–75, 193, 240
New York Tribune, 223
New York World, 39–40, 196
Newcomb, Abner B., 109–10, 141, 233, 253, 258, 268
Newcomb, Lizzie W., 268

P

Palmer Raids, 266
pardons, push for, 196–204
Patterson, Amanda, 64–65, 70–75, 78–79, 88
Peel, Robert, 38
Perry House hotel, 22
Philadelphia Inquirer, 246
photography, as crime fighting tool, 141, 169, 215
Pierrepont, Edwards, 123–24, 130–31, 254–56
Pinkerton, Allan, 39, 106, 270
Pittsburgh Chronicle, 136
Poe, Edgar Allan, 38
Pool, John, 149–54, 168, 191
Pope, Gen. John D., 79, 186, 191
"puker" (KKK oath violator), 171

R

Raleigh Sentinel, 169–70, 174
Reconstruction, 22–27, 30, 32–33, 60, 65, 75, 77, 144–46, 150, 187–88, 194, 238, 248–49, 259–60
Reconstruction Acts, 1867, 24, 26, 32–33, 67–68, 91, 93, 152
Red River steamboat trade, 53–54
Red Shirts, 260
Reed, William H., 35, 64, 66–69, 79, 83, 85, 101, 222–24
Republican National Convention, 1872, 194, 198
Republican Party, Georgia, 21–23
Republicans
anti-Grant faction, 193, 213, 237–38
Ashburn murder, 64
attacks on black Republicans in GA, 145
campaign theme, "waving the bloody shirt," 196
create centralized federal government, 98
Democratic attacks on, 259–61
expelled from Georgia state legislature, 144–45
fear of white supremacists after Grant's pardon of Klansmen, 203–204
John Pool and. *See* Pool, John
Klan infiltration plans, 155
Liberal Republicans faction, 187–88, 193–94, 196–97, 245
list of, demanded from Bennett, 71–72
lose House in 1874 midterm elections, 253
response to Ashburn murder, 31
and resurgence of Klan, 258–59
retake seat in North Carolina, 1872, 199
threats in the night, 20–22, 27–28
and undercover operations, 246–47
win White House and Congress, 1868, 145–46
See also Ashburn murder; Grant, President Ulysses S.; Southern Republicans; Whitley, Hiram Coombs
response to KKK arrests, Ashburn murder, 79–80
Richardson, William A., 237
Rivarol, Antoine, 140
"rogues' gallery," 141
Roper, Alva C., 79
Rosecrans, Gen. William, 21

S

"salary grab," 237
Sanborn, John B., 237
"Sanborn Affair," 237
Saxton, Gen. Rufus, 87
Schofield, John, 81
Scott, John, 154–56
Secret Service
    adversaries in Congress, 213–14
    attacks by Southern Democrats,
        260–61
    authorized by Congress, 1882,
        262
    Bristow calls for reform instead
        of abolition, 246–47
    capture of Joshua Miner, 111–
        33
    captures Fred Biebusch, 110
    captures Jim Boyd, 110–11
    "Circular of Instructions," 215–
        17
    effects of Judge Benedict's in-
        structions, 133–34
    intelligence-gathering in World
        War I, 265–66
    investigations, 210–11
    as leading U. S. detective agency,
        158
    move to Bleecker Street, 102–
        103
    receives mandate to act as presi-
        dential bodyguards, 265
    reduced to counterfeiting cases
        only, 261
    renewed by Congress, 1873,
        209–10
    revamped by Whitley, 103–10
    "special reports" on elections
        ordered, 194–95
    Whitley announced as chief,
        16–18, 96
    Wilson calls for abolishment of,
        242–45
    under Wood, 100–101
    Senate Committee hearings, 136–
        39
7th Cavalry, 147, 181, 184, 205
7th Louisiana Volunteer Infan-
    try, 57
Sherman, Gen. William Tecum-
    seh, 27, 98
Sherman, John, 98
Shotwell, Randolph A., 201–203,
    259
Sibley, Gen. Caleb C., 87–88
16th Infantry Regiment, 31–34
"slave-hunting," 41, 61
Smith, Gerrit, 197–200, 202–203
Smith, Joseph, 43
Snow Camp, 174
Southern Democrats, 23, 81, 259
Southern Republicans, 189–90
Spanish-American War, 265
Stanton, Edwin, 39
Stapler, John, 83–86, 94
Starlight, 53
Stella, Jean Louis, 56–57
Stephens, Alexander H., 23, 88–92
Stevens, Wade, 82–83
Sumter, 154

T

Tammany Hall political machine,
    112, 117, 123, 130–31
Tammany Hall scandal, 136
Taylor, Dick, 173
Teal, William, 203
Temperance Hall, 28, 32, 74, 79

Thirteenth Amendment, 159
threats in the night, 20–22, 27–28
torture stories, Ashburn investigation, 80–81, 85–86
Treasury Department's Secret Service Division, 15–19, 37
Turner, Henry McNeal, 28, 31–32
Tweed, William M. "Boss," 112, 128

U

Underground Railroad, 41
United States Army, 37, 53, 62, 68–79, 144, 153–54, 164, 166, 182, 205, 260
See also Marshall, Sgt. Charles; 7th Cavalry
United States Marshals, 37, 41, 99–100, 126, 148, 170, 182, 184, 218, 243–45, 254, 260, 263

V

Vanderbilt, Cornelius, 128
Vidocq, Eugène François, 38, 140, 213, 270

W

Walkinshow, James, 62, 86
"wanted" poster for Ballard, 211, *212*
War of 1812, 43
war on terror, 266
Washington, President George, 97
Washington Daily Critic, 197
Washington Safe Burglary Case, 225–37, 245, 250–52, 254–56
Watson's Photograph Studio, 168

Wells, John, 83, 85, 94
Western Reserve Seminary, 43–44, 60
Whiskey Ring, 253, 255
White, William Allen, 249
White League, 260
white supremacy. *See* Ku Klux Klan
Whitley, Catherine Webster Bates, 45, 49, 51–53, 61, 102, 208–209, 258, 268–69
death of, 274
Whitley, Hannah Dixon McCoombs, 43, 258
Whitley, Hiram Coombs
"adopts" a child, Marie Louise Gladde (Kittie Whitley), 208–209
adopts second daughter, Sabra, 268–69
and *Appletons' Journal* interviews, 211–13
appointed Secret Service chief, 13–19, 96, 101–102
arrested for kidnapping and highway robbery, 48–50
Ashburn case, confessions and trial, 78–95
asked to handle Williams's personal matter, James Ivins, 218–19, 221–22
assigned to provost marshal's office as spy, 55–56
autobiography, *In It*, 270–72
Biebusch investigation and arrest, 110
Bristow's appointment and investigation, 238–42
buys hotels and builds Opera

House, Emporia, Kansas, 249–50, 267–68

as cattle driver, 44–45

and constraints by Williams, 188–95

convinces Boutwell and Banfield to set up sting for Miner, 117

counterfeiter arrests, 157

death of, 274

disguises, *125*

early background of, 43–44

enrolled as Army major, 57–59

evaluates pardon requests at Albany Penitentiary, 199–202

excesses in obtaining confessions, 80–81, 85–86, 89, 94–95

frustration with New York justice system, 103

Gurney arrest, 111–12

hired by Treasury Department as agent, 60

hired to combat illegal whiskey epidemic, 60

hires Burnham to write *Memoirs of the United States Secret Service*, 139–43

indicted in burglary case, 246–47

Klan investigation update to Akerman, 180–83

letter/pamphlet against Judge Benedict's jury instructions, 134–36

marries Catherine and opens saloon, 45–46

methods compared to modern agencies, 266–67

Miner investigation and arrest, 114–24

Miner trial, 124–33

moves to Kansas after trial, 257–58

moves to Lawrence, Kansas, 46–47

in New Orleans, 50–55

ordered to investigate Klan, 158–63

ordered to investigate Klan in KY, 210

photographs of, *58, 269, 270*

pressures Babcock for job, 252–54

proven correct about need for Secret Service, 261–62

publishes *The Nation's Peril*, 195–96

rebuttal to Wilson, defense of Secret Service, 243–44

and reduction of Secret Service in the South, 205–207

on reticence of Klan victims to testify, 172

revamps Secret Service, 103–10

rumors of replacement, 224–25

Senate Committee hearings, 136–39

sends Knight's report to Akerman, 187

sends Nettleship to GA to investigate Klan, 184–85

sent to investigate Ashburn assassination, 36

shoots Capdeville, 56

as slave catcher, 42–43, 47–48

solves Ashburn assassination case, 63–95

submits letter of resignation, 245–46

testifies to Judiciary Committee against Babcock, Burglary Case, 254

trial, "Washington Safe Burglary Case," hung jury, 250–52

as undercover operator, 37, 40, 59

and "Washington Safe Burglary Case," 225–37

watches and denounces *The Clansman*, 249–50, 272–73

writes "Circular of Instructions," 215–17

Whitley, Kittie, 209, 258, 268, *270*

Whitley, Sabra, 268, *270*

Whitley, William, 43

Whitley home, Emporia, Kansas, 268–69, *269*

Whitley Hotel (former Coolidge House Hotel), 267, *268*

Whitley Opera House, *251*, 267

Wicker, William Washington, 171

Wiggins, James L., 79

Williams, George H., 189–95, 199–200, 203–204, 207, 216, 221, 236, 242, 255

asks Whitley to investigate a personal matter, 218–19, 221–23

orders Whitley to investigate Klan in KY, 210

scandal involving Kate's expenditures, 237

uses Secret Service to gather political intelligence, 217

Williams, Kate, 218–19, 221–24, 237, 252

Willis, Benjamin, 260–61

Wilson, Bluford, 239–46, 252–53, 255, 257, 259, 263, 267

Wilson, James F., 159

Wilson, James H., 239, 241, 246

Wood, Robert A., 79

Wood, William Patrick, 99–102, 107–10, 112, 114–15, 241, 244

World War I, 265–66